DEMOCRACY
IN CRISIS

Sortition and Public Policy

Barbara Goodwin, *Justice by Lottery* (2005)

Anthony Barnett & Peter Carty, *The Athenian Option* (2008)

Thomas Gataker (ed. Conall Boyle)
The Nature and Use of Lotteries (2008)

Keith Sutherland, *A People's Parliament* (2008)

Ernest Callenbach & Michael Phillips, *A Citizen Legislature* (2008)

Oliver Dowlen, *The Political Potential of Sortition* (2009)

Conall Boyle, *Lotteries for Education* (2010)

Gil Delannoi & Oliver Dowlen (eds.)
Sortition: Theory and Practice (2010)

Peter Stone (ed.), *Lotteries in Public Life* (2011)

John Burnheim, *The Demarchy Manifesto* (2016)

Liliane Lopez-Rabatel & Yves Sintomer (eds.)
Sortition and Democracy (2020)

Jeff Miller, *Democracy in Crisis* (2022)

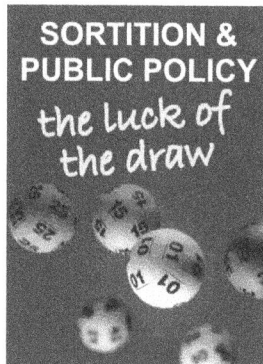

Series Editor: Barbara Goodwin, University of East Anglia

DEMOCRACY
IN CRISIS

LESSONS FROM
ANCIENT ATHENS

Jeff Miller

ia

imprint-academic.com

Published in the U.K by
Imprint Academic, PO Box 200, Exeter EX5 5YX, U.K

Distributed in the U.SA by
Ingram Book Company,
One Ingram Blvd., La Vergne, TN 37086, U.SA

ISBN 9781788360630 (cloth)

A CIP catalogue record for this book is available from the
British Library and U.S. Library of Congress

Acknowledgements

Many people helped the writing of this book. First off, let me thank Sara Bilik, who—after listening to me talk about ostracism at a cocktail party for a good half-hour—encouraged me to put what I was saying down in writing, assuring me that other people would also be interested. Thanks to Keith Sutherland, at Imprint Academic for his patience and excellent, scholarly advice. The interlibrary loan staff at the Sojourner Truth Library at the State University of New York, New Paltz have been fabulously quick at getting books and articles for me; this book would not have been possible without their help.

There are many colleagues and teachers to whom I owe a debt of gratitude. Here I'd like to single out David Thomas, who first showed me how important history is to thinking about politics.

And many thanks to Sarah, my partner in so many things, for unfailingly supporting me during the writing of this book. Finally, let me dedicate this book to my daughter Clio, our own muse of history. The future of democracy matters most for her and future generations; I'm hoping this book can nudge things in the direction of a better world.

Contents

Introduction

Liberal democracy in the twenty-first century is under threat. Whether looking abroad or within, we see mounting challenges posed by a range of alternative ideologies and approaches to governing, increasingly dire environmental crises, as well as more direct and traditional conflicts over trade, territory, and influence.

Externally, one-party states — like China under Xi Jinping — pose powerful alternative models to liberal democracy, harnessing impressive economic growth, world-dominant production capabilities, and a growing sphere of political influence. Chinese citizens lack many of the key protections and powers that citizens in much of Europe, the United States and other liberal democratic governments take for granted. In their place China offers better economic and institutional performance, which the government seems to have successfully delivered over the last half century by lifting a large portion of their population out of poverty and generating huge trading surpluses. In a modern, economically complex world, countries like China are betting that future success will be linked to uncontested political control, which allows them to plan decades into the future, unlike liberal democracies, where policies shift according to the party in power.

Other alternatives to democracy seem to look backward instead of forward. The religious fundamentalisms of the Islamic State, al-Qaeda, Ansar al-Islam, and the new Taliban regime in Afghanistan pose a more direct challenge to not only liberal democracy but modernity in general. They appeal to a narrow and austere form of Islam which—while rejecting democratic mechanisms of accountability as well as human rights—does not rely on the promise of economic success like China, but rather the imperative of a life lived according to their theological tenets.

We sometimes like to imagine that these regimes are imposed on their subjects unwillingly. And, indeed, by liberal democratic standards there are few formal mechanisms by which Chinese citizens (let alone those ruled by Islamic Fundamentalist regimes) can indicate their dissent from the Communist Party's dominance. But it is not at all clear that the majority of Chinese do not consent to the government. A recent Harvard study shows broad support for Xi Jinping and the Communist Party.[1] Similarly, there is evidence for some support for the Taliban, at least outside heavily urban areas.[2] Many people are more than willing to trade the vote or political rights for economic prosperity or—in the case of many Afghans—simply security. Advocates of democracy should not delude themselves into thinking that democracy is somehow a default or even preferred position for human societies.

Internally, liberal democratic societies have suffered a massive crisis of trust over the past two decades. The gap between the very wealthy and the rest of society has grown substantially, and the growing political and financial power of the economic elite in turn leads to suspicions that politicians serve the interests of large business and multinational corporations at the expense of average people.[3] Citizens feel powerless; the work of legislation and policy-making seems distant and captured by elites. The nation state, of course, has always been subject to a continual tension between, as Manuel Castells puts it, 'acting as a node within the global networks, where the fate of its people are decided, and in representing its citizens who refuse to give up on their historical, geographical and cultural roots, or to lose control over their work.'[4] But recent difficulties have amplified this problem, making it a crisis. In addition to the difficulties already mentioned, a belief in the efficacy of state action and capacity has diminished along with aging and failing infrastructure, an inability or unwillingness to curb pollution, a lack of significant movement in fighting global warming, and most recently difficulties dealing with the COVID-19 pandemic. Social media and aggressively partisan news sites compound the problem.[5] Trust in government in countries like the United States is low at all levels. And trust in multinational institutions like the European Union has cratered, as evidenced by Britain's 2020 departure — the first state ever to leave the EU.

In response, citizens in the largest democracies — the United States, Brazil, and India — have turned to new quasi-authoritarian leaders like Donald Trump, Jair Bolsonaro, and Narendra Modi, who are openly contemptuous of democratic elections, due process, and checks on power. These leaders support a return to nationalism and build cults of personality around themselves while simultaneously eroding democratic norms. In some states, liberal democracy has virtually vanished. In the twentieth century, repressive dictatorships were the most common form of authoritarian regime. Today, by contrast, we have electoral autocracies like those found in Hungary under Viktor Orbán, or in Turkey under Recep Tayyip Erdogan. These leaders have transformed liberal democratic societies by gutting checks and balances on their power and ignoring human rights. They tolerate some limited space for civil society, in order to maintain the appearance of openness and democratic accountability.

Even in relatively stable liberal democracies, acute and mounting problems threaten political stability. The biggest of these is the existential challenge of unchecked global warming. At the time of this writing, a significant portion of the western United States was on fire, something Australia and other countries experienced in 2019 and 2020. Germany, the Netherlands, and Belgium suffered massive flooding this summer.

Temperatures are reaching record levels each year across the globe. Changing weather patterns, rising sea levels, increased weather volatility, and the desertification of once arable land pose immediate and future problems for us. Some of this manifests itself in the form of straightforward disasters, like 2011's Hurricane Irene. But the effects of climate change also combine with other crises, amplifying them. In the past decade European states have faced a refugee influx which threatened to overwhelm not only their logistical capacity to cope with the problem, but also fertilized a virulent xenophobia that cashed out in right-wing and populist electoral gains. The United States has seen a similar flow of economic and political refugees from Central and South America which sparked a rise in white nationalist violence, capitalized on by populist politicians like Donald Trump. Increased racial and ethnic diversity in both Europe and North America tracked the rise of identity politics and claims for equal recognition on the part of growing non-white communities, aggravating and playing into older racist paranoias.[6]

Liberal democracies are relatively new in historical terms. Understood generously, they date back scarcely two hundred years, with their philosophical roots going back perhaps to the 1600s. In the recent past there has been a tendency to see them as natural or as a sort of default position for human communities. In 1989, after the break-up of the Soviet Union and the collapse of communist regimes in Europe, Francis Fukuyama notoriously argued that liberal democracy represented the 'final form of human government', and that the following decades would see a gradual expansion of it.[7] Of course, the post-Soviet world has witnessed anything but that.

It is the argument of this book that liberal democracy — and democracy in general — needs some rethinking, expansion, and retooling to help it adapt to and deal with the many challenges briefly outlined above. Democracy is not a default position for human communities. It is historically rare, and when subjected to pressure it can collapse or devolve into some other regime type, as we are witnessing in Hungary and Turkey today. Democracy is also not simply one thing. Etymologically, the word derives from two Ancient Greek words: *demos,* the word for 'people', and *kratos,* which means 'power' or 'force'. The word is sometimes glossed as 'people power'. But what exactly constitutes 'people power'? Who *are* the people? What kind of power do they wield? How may they use it, and to what end? Today, many states around the world claim to be democratic, and the widely accepted standard to qualify as a democracy is regular, free, and fair elections, though what those three terms mean is disputed. Even countries which no one would reasonably admit into the club of democratic nations sometimes feel the need to at least *claim* to be democratic, testifying to the normative power of the term. The formal title of the North Korean regime is 'The Democratic People's Republic of Korea', and while Russia might hold elections, they are anything but free and fair.

Most recognized democratic regimes today are representative democracies, where the people vote into office legislators who then do the work of governing for them in either a parliamentary or presidential system. And even after laws are passed, large bureaucracies and regulatory agencies must go through the complex process of setting policies, procedures, and implementation guidelines. Governing in liberal democracies today is always several steps removed from the governed, regardless of election frequency.

Political thinkers sometime regard representative democracy as a sort of compromise made necessary by the size of modern nation states. While ultimate power resides in the people, their representatives exercise it on their behalf because of the logistical difficulties of everyone deliberating and voting on every issue. Over time, representatives gain expertise in certain areas, presumably providing for better legislation and policies. This division of labor also frees up the larger part of the population for pursuits outside of the political sphere, which may hold more interest. While periodic elections theoretically allow the peoples' preferences to work their way into the law, political scientists debate the extent to which democratic preferences actually translate into policy. A quick survey of some alternative labels for liberal democracies today—spectator-democracy, mediacracy, drama democracy, audience democracy—give some sense of where the real power in 'democratic' regimes might lie.

Setting aside its usage today, the term democracy itself has its origins in a more radical form: direct democracy. In Ancient Athens the term *demokratia* appears in the fifth century BCE as a way of distinguishing a democratic government, in which the real governing power rested in the hands of all citizens, from oligarchic or monarchical regimes where power was restricted to a few families or single individuals.[8] For nearly two centuries in the fifth and fourth centuries BCE, Athenian citizens governed themselves directly, voting on laws and policies, serving in the law courts, public magistracies, and other civic institutions. In Classical Athens the power of the people was unchecked by a written constitution, human rights, or any of the other constraints liberal democratic theorists today see as crucial.[9] Instead, each individual citizen had the duty to deliberate on and evaluate legislative proposals, treaties, budgets, as well as crucial decisions about war and peace. The primary legislative body, the *ecclesia,* or assembly, was open to all adult male citizens, and had final authority to enact binding legislation on a simple majority vote. Additionally, as we will see in detail in Chapter Three, political and administrative offices—positions we might identify as bureaucratic—were distributed broadly across the citizenry. At Athens, the political was a collective effort and exercise of the citizens.

Athenian democracy, however, was not universally inclusive. Like all societies in the ancient world, Athens excluded women from virtually all civic offices, as well as much of the economic

Philipp von Foltz, *Pericles Gives the Funeral Speech* (1852)

Democracy: Ancient . . .

US Capitol attack (6 January 2021)

. . . and Modern

life of the city. The Athenian politician and general Pericles claims in a speech that the best woman is the one about whom nothing was known, either in praise or blame.[10] Politics, especially, was an affair between men, and even then not all men, but rather only those who were citizens. Athenians were proud of their city and their form of government. Citizenship was a closely held prerogative, one that individuals sometimes counterfeited, and one they sometimes lost as a penalty for misfeasance. In addition to being a source of pride, citizenship also brought concrete benefits, both legal and economic. Some of these were the results of the substantial empire Athens acquired in the fifth century (and then subsequently lost), which generated considerable revenue widely shared by the population. We should finally note that Athens was a slave-holding society, like all political units in the ancient world. At Athens, however, the substantial slave population helped underwrite democratic practice, freeing citizens from the labor that might otherwise have prevented them from fulfilling their civic responsibilities. By modern standards, democracy in Athens fails dramatically in terms of inclusivity and exploitation.

But these facts should not diminish the truly radical nature of the Athenian experiment. Extending real political power so broadly through a population was new, and relatively rare even in the Hellenic world, where monarchies and oligarchies were the norm. Indeed, Athenians themselves were acutely aware of the constant vigilance required to maintain their form of government in the face of both internal and external pressures; the threat of an oligarchic or tyrannical coup was never far from their thoughts. And, in fact, the Classical Period saw several dramatic attempts to overthrow or replace the democracy with more restrictive forms of government, but none of these were long successful. It was only with the break-up of the Macedonian empire that democracy was finally snuffed out when a successor kingdom to Alexander the Great absorbed Athens and moved political control out of the city in the 330s BCE.

In retrospect, the durability and tenacity of the Athenian experiment represents a significant achievement. For a democracy to work, and to persist, it needs the full resources of its citizen body. We can catch a glimpse of the Athenian citizen in an often-cited speech given by a Corinthian ambassador to the Spartans as represented by the historian Thucydides, himself an Athenian:

> Their bodies they spend ungrudgingly in their country's cause; their intellect they jealousy husband to be employed in her service ... they toil on in trouble and danger all the days of their life, with little opportunity for enjoying, being ever engaged in getting; their only idea of a holiday is to do what the occasion demands, and to them laborious occupation is less of a misfortune than the peace of a quiet life.[11]

In this speech, the Corinthian ambassador emphasizes the threat Athens poses to Sparta in an ultimately successful attempt to draw Sparta into war. Even allowing for exaggeration, the portrait is striking. Devoted Athenians give themselves over entirely to their city and its way of life. In the words of Thucydides' Pericles, they became 'lovers of Athens'. How did the democracy produce citizens like this? By what means did they maintain their form of government for so long? In this book we will investigate how the internal structures, procedures, and civic ideology used by Athenians operationalized the power of the people to stabilize the regime and its values over the course of several generations.

Since the Classical Period few other peoples have attempted similar experiments, and certainly not at the scale or duration of the Athenians. Athenian democracy, in fact, played the role of a cautionary tale until relatively recently in political thought. The mass of people were thought too fickle, uneducated, and gullible for power to rest securely (or safely!) in their hands.

This was a common view during the American founding debates. James Madison, for example, rejects democracy as dangerously conducive to faction, arguing instead for a republic: 'Men of factious tempers, of local prejudices, or of sinister designs', he writes in *Federalist* 10, 'may, by intrigue, by corruption, or by other means, first obtain the suffrages, and then betray the interests, of the people.' Democratic passions needed to be tempered, moderated. Even the directly elected U.S. House of Representatives seemed too close to popular passions and needed the sobering restraint of the Senate, whose members were originally appointed by state governments, not by popular election. A perhaps apocryphal story has George Washington tell Thomas Jefferson that the Senate was the cool saucer into which the hot tea of the House of Representatives was poured. In rejecting direct democracy, the American founders turned instead to the mixed regime of the Roman Republic for a governmental model — where the people had a voice, but a diminished one relative to elite authority.

Democracy returned as an affirmative political value only recently. However this book argues that, despite widespread adoption and valorization of the term, our political imaginary has yet to fully explore the possibilities of democratic government. Literary critics, philosophers, historians and others still find valuable resources in the major intellectual figures of the Classical Period. Plato, Aristotle, and Thucydides, among others, appear regularly on college course syllabi, in international relations journals, and forums for public intellectuals like the *New York Review of Books*, or *The London Review of Books*. Melissa Lane, for example, has fruitfully described the philosophical roots of our contemporary basic political vocabulary in *The Birth of Politics*.[12] Theater companies produce new performances of plays by Sophocles, Euripides, and Aeschylus. But few sources explore what actual Athenian democracy might have to offer contemporary democratic societies.[13] This book takes up that challenge by exploring several actual political institutions from democratic Athens, and considers how we might incorporate some lessons the Athenians learned about how to generate, expand, and maintain a truly democratic regime.

The differences between Ancient Athens and modern liberal democracies, of course, is vast. We have already briefly mentioned slavery and the treatment of women. But many other factors separate the ancient Mediterranean from today. Classical Athens—even at its zenith—scarcely would rate as a mid-size city in most nations today. Its relative ethnic and cultural homogeneity distinguish it from the diverse multicultural societies of today's developed world. And while the scope of Athenian democratic government was expansive in the context of the ancient world, today's governments are far larger and deal with issues of considerable more complexity: our economies are larger, our technologies far more sophisticated and specialized, and the sheer range of problems addressed by the state outstrip those within the ambit and ability of the ancient city state. Technology, the complexity of government, and population diversity all clearly set modern democracies apart from their ancient counterpart.

But the purpose of this book is not to suggest that we can directly adopt Athenian practices or institutions in states today. We are not Athenians, and this is not the Ancient World. Instead, it argues that a consideration of Athenian civic life can help expand the horizon of our thinking about the possibilities for democracy. It can point away from a simple equation of voting with democracy and toward a more robust vision of people power. It can direct us toward untapped and unconsidered resources which lie dormant in democratic states today, and help us re-think and perhaps alter our own political assumptions, procedures, and processes. Most importantly, we can use Athens to reimagine the way democracy works and hopefully address the not insignificant challenges outlined at the beginning of this introduction. We may not be Athenians, but we can begin to think and act more like them.

The following chapters each take a particular institution or aspect of Classical Athenian civic life, examining how it worked and then considering how we might reimagine it in the context of contemporary liberal democracies. We begin with an overview of some of the important theoretical and ideological differences between Athens and today's liberal democracies. Athenians held very different views about key political values like freedom, equality, the relationship between the individual and wider community, and even the understanding of the self. Clarifying these differences will help us to understand how some of the specific institutions discussed in later chapters functioned and were broadly supported by Athenian citizens. Indeed, many aspects of this deep ideology allow for the specific institutions discussed later in the book. They will also allow us to see how our parallel set of beliefs — our liberal democratic ideology — often presents obstacles to substantive political and social improvements. One of the key lessons of the discussion of Athenian civic ideology is that human beings are somewhat more flexible that liberalism often allows. We are not born liberals or capitalists any more than we are born Christian, Muslim, or Buddhist. Rather we are made or become that. Our very ideas of ourselves come from an imagined community, and the boundaries and aspects of that sense of self can — albeit within limits — be shifted.

Following the theoretical overview, four subsequent chapters examine specific Athenian institutions and practices. Readers already familiar with Athenian civic ideologies may want to skip ahead to topics of particular interest, since each individual chapter can be read on its own.

Chapter Two, on ostracism, the first political practice examined, takes up the legal process and justification of one of Athens' most (in)famous political traditions: the annual decision as to whether to send into exile one member of the political community for a decade. We will look at the roots of this fifth century BCE practice, and then consider arguments for and against it as they appeared in the Classical Period and in the later tradition of political thought. Importantly, we will try to reconstruct how and why ostracism was so important to the early democracy as it emerged from oligarchic domination, and how analogues to the Athenian practice might be used as resources today.

Following the discussion of ostracism we turn in Chapter Three to another specific and distinctive practice: the use of chance to fill political offices. Like ostracism, sortition evoked significant principled and philosophical opposition in both the Ancient and Modern worlds, and as a practical matter was often linked to poor or inefficient governmental functioning. The use of lotteries to distribute offices, however, was a widely-endorsed, complex and well-oiled mechanism in Athens. It also had powerful ideological justifications and practical benefits. Unlike ostracism, interest in the use of sortition has undergone a renaissance in the last few decades, with many real-world experiments demonstrating clear implementation paths. At the end of the chapter we will briefly consider this growing body of literature and some recent real-world examples of sortition in action.

Chapter Four takes up the question of Athenian finances, specifically ways in which Athens paid for its expensive and demanding form of democracy. The discussion explains how how revenues were raised, but more importantly addresses the question of which parts of the body politic should bear the primary burden of taxation and why. Like many other ancient practices, revenue generation in Athens challenges some of our own basic assumptions and procedures, including important aspects of liberalism and capitalism like the protected nature of private property. And as with sortition and ostracism, we will discuss how taxation in Classical Athens worked to reinforce and operationalize certain assumptions about political equality important to the democracy.

The final chapter turns away from specific legal procedures and considers the sorts of cultural practices which supported and continually reinscribed democratic practices. Athens provides us with examples of many of these, but we have by far the most evidence for the City Dionysia, an annual theater festival which folded into several days both a (re)education about democracy and a theoretical space within which members of the community could critically reflect on and confront basic aspects of their civic ideology and attending complications. We will review how the City Dionysia worked, and look at examples from specific plays to imagine what lessons viewers took away from the festival. As in all the chapters in this book, the importance of festivals — moments when the people of Athens assembled together as an imagined whole — highlight our own lack of civic cohesion today and offer some hints as how to move forward. As in the other chapters, the goal, again, is not to adopt Athens' particular practices, but to expand the range of the possible in our democratic thinking to deal with the existential threats we face today. Athens has much to teach us about democracy.

Chapter One

Theoretical Foundations

Fairly early on in the COVID-19 pandemic, mask wearing took on a charged political valence. In the U.S., President Trump's initial mishandling and continued denial of the magnitude of the crisis led him to refuse to endorse the importance of masking in order to downplay the scale of the growing medical disaster. For many in the U.S., refusing to mask up became a sign of political identity, justified by an appeal to personal freedom. Mask wearing was a choice. Each person, they claimed, could evaluate the evidence and decide whether the risk was real and merited additional precautionary steps. As we all know, many people opted not to wear masks. High rates of hospitalization, deaths, and new COVID variants quickly followed, with little effect on the anti-masking movement.

The astonishing capacity of one political party to politicize a lethal public health crisis offers a sober warning. It should make us reconsider our faith in the efficacy of rationality and scientific explanations in public discourse. But I want to focus here on how the liberal conception of the self provides a justification for refusing to comply with sound advice. Setting aside some of the wilder conspiracy theories about pandemic lockdowns, home remedies, PPE, masks, and vaccines, the mask and vaccine skeptics repeat one word again and again: *freedom*. Many Americans refuse to wear masks on the grounds of personal freedom. The government, they claim, has no more right to tell them to wear a mask than it has a right to tell them to wear a jacket or get a haircut. Nor can it compel them to get vaccinated, which involves even deeper concerns about bodily integrity and autonomy.

On the face of it, this appeal to freedom is absurd. Wearing a mask or getting a vaccine to prevent the spread of COVID certainly does protect the individual. And if failure to comply with masking requirements harmed only the non-compliant, perhaps no governmental mandates would be justified. But importantly, masking and vaccination also protect other people and that additional benefit, ultimately, justifies lockdowns and mask mandates; it justifies restrictions on the freedom to *not* wear a mask. The government, after all, restricts liberty in some formal sense all the time. I must drive on the right side of the street, stop at red lights, and ensure my automobile has working brakes, steering, and lights. Similarly, I am not free to dump my used motor oil in the local river. In the abstract, these prohibitions restrict my ability to act as I like, yet we accept these restrictions because of the protections they provide to others and because they allow us to maximize other more important liberties like life and health.

The inability to recognize or acknowledge the effects our actions might have on others is underwritten by a distinctive, and relatively recent understanding of the self—prominent in contemporary liberalism—which imagines human beings as separate from each other and conceptually prior to the societies in which they live. Early Modern political theorists such as Thomas Hobbes, John Locke, and Jean-Jacques Rousseau grounded their political theories of human behavior in a state of nature, which Locke described as human beings 'living together according to reason, without a common superior on earth, with authority to judge between them.'[14] In these states of nature, human beings interact without the protection of law, the state, or any other point of appeal to resolve disputes. Inevitably, violence erupts in the state of nature, and human beings agree to establish government, which regulates their actions and stems violence. For thinkers like Hobbes and Locke, this movement from the state of nature into civil society provides both a justification for government as well as the theoretical scope and limits of state power. They describe the relationship between the individual and the state as contractual: the individual owes the state allegiance so long as the government protects him; if the state should fail in this basic task, the individual returns to the state of nature and reclaims his original liberty. Hobbes and Locke differ greatly in the amount of power and authority they afford the state, but crucially, they agree in their description of human beings as having this antecedent existence, where they are imagined as rational and fully formed. Importantly, individuals in the state of nature have the ability to determine and pursue their own conception of the well-lived life, what political theorists call 'the good life'. Each person has the capacity to determine how to live their life, and provided they do not harm others in this pursuit, no interference is justified, especially on the part of the state. Setting aside the problem of determining what counts as 'harm' — a truly vexing question, when stated at this level of generality — the liberal state adopts a posture of neutrality on the question of the good life. We can see this in basic elements of the U.S. Bill of Rights, which prohibits the government from interfering with freedom of speech, association, movement, conscience, *etc.* We are free to exercise these liberties or not, as we choose. The state cannot tell us what to say, where to live, or what to think.

For Locke, who was a pivotal influence on the development of contemporary liberal democratic constitutions, individuals also have a natural moral sense. Locke argues that while the state of nature is 'a state of liberty, yet it is not a state of license', in that people are able to discern natural rules of conduct — natural laws — given by God, which help regulate conduct and determine right from wrong.[15] These natural laws often protect parallel natural rights — what we today call *human rights*. These important protections, including the right to property, speech, or conscience, delineate a space within which the individual can act unconstrained by others. Because these rights are said to inhere in individuals, they require a theoretical pre-political status for human beings similar to that provided by Locke's state of nature. In this sense, rights not only protect individuals, however, they also separate them.[16] Their crucial position in the architecture of liberal theory generates a discrete and autonomous self, that needs protection from others, and a self which cannot be obligated to others except through consent. To understand the implications of this, consider the distinction political theorists often make between obligations and duties. Obligations are those responsibilities one agrees to assume through either express or tacit consent. Locke argues that the legitimacy of laws rests in the consent of the governed; if we cannot demonstrate consent on the part of the governed, governments cannot *legitimately* enforce the laws. Locke, of course, problematically argues that most of us have consented to the state, if only tacitly. Duties, by contrast, consist of those responsibilities we have regardless of whether we have agreed to them. Responsibilities to parents, family members, the duty to aid others, for example, are all typically recognized duties. They come with being human or being a member of a particular family or community. Philosophers refer to duties as 'positional' because they adhere to individuals contingent on where they find themselves in society, or most broadly, in their status as a human being. Crucially, while liberalism allows for the existence of these duties, we rarely codify them legally, preferring instead to allow individuals to decide whether to act on them. For liberals, our reluctance to require adherence to, say, the duty to care for one's parents stems from the fact that we did not *consent* to being born. If I refuse to assist a sibling or other relative in need, my friends and family might think poorly of me, but I would suffer no legal penalties. My legal obligations to others derive, rather, from verbal or written agreements into which I have entered, and not from my status as a human being.

We can see from this brief overview that the liberal conception of the self carries with it a sense of separateness that effectively acts as a barrier between us and our fellow citizens and the outside world. And while many of us appreciate the protections such insulation affords us (like human rights), this idea of the self impedes the development of community and abets the sense of isolation and alienation common in contemporary liberal democracies. Outlier versions of this extreme autonomy also partly explain the appeals to freedom on the part of anti-maskers; they are unwilling to recognize many important duties to other people. Furthermore, those obligations they do recognize are 'supererogatory' (beyond the call of duty), and not for the government to enforce.

We should also remember that the liberal sense of self appears relatively recently in historical terms, finding its origins in thinkers like Hobbes and Locke in the sixteenth and seventeenth centuries, and is only fully politically articulated in the twentieth century. For much of occidental history, in fact, a very different sense of self appears to link the individual to her wider community and society, one which foregrounds duty and connection to others. We have our first clear view of this in the Greek philosophical and political tradition, which we will investigate in this chapter.

In Book II of Plato's *Republic*, Socrates introduces what scholars refer to as the 'city–soul analogy'. In response to requests from other characters in the dialogue to supply a definition of justice and explain why we should act according to its tenets, Socrates responds that justice in individuals is hard to discern, and that if they can locate justice in a larger space where it could be seen more clearly, like a city, they could then look for parallels in the individual. Socrates and his interlocutors then spend the next several books of the dialogue outlining a 'city-in-speech' which, while not practically realizable, embodies an ideal form of justice to which one can aspire. Along with the *kallipolis* or beautiful city, they develop a parallel structure of the human *psyche*, or soul, determining that a particular arrangement of the different parts of each—the city and the soul—produces justice. Moreover, a just city, Socrates argues, fosters just individuals. The city and soul, it turns out, are mutually interdependent and closely related to one another.

The details of Socrates' *kallipolis* and his definition of justice as well as his discussion of the soul, are less important for our purposes here than his comparison of the city to the soul, or individual. This analogy strikes many modern readers as highly problematic at best. Why should we think that the individual and her wider community are connected in this sort of way? Do the internal parts of a human being parallel the parts of a city? Is justice in the individual contingent on justice in the city, or vice-versa? Some contemporary liberal thinkers might reject this comparison out of hand, but for the Greeks, these comparisons seemed obvious—Socrates' interlocutors accept it without dissent.[17]

Socrates' connection between the city and the soul in Book II of the *Republic*, taken loosely to mean the deep and constitutive connection between the individual and wider community, echoes widely-held assumptions in Athenian political and philosophical discourse. Late in the *Republic*, Socrates links the decline of the *kallipolis* to changes in the souls of the citizens. Slight errors by the philosopher-rulers of the city lead to excessive emphasis on honor in the souls of some citizens, soon transforming the city into timocracy—or rule by the honorable—and then oligarchy. From there, the city and its occupants are further corrupted, with lower appetitive forces leading the city into democracy and eventually tyranny. Each stage represents a parallel process of deterioration both civically and psychologically.

Aristotle, writing late in the Classical Period, supplies us with concise theoretical summaries of the Greek position. Early in the *Politics*, he famously describes the origin of the city as natural: 'the city belongs among the things that exist by nature, and man is by nature a political animal.'[18] Unlike Social Contract thinkers Hobbes and Locke, Aristotle argues politics and the state arise naturally, not as a result of a contractual arrangement from some pre-political state of nature. Human beings find themselves always already embedded in a political and social context, with laws, norms, customs, traditions, and language already in place shaping who they are and how they understand themselves in relation to the whole. Something like the liberal alternative—that the state is a matter of convention, or agreement to protect preexisting interests and capacities—appears occasionally as a possibility in Plato and Aristotle, usually attributed to sophistic figures who are dangerous, and eager to challenge the stability of the law or custom. In another passage from the *Politics,* Aristotle notes the connection between the *arete* (excellence or virtue) of a citizen and a good regime as well as the sophistic alternative:

> Whoever takes thought for good management [of the city], however, gives careful attention to political virtue and vice. It is thus evident that virtue must be a care for every city, or at least every one to which the term applies truly and not merely in a manner of speaking. For otherwise the partnership becomes an alliance which differs from others . . . only by location. And law becomes a compact, and, as the sophist Lycophron says, a guarantor among one another of the just things, but not the sort of thing to make the citizens good and just.[19]

Good cities and good laws, in other words, make good citizens, and the failure to attend to them properly potentially degrades both. We see a similar debate in Plato's *Republic,* where the character Glaucon suggests early in the text that justice, and hence law and the city, arise when people experience the unpleasantness of other individuals harming them: 'that's how they come to start making laws and agreements with one another', he argues.[20] Glaucon emphasizes the artificial or constructed nature of politics, and his description anticipates, in a rudimentary way, the social contract argument found later in Hobbes and Locke. Socrates' response through much of the rest of the dialogue can be read as a rejection of Glaucon's position: an emphasis on the connection between the laws, norms, and traditions of the city and the quality of its inhabitants, as well as the importance of a sense of common purpose and community. Indeed, one of the striking aspects of the *kallipolis* developed by Socrates and his interlocutors is the fact that good citizens need few laws to regulate their behavior. Most do the right thing by instinct and habit, not through rational calculation or conclusions.

Greek thinkers often referred to the responsibility the city as a whole has to each individual: how the laws, city, or *demos* shape the individual. But this responsibility could also appear as an individual duty. The Athenians Anytus and Meletus successfully prosecuted Socrates for 'corrupting the youth', a vague and easily abused charge, but one which underlines the Athenian belief that each individual has some responsibility to properly educate citizens. In Plato's imagined version of Socrates' defense speech, he questions Meletus about who, specifically, improves the youth of the city. The rather befuddled prosecutor first responds 'the laws', then under further questioning adds the members of the jury, followed quickly by the members of the *Boule*, the assembly, and finally the whole population of Athens. Socrates responds dryly: 'Then it would seem that the whole population of Athens has a refining effect upon the young, except for myself.'[21] Anytus' almost comic inability to answer precisely reflects a broadly held serious belief among Athenians about the wide-spread burden all parts of the city had to ensure that Athenian youth were properly guided to adulthood.

Plato's *Apology* portrays Anytus as seriously misguided in prosecuting Socrates. Indeed, one suspects that *he* might have been corrupted as a youth. The blame in his case, however, rests

not with Socrates, but in the democracy itself, which is portrayed in philosophical sources as providing a flawed form of
education and preparation for the necessities of governing.
Indeed, conservative critics of the democracy sometimes argued
that the basic premise of democracy — that all citizens could
participate meaningfully and productively in governing the
city — was fundamentally flawed. Rule should, instead, be
reserved for those with the proper knowledge and disposition,
an extreme example of this being the philosopher-rulers of
Socrates' *kallipolis* in Plato's *Republic*. But such rulers are
difficult — and maybe impossible — to find in practice, so actual
monarchies are not necessarily a solution. In Plato's *Laws*, for
example, the Athenian Stranger argues that Persian monarchs
such as Darius and Xerxes tend towards tyranny because their
education has been neglected: they have grown up in the care of
women and eunuchs, are extremely wealthy, and are taught that
wealth is to be honored instead of excellence.[22] The close
connection between regime and individual, however, links these
examples. In both cases, the city fails to properly shape its
citizens and rulers.

Contrary to the arguments found in philosophical sources,
most Athenian politicians connected democratic rule and
procedures *to* individual excellence. Sometimes this connection
was made through very specific democratic practices. The
fourth century orator Demosthenes, for example, connects the
Athenian practice of *parrhesia* – free speech — with making 'even
stupid people tolerable'.[23] More gracefully, Pericles notes that
every citizen has something to offer the city, even the poorest:
'nor again does poverty bar the way, if a man is able to serve the
state, he is not hindered by the obscurity of his condition.'[24]

At a deeper level, democrats endorsed the idea that regime-
type marked and shaped the moral character of the individual.
We can see this clearly in the distinction Classical Athenians
made between citizens in a democracy and subjects in more
despotic forms of rule. Isocrates, for example, clearly states in

the *Panegyricus* that Persian inferiority originates in a lack of political education and political freedom. Even those in high position — presumably well-educated and accustomed to rule:

> have never lived their lives by dictates of equality or of common interest or of loyalty to the city [οὐδὲ κοινῶς οὐδὲ πολιτικῶς] . . . their whole existence consists of insolence toward some and servility toward others . . . nothing could be more demoralizing to human nature. Because they are rich, they pamper their bodies; but because they are subject to one man's power, they keep their souls in a state of abject and cringing fear . . . falling on their knees before a mortal man, addressing him as a divinity, and so thinking more lightly of the gods than of men.[25]

This passage from Isocrates' *Panegyricus* parallels the description of the Chorus in Aeschylus' *Persians*: cringing and bowing down before the Persian kings Darius, Xerxes, and the Queen-mother Atossa, as well as the lavish description of wealth (mostly in the form of clothing), and imperial hubris in Persia. But Isocrates' argument also emphasizes the fact that the Persian social and political system makes the Persians unfit, not their ethnicity or some other natural cause. The passage represents an oblique endorsement of democratic practice. Demosthenes agrees. When commenting on the wrongs done to the Greeks by the Persian Satrap Ariobarzanes, he explains the behavior by saying '[Ariobarzanes] had been brought up where there were no laws [ἄνευ νόμων] and none of the advantages of a free constitution [πολιτεία καλῶν].'[26] For Demosthenes, regime type explains why the Greeks import slaves from barbarian neighbors: they tend to be cowardly and they are always ready to serve because of the norms of the regime in which they were raised.

We can see a good example of the range of characteristics Athenians thought were inculcated by democracy in the just-mentioned play *Persians*. Edith Hall identified a readily visible series of binary oppositions between the Persians and Greeks that surface throughout the play. Some of the opposing terms apply broadly to the Greeks; some seem more specifically to represent Athenian characteristics. Persians are ruled by a king, Athenians live in a democracy. Persians are described as subjects or slaves, while Greeks have freedom. Persian opulence, decadence, and wealth take the form of gold, while a more sober Athenian wealth derives from the silver mines at Laurium. Aeschylus emphasizes Persian emotion in contrast to the firmness of Greeks. The Persian army rapidly disintegrates into disorder and chaos during battle, while the Athenians maintain discipline and order. The Persian army, made up of contributions from across the empire, speaks a confusing polyglot of languages, while the Greeks speak in one language. The Athenians use spears, which are associated with bravery and masculinity, while the Persians use more cowardly bows (Xerxes returns to Persia with his quiver empty). Even nature is recruited in the division between the Persians and Greeks: night and darkness, symbolizing ignorance and associated with Persia, are contrasted with the Greek characteristics of daylight, heat, and fire. Finally, Xerxes himself, in contrast to Greek *sophrosune*, wisdom and temperance, makes a number of decisions easily described as hubristic. This is probably best symbolized by the floating bridge he builds over the Hellespont for his army to cross — thus negating a division between east and west decreed by nature or the gods.[27]

Regime type, then for Athenians, was thought to shape character and hence behavior throughout life. Laws, customs, and traditions consequently maintain immediate importance in the political thought of the time. It is not enough for the government to take a laissez-faire attitude toward culture, given its role in shaping citizens. Rather, the people should craft laws and customs consistent with the goal of producing virtuous citizens. We will see that this position affords the Athenian government a far more active relationship in regard to individual citizens, not only when they are young, but throughout their lives.

The contrast on this point between the Athenian and contemporary liberal position could not be clearer. Liberalism calls for the state to be neutral on questions of how one should live one's life. For liberals, arguably the most important capacity held by individuals consists of the ability to choose, and liberal freedom orients itself around this capacity. Because individuals are imagined to determine their own idea of the good life outside of any social or political influence, the liberal state strives for neutrality on this question, thus maximizing choice. In practice, this means that in a liberal democracy, the state should not make laws favoring a particular religion, lifestyle, or moral code. Society should allow individuals as much choice as possible, consistent with a parallel degree of choice for others.

Like the liberal conception of the self, neutrality on the question of the good life appears fairly recently in both theoretical approaches and actual political application. Before liberalism — and still in many parts of the world today — states had and enforced a clear view of the good life. We can see this most easily in legislation or moral codes shaped by theological concerns. Medieval European governments did many things that modern liberals would recognize: regulating commerce, providing for military defense, building and maintaining basic infrastructure, etc. But another key goal of most regimes, in theory if not completely in practice, was the maintenance and spread of Christianity. Part of the job of a good prince was ensuring that his subjects abided by Christian tenets and prepared themselves for the afterlife. No doubt, concern for the souls of subjects often thinly masked forms of domination and exploitation, as it did when underwriting large-scale colonial and imperial exploitation of non-Europeans. But we should not discount the ideological power of a widespread agreement about the ultimate ends and purpose of human life. Catholic Spain and Protestant England might disagree on the particular rituals and rites necessary for the salvation of souls, but little disagreement existed on the question of the reality of the soul or the necessity of preparing for eternal life. Human beings had a goal in life and an end — hopefully — in heaven after the Last Judgement.

In terms of the question of the good life, Medieval Christian Europe had more in common with the Ancient Greeks, who, like most pre-Modern civilizations, endorsed the idea of a *telos*, or an end for human beings. How they articulated this as well as the specifics about what constituted the appropriate end varied. For clarification, we can turn to Aristotle, who provides us with some framing arguments. In the *Physics*, he identifies the nature of a thing with its fullest and final development, and internal causal principles push the thing forward toward that end.[28] As he puts it at the beginning of the *Politics* 'the nature of a thing is its end [τέλος]. For what each thing is when fully developed, we call its nature.'[29] Turning to a well-used example, we can say that the end of an acorn is a full-gown oak tree. The acorn is on a natural trajectory to develop into a mature oak tree, though insufficient soil, disease, or predation may prevent it from fully developing. Similarly, human beings have both a nature and a *telos*. Aristotle tells us that the distinctive capacity for human beings consists of *logos*, a very flexible term which ranges in meaning across 'word', 'argument', 'discussion', and 'account'. Fortunately, Aristotle helps with further clarification. *Logos* represents the 'power to set forth the expedient and inexpedient, and therefore the just and the unjust. And it is a characteristic of man that he alone has any sense of good and evil, of just and unjust and the like — and the association of living beings who have this sense makes a family and a state.'[30] This passage packages the Greek perspective in a nicely compressed manner. The distinctive capacity of human beings consists in the ability to argue, to deliberate about right and wrong, and this capacity to deliberate develops within a wider community. The good life for human beings, then, is developing one's rational and communicative faculties within a wider community. Aristotle underlines the necessity of the community a few lines later, noting that

> the individual, when isolated, is not-self-sufficing; and therefore he is like a part in relation to the whole. But he who is unable to live in society, or who has no need because he is sufficient for himself, must be either a beast or a god.[31]

Aristotle's formulation in this passage helps explain the Athenian conception of the relationship of the individual to the wider society—the city to the soul. To reach their fullest form of development, their *telos*, human beings live together in communities and develop their *logos*, or rational capacity. The self finds its origins, development and reaches its end only in the context of others. This is one reason why he defines citizenship in the *Politics* as the act of 'ruling and being ruled in turn.' The process of deliberation and judgment characterizing citizenship allows for a qualified endorsement of democratic elements in his realizable political ideal of a mixed constitution.[32] Full development of the self is difficult and unlikely outside of political community. Aristotle's formulation also clarifies the importance Athenians place in embedding moral guidance in the laws, customs, and traditions of a *polis*. Because of their unavoidable entwinement in our development as human beings, communities have a compelling interest to get them right so they offer proper shaping and guidance. Setting aside the question of guilt or innocence for the moment, the prosecution of Socrates for 'corrupting the youth' appears more intelligible in view of the responsibility of the laws to ensure a space for the self to develop.

   This sense of self represents a much more plastic and permeable conception of human development and nature than usually admitted in liberal thought. The Greek idea of the self develops and entangles itself within community. Liberals imagine the self as standing outside of and antecedent to society, able to disaggregate societal pressures from deeper authentic and perhaps unique desires. Advisors at my university urge students to 'discover their passion', and faculty members to meet their students 'where they are.' High school guidance counselors across the country tell students to consider the range of possible career choices the modern economy offers. The underlying message presents the conception of college, major, career, lifestyle, as one of selection, of choice across a wide range of possibilities—the wider, the better. But a moment's reflection should tell us that things are not so simple. Our choices of where we go to school, our career, what we value in life and so forth emanate not from some abstract position of choosing between many alternatives, but rather from our upbringing, what our parents, peers, and families value. Our choices, in short, are the products of who we are and from where we come. None of this means that our choices are predetermined in any strict sense, but rather that the range of good choices is far more constrained than liberalism often imagines it, and we are far more embedded within our communities than we realize. Determining what a good life looks like means, then, considering oneself in the context of—and as a product of—a particular time and place.

Aristotle's argument that human beings need to exercise and develop their rationality in order to reach their *telos* reflects a broad agreement among Greek thinkers when formulated at this level of generality. The Socrates of Plato's early dialogues best embodies this in his perpetual epistemic agnosticism.[33] In his defense speech in the *Apology*, Socrates repeats the story of the oracle at Delphi, which announced that he was the wisest man in Athens. Claiming not to believe this, he spends the rest of his life testing the veracity of Apollo's oracle, asking people in Athens what they know and how they know it. Socrates discovers himself wiser than the men he questions, but only marginally. As he puts it in his defense speech:

> it is likely that neither of us know anything worth-
> while, but he thinks he knows something when he
> does not, whereas when I do not know, neither do I
> think I know; so I am likely to be wiser than him to
> this small extent, that I do not think I know what I
> do not know.'[34]

Scholars debate how seriously we should take Socrates' claim that he knows nothing. Indeed, he seems, at minimum, an expert in argument and exposing fraudulent claims to knowledge. But what Socrates knows seems less important in dialogues such as the *Apology* and *Euthyphro* than the process of constantly *questioning* what he knows and *how* he knows it. Socrates spends his life not in passive, abstract contemplation, but rather thinking and talking about exactly those characteristics Aristotle identifies with the distinctive human capacity for *logos*: examining and articulating rationales for important human activities. As Socrates himself puts it, 'The unexamined life is not worth living.'[35] The Socrates of the *Apology, Crito, Euthyphro,* and other early dialogues, additionally, refuses to rest secure with any conclusions he reaches in the course of the dialogues. Rather, he remains ready to re-examine conclusions, on the chance that new information or arguments might change his mind.[36] The provisional quality of Socratic knowledge points to the continued necessity of revisiting conclusions we might think are secure and helps explain the restless nature of Socrates' intellectual life, continually honing his arguments and intellect over time. This, for Socrates, moves human beings toward their *telos*.

Socrates' method, as described in Plato's early dialogues, fits well with the democratic ethos of Classical Athens, which valued free speech, deliberation, and discussion, linking these to the production of good citizens and the success of the city. Not all paths in life were considered equal, or equally beneficial for the life of the city, and the citizen's first responsibility was his civic one. As Thucydides has the Athenian politician Pericles emphasize, 'we regard the citizen who takes no part in his duties not as unambitious but as useless [ἀπράγμονα].'[37] Conceptualizing human beings as having a *telos* and linking it to cooperative endeavors in the city, not surprisingly, justifies strong normative (and legal) imperatives to conform.[38]

Taken to an extreme, of course, the Greek position implies or authorizes strict controls on the development of individuals. The clearest example of this comes from the already mentioned *Kallipolis* of Socrates in the *Republic*. There, Socrates and his interlocutors imagine an elaborate system of controls which collectively shape all aspects of the lives of the city's citizens. Premised on the idea that individual people have disparate and varied capacities (and that these are discernible at birth), a strict class system divides the citizens up, assigning a role consistent with their abilities and true desires. Those who are capable of the most demanding intellectual work, after successfully completing a fifty-year educational program, become philosopher-rulers, in charge of administering the city on a rotating basis. Other citizens become soldiers, or work as artisans. Aware of the subconscious effects of art and music, Socrates argues that the city should regulate both, as well as poetry, an important means of conveying cultural norms in the Classical Period. Fearsome images of death or Hades in Homer's *Iliad* or *Odyssey*, for example, would make soldiers cowardly, and so those portions of the text are excised. Similarly, certain forms of music are appropriate for citizens and others not. Socrates speaks of the Lydian and Dorian 'modes' of music, but we can think of the difference between a J. S. Bach canon and the Dire Straits single, 'Money for Nothing.' The discerning reader can guess which one would fall under the ban. The lives of the soldier class are the most regulated; they live together in barrack-like structures which are open to the public. They own no property and are not allowed to touch money to minimize the seduction of privately held goods and wealth.

The philosopher-rulers maintain the regulations of the city through a series of 'useful' falsehoods and tricks. Members of the city are told that their souls contain a mixture of gold, silver and bronze, which the philosopher-rulers know correspond to the relative dispositions of their souls. Those with gold in the souls are the true intellectuals, and are tracked to become philosopher-rulers. Those with silver love honor and competition, and so become soldiers. The lowest class of the city, the artisans, have mostly bronze in their souls, and are dominated by the appetites. They will be happiest acquiring and seeking after material goods. Importantly, each class of the city is allowed to pursue its deepest desires, and so, Socrates argues, what will make them happiest.

Sex and procreation are regulated through a fixed lottery, which only allows the best to breed with the best (Socrates and his interlocutors refer to the citizens as a 'herd,' underlining their selective breeding efforts). Similarly, to ensure emotional attachment to the city as a whole instead of family groups or individuals, residents of the *Kallipolis* are collectively raised and do not know who their parents are. Thus, Socrates argues, the city as a whole makes up a family, and those protective impulses normally directed toward one's immediate family get redirected to the community as a whole.

Not surprisingly, many contemporary liberals take Socrates' *Kallipolis* in the *Republic* as an example of regulation of the self taken to dangerous political extremes. Most famously, philosopher Karl Popper argues the roots of twentieth-century totalitarianism are found in Socrates' city.[39] The Athenians themselves parodied the sorts of ideas found in the *Republic*. Aristophanes' play, *Assemblywomen*, for example, has the women of Athens, disguised as men, vote themselves into power. Once in control, they communize private goods, making the entire city into one large family, sharing meals and using goods from a communal storehouse. Most hilariously, the women attempt to equalize sex, permitting sexual activity between the young and beautiful only after the old and the ugly get theirs. Intriguingly, Aristophanes' play may have been directly responding to Socrates Kallipolis. The *Assemblywomen* dates to 391 BCE, around the same time we think Plato wrote the *Republic*.[40]

As Aristophanes' parody suggests, the Athenians themselves generally rejected the degree of intrusion and control prescribed in the *Republic*, though other city states, especially Sparta, came closer to that model. If an Athenian citizen fulfilled his civic responsibilities, he was accorded some degree of latitude in his private life, as Pericles claims in his Funeral Oration:

> Far from exercising a jealous surveillance over each other, we do not feel called upon to be angry with our neighbor for doing what he likes, or even to indulge in those injurious looks which cannot fail to be offensive, although they inflict no real harm.[41]

Athenian ideas about the good life established a general tone and norms for citizen behavior, setting up markers for judging behavior and encouraging a commitment to the public sphere and wider society. Where the modern liberal leans toward the private life and her own idiosyncratic interests, the Athenian leaned toward the community, and the collective good.

The question, then, is not so much whether an affirmative view of the good life leads inevitably to a totalitarian regime so much as whether neutrality on the question of the good life is both possible and desirable. First off, we should remember that liberal values are plural and in this broad sense, liberalism also imposes a particular idea of the good life, one which privileges the individual and autonomy. Liberalism developed against the backdrop of strong monarchical claims of political authority, and European wars of religion in the Early Modern period. Religious tolerance and pluralism as well as freedom of conscience, for example, begin as a means of mitigating the danger of further conflicts and later harden into rights. Today we allow freedom of speech, religion, association, movement, diversity of opinion, and endorse forms of representative government and accountability. No doubt most of us regard these generally as good things, but we should not lose sight of the fact that they do represent a particular, and historically locatable, set of norms. If your idea of the good life involves living in a society in which women must remain covered when they go out in public, or where children are married off by their parents, or where speech rights are restricted, you cannot do that in a liberal democracy.

Setting aside the formal structure of the state and laws, no society is truly neutral on the question of the good life. Consider the number of messages people receive throughout their lives from friends, family members, religious and educational institutions, not to mention the pervasive reach of advertising and social media. From ideal body types to consumer and career choices, people receive both direct and indirect messages about what to value, what to pursue, and how to live their lives. In most liberal democracies, the default position is for the state to cede this space to the market, allowing people to navigate these choices on their own, remaining formally neutral beyond the important admonition that one's choices and actions should not harm others. Formally, the state has no opinion on the relative merits of differing individual pursuits. So long as I don't get in my car and drive, I am free to drink a pint of whisky and play Grand Theft Auto every night. The utilitarian philosopher Jeremy Bentham, though no liberal himself, influenced the development of liberal ideas of neutrality, ranking pursuits along the lines of the amount of pleasure they generated:

> Prejudice apart, the game of push-pin is of equal value with the arts and sciences of music and poetry. If the game of push-pin furnish more pleasure, it is more valuable than either. Everybody can play at push-pin; poetry and music are relished only by a few.[42]

Were he writing today, Bentham might defend the relative pleasure millions of viewers of 'The Real Housewives of New Jersey' enjoy favorably in comparison with programs on PBS, or readers of Jane Austen novels. But crucially, Bentham *had* a criterion for making this distinction: utility. Liberalism lacks even this, since individual choice, not utility or pleasure, is the standard.

The problem with liberal neutrality seems clear. Some pursuits, careers, decisions simply *are* better than others. We all recognize this at some level. Even a staunch defender of state neutrality on the question of the good life like John Stuart Mill — a student of Jeremy Bentham — recognized that living a good life required some conception of a developmental trajectory, grounding his utilitarian liberalism 'in the permanent interests of man as a progressive being.'[43] For Mill, this meant some form of continuing intellectual development, experimenting with new ideas, and learning from failure.[44] In a memorable aphorism he wrote:

> Thus it is better to be a human being dissatisfied than a pig satisfied; better to be Socrates dissatisfied than a fool satisfied. The fool and the pig might not agree but that is because they only know their own side of the question. The other party knows both sides.[45]

Simply put, Benthamic pleasure is not sufficient for a full life. Human beings require developmental challenges and complexity, not merely pleasure or satiation. Despite this recognition, Mill rejects interference from the state and society, arguing that freedom best promotes human flourishing. Mill's utilitarian arguments for state neutrality on the question of the good life are highly problematic. For one thing, it is not clear that individuals living in non-liberal regimes fail to fully develop, nor is it clear that the space generated for choice within liberal regimes promotes such development. In fact, Greek philosophers would likely argue that state neutrality inhibits the full development of the self. This argument appears most clearly in the different ways in which the Athenians and liberals today understand a fundamental concept, *freedom*.

Scholars generally credit Benjamin Constant, in 1819, with first clearly distinguishing the modern liberal conceptions of freedom from those found in Classical Greece and Rome. Modern liberty, Constant writes:

> is the right to be subjected to the laws, and to be nei-ther arrested, detained, put to death or maltreated in any way by arbitrary will of one or more individ-uals . . . Now compare this freedom with that of the ancients. The latter consisted in exercising collec-tively, but directly, several parts of the complete sovereignty; in deliberating in the public square, over war and peace . . . But if this was what the an-cients called freedom, they admitted as compatible with this collective freedom the complete subjection of the individual to the authority of the community. You find among them almost none of the enjoy-ments which we have just seen form part of the freedom of the moderns. All private actions were submitted to a severe surveillance. No importance was given to individual independence.[46]

Constant argues that modern conceptions of liberty involve the absence of interference with the individual, especially on the part of the state, while the Greeks and Romans saw it as participation in collective rule. Moreover, Constant argues, liberty in the modern sense was entirely absent from the Ancient World. Setting aside the accuracy of this division, we can adopt the labels popularized by 20th century political philosopher Isaiah Berlin, who called these forms of freedom negative and positive, respectively.[47] Berlin follows Constant in seeing Ancient—or positive—liberty as dangerous. And like Karl

Popper, he finds the roots of twentieth century totalitarianism in the Greek concept.

For Berlin, negative liberty, freedom *from,* which he rightly associates with liberalism, involves establishing spaces within which individuals may act or not without coercion from the law. I may or may not join a religion, live on a commune, exercise my right to freedom of speech, and so forth. Thomas Hobbes formulated one of the earliest — and most extreme — versions of it in 1651, defining liberty as 'the absence of external impediments'.[48] Notoriously, Hobbes argues that coercion or necessity does not obviate consent, provided one still has a choice. When passengers on a foundering ship throw their goods overboard in order to reduce the chances of sinking, for example, they do so freely.[49] For Hobbes, the mere possibility of an alternative action makes an act free. Few people accept Hobbes' definition of liberty today, agreeing that significant coercion (and certainly the threat of death or bodily harm) obviates free choice. Hobbesian 'impediments' now refer to laws, and to a lesser extent social pressure. I am not free to drive on the left side of the road in France, though I am able to in Great Britain. As its name implies, a primary goal of liberalism is to minimize the intrusiveness of the state — more laws generally mean less freedom.

Advocates of negative liberty think *what* we do with our capacity to act is less important that preserving the space within which we might act. So long as my activities do not harm others, I may engage in them. We see negative liberties embedded in the legal codes of most liberal democracies. When the First Amendment of the U.S. Constitution restricts the government from prohibiting the free exercise of religion, what is being protected is a negative liberty, in this case, the right to worship (or not) as one chooses. Similarly Article 10 of the 1998 Human Rights Act protects freedom of expression in the U.K. Importantly, negative freedoms are not premised on actions, but rather the capacity *to* act. In generating this space of freedom, individuals can best choose which form of the good life they wish to pursue.

Positive liberty, freedom *to*, by contrast, involves action, and at a deeper level, some capacity to act. Advocates of positive freedom argue negative freedom alone is insufficient. We might, for example, say that a wheelchair bound paraplegic possesses negative freedom to walk: no person or state prevents her from doing this. But this seems absurd, since she clearly lacks the ability to do so; she is not free in any reasonable sense of the word. Similarly, a person with a stutter or severe agoraphobia is not physically or legally prevented from giving a public lecture, but they nonetheless lack the capacity to do so. More controversially, we might argue that an illiterate person in modern society lacks the sort of freedom of the fully educated and literate; lacking certain capacities, the illiterate cannot move about freely in modern society. By restricting freedom to external constraints, negative freedom fails to account for significant other impediments to action which contribute to a more robust understanding of freedom.

Philosopher Charles Taylor helps explain this problem in an often cited example using the Soviet-era East Bloc capital of Albania. Tirana had fewer stop lights than London, so in this specific sense, the Albanian government placed fewer constraints on its citizens. But, again, we would not say that the people in Tirana were more free than those in London; the kind of governmental restriction matters.[50] Positive liberty, then, involves not just concern about the capacity *to* act, but also involves making a choice between relevant actions: ranking them according to their importance. As Taylor puts it, applying any sort of conception of liberty:

> requires a background conception of what is significant, according to which some restrictions are seen to be without relevance for freedom altogether, and others are judged as being of greater and lesser importance.[51]

Critically, while most liberals would acknowledge that we rank freedoms in terms of their importance, their commitment to neutrality on the question of the good life restricts the legal or social operationalization of those evaluations. Human beings need, they argue, the negative liberties of free speech, conscience, association, etc., because how we choose to use those capacities allow us to shape our idea of the good life. But at the same time, liberalism refuses to encourage or foster the development of our capacities to act in these spaces of freedom.

In Book 8 of Plato's *Republic*, while evaluating different regime types, Socrates identifies democracy with negative freedom: 'Isn't the [democratic] city full of freedom [ἐλευθερία] and free speech [παρρησία]? And isn't there license in it to do whatever one wants?'[52] For Socrates, Pericles' boast that Athens allows its citizens considerable freedom to live as they like is not an unadulterated good. Despite the fact that many regard democracy favorably, even as the 'fairest of the regimes', Socrates argues that the democratic conception of freedom fails its citizens in a crucial way. The democratic citizen, Socrates reports:

> lives along day by day, gratifying the desire that occurs to him, at one time drinking and listening to the flute, at another downing water and reducing; now practicing gymnastic, and again idling and neglecting everything; and sometimes spending his time as though he were occupied with philosophy. Often he engages in politics and, jumping up, says and does whatever chances to come to him; and if he ever admires any soldiers, he turns in that direction; and if it's money-makers, in that one. And there is neither order nor necessity in his life, but calling this life sweet, free [ἐληλυθότες], and blessed, he follows it throughout.[53]

Democratic citizens flit from one activity to another without developing and deepening any of their skills. Moreover, they lack the critical apparatus which would allow them to distinguish appropriate from inappropriate ways of life, regarding all of them as equally choiceworthy. For Socrates in Plato's *Republic,* a life guided by true knowledge gained through philosophical inquiry, and ultimately contemplation of the Forms, orients humans to their ends. But we need not adopt Socrates' controversial metaphysics here to see that his critique applies equally to liberal democracy's emphasis on negative liberty and neutrality on the question of the good life.

The size, diversity, and complexity of liberal democracies today effectively rule out the sorts of uniform understandings of the good life we can see in earlier societies. Ancient Athens was small and relatively homogeneous; modern liberal democracies are anything but. Adherence to any one version of the good life would likely threaten many of the liberties we enjoy. But imposing a particular set of ideas regarding the good life is not the only option open to modern societies. Isaiah Berlin implies that a small move away from strict negative freedom opens up a slippery slope toward the political re-education camps of Maoist China or the Soviet Gulag. But we must resist this overly simplistic argument.

We can frequently identify an overlapping consensus that certain practices or choices are problematic or simply bad — individuals and the wider society benefit from their reduction or elimination. Health issues represent the clearest examples of these. Over the past fifty years, rates of smoking have dropped dramatically in most industrialized economies — the result of concerted public health campaigns, increasing restrictions on advertising, and higher taxes. Smoking remains legal in most countries, but the practice is diminishing because our norms surrounding the practice have shifted. In the case of smoking, as with obesity, heavy drinking, and various forms of unhealthy eating, medical studies clearly indicate better and worse choices, making regulation and efforts to direct people toward better choices easier to enact. In other areas, we lack a clear scientific consensus on bad effects even though we might intuitively understand the problem and recognize a need for some form of stronger regulation. Certain forms of pornography, for example, are linked to objectification and violence against women (not to mention unrealistic and often unhealthy sexual expectations). Heavy usage of social media apps is linked to depression and lower self-esteem, especially in teens, but also in the adult population. The wild-west style unregulated free speech zone on the internet has produced dangerous forms of extremism and political division. More broadly, many forms of advertising encourage unsustainable consumption patterns, and contribute to a whole host of environmental problems.

Regulating these latter categories of problems presents real legal difficulties in liberal democracies because restrictions run directly into rights claims. Earlier in this chapter, we discussed the atomizing and isolating effect rights have on societies. Now we can consider their role in regard to a more explicitly political problem. Especially in countries like the U.S. under the current Supreme Court, speech right claims trump almost all other concerns. Natural or human rights are the underwriting concept behind free speech and they act as an effective and powerful ideological barrier between the individual and the state in modern liberal democracies. This presents certain practical problems, such as how to rank conflicting rights claims.[54] But, as political theorist Wendy Brown points out, rights also tend to depoliticize important issues and obscure their own contested — and political — origins.[55] To make a claim that something is a natural or human right is, in effect, to an attempt to eliminate it from political debate and discussion. Rights claims mark off areas into which the state cannot intrude, and that state activity should not violate.[56]

Interestingly, the Ancient Greeks lacked a parallel conception of human or natural rights, the latter of which arguably appears

first in Late Antiquity among Roman jurists and Stoics, and
which more fully develops in the Early Modern period with
thinkers like Jean Gerson, Thomas Hobbes, and John Locke.[57]
Instead, Athenians spoke of citizens having a 'share' [μοῖρα] in
the city, something closer to our conception of a legal right or
privilege today. The share, or privilege, was attached to citizenship, not to one's status as a human being, and so was protected
only within the boundaries of the *polis,* and, of course, did not
extend to all its members, but only adult male citizens. Part of
the reason the Greeks did not think in terms of rights stems
from the embedded nature of the self discussed earlier in this
chapter. A fully developed conception of natural or human
rights requires an antecedent conception of the self—the sort of
self the Social Contract theorists imagined existed in the state of
nature. Only there can we theorize a self with attributes originating in and belonging solely to itself, and not dependent on
the wider society. But, as previously discussed, the Greeks
generally saw human beings as products of the society around
them, and so attributes of the self were either given by the
community, or enmeshed in the social and political realm.
Rights in the strong sense—protections held by the self over and
against the state and wider society—cannot conceptually exist
because the individual comes into being within that society.

Although it may seem obvious, it is worth stating clearly here
that the idea of the self at the root of liberalism seems almost
fantastical. As Aristotle points out, as human beings we find
ourselves always already in society with others. Every step of
our development is mediated by the world in which we live. We
may have rights, but those we hold are generated within,
respected, and enforced by particular states. This realization
alters the unique status rights claims have within liberal
democracies. If these sorts of protections are extended by
societies and states and do not derive from some independent
source, they can be retracted or modified. Rights disputes need
not necessarily lead to impasses on important issues.

All this is not to say that we should eliminate or dramatically curtail rights, only that other collective concerns should have standing when it comes to their implementation. In practice, Athens can serve as a model along these lines. Benjamin Constant was right to say that the Ancient World lacked the sorts of formal protections rights afford us today. In practice, however, Athens seemed to endorse a *de facto* recognition of many important liberties such as freedom of speech and association, as well as a general agreement to allow citizens to live as they like. Certainly there were exceptions.[58] But famous examples to the contrary often prove the rule. Socrates, notoriously executed by Athens in 399, lived seventy years, freely circulating in the city, unrestricted in his ability to question, pester, and embarrass important figures in the city. And when he finally was brought to trial, the actual cause was likely less a matter of his philosophical approach, speech, or beliefs than his association with anti-democratic forces in the city, especially Alcibiades and later the short-lived and brutal regime of the 30 Tyrants.[59]

Liberal democracies today face a host of very real and pressing problems with which absolutist conceptions of rights are ill-suited to deal. Free speech claims in particular demonstrate the stakes. A common assumption among free speech advocates is that the practice yields particular benefits. John Stuart Mill's classic text *On Liberty* is a good example. Incorrect or false claims, Mill argues, will be refuted in a free exchange of information, allowing the truth or best view to eventually come out. Allow people to debate and discuss freely and you get the benefit of understanding your own position better, you are better prepared to navigate complex claims, and eventually someone will get the right answer.

While these arguments seem plausible and intuitively correct, it is actually not at all clear that Mill is right about many of these claims. Take, for example, the problems raised for the free speech argument by the well known tendency toward confirmation bias, where people selectively interpret information or arguments to fit their own pre-existing opinions or beliefs. Free speech is premised on the ability of human beings to rationally (and dispassionately) evaluate the evidence. This capacity — while certainly important — may have been oversold given that we are subject to so many influences, many of which can be quite subtle. And even if only unconsciously, we are — as Plato and Aristotle thought — partly products of the social and political forces around us.

Or consider the fact that while truth, as Mill says, clearly has the advantage of rediscoverability, it is not at all clear that the rediscovery of an obscured truth will appear in a timely manner. Sometimes false speech (whether intentionally so or not) causes real problems. Consider how effective tobacco lobbyists were for decades, or — for a more immediate and pressing example — consider the current confusion in the public regarding climate change or the validity of the 2020 U.S. elections.

We might also consider the fact that free speech arguments first appeared and matured in a very different time period. In the last thirty years, the media and internet have balkanized public debate and discourse. Most people visit websites or chatrooms that reflect their own views and hear little real debate or challenge, but rather see their own positions repeated and reinforced. Individuals with dangerous viewpoints in the past usually found themselves alone in larger communities, which tended to have a moderating influence. Today, though, they can find a sizable group of similarly minded people online. Anonymity licenses and normalizes views people would not otherwise admit to in public, and often shields the worst offenders from consequences. Conspiracy theories can intensify, and political extremism in this sort of atmosphere can move from theoretical discussions to real-life actions, as we all have learned recently. Appeals to rights like freedom of speech seem at best ill suited to deal with this new reality.

The most compelling argument for free speech today concerns the dangers of letting any one person or governmental agency determine what counts as acceptable or unacceptable speech. Even setting aside political and personal biases, it is difficult to know what sorts of speech are actually dangerous. Epistemological humility would have us err on the side of generosity. But this concern needs to be weighed against the very real danger (and demonstrable harm) from unrestricted speech by COVID or climate change deniers, Q-Anon conspiracy theorists, and white nationalists, among others. In these areas where we can find an overlapping consensus on both the danger and falsity of the view, some diminishment of speech rights seems not only reasonable, but crucial. And we can base the restriction on a more embedded or contextual view of the self, something more in line with the Ancient Greek view on this matter.

I want to circle back at the end of this chapter to the advantages of understanding human beings according to the Ancient Greeks, as always already embedded within a social and political matrix, as creatures with a developmental path and *telos*. At a minimum, tempering the basic assumptions of liberalism with the Athenian position would prompt us, as a community, to consider more seriously what it means to live a good life, and what sorts of goals we, as human beings, living together, should pursue. Perhaps we should not leave this development up to the advertisers and social media apps, but rather foster these sorts of conversations both locally and nationally about what we value, and what we owe to one another. This is not, of course, to say that we can either finally resolve these conversations nor can we expect to all agree on a single understanding of what it means to be a human being. But we can certainly exclude or marginalize unhelpful and dangerous views.

Having these conversations as a community has additional benefits. One of the founders of modern conservative political thought, Edmund Burke, was right when he argued that society should not be imagined as a social arrangement into and out of which we can step, but as a different kind of contract:

> Society is indeed a contract . . . not a partnership in things subservient only to the gross animal exist-ence of a temporary and perishable nature. It is a partnership in all science; a partnership in all art; it is a partnership in every virtue and in all perfection. As the ends of such a partnership cannot be ob-tained in many generations, it becomes a partner-ship not only between those who are living, but between those who are living, those who are dead, and those who are to be born.[60]

Liberals would do well to adopt this viewpoint, and think about the individual as always already connected to the past, and having duties to the future. If we think of our selves as liberal individuals, connected to our communities only by virtue of obligations we have taken on, discussions of responsibilities to future generations become exceedingly difficult.[61] The worst effects of carbon emissions, resource consumption, and other forms of environmental degradations lie elsewhere or far off in the future, affecting people to whom we have no relation, or who have not yet been born. Moreover, the real and perceived benefits of individual consumption are immediate and tangible. Only when we see ourselves as morally and communally linked to the future as well as the past can these sorts of duties to the distant or yet to be born come into clear view. Indeed, the liberal sense of self complicates discussion of many of our current social justice conundrums. Consider the issue of race and reparations. Liberals might correctly say that they themselves did not take part in slavery, Jim Crow laws, or other forms of discrimination. As a result, they do not see themselves as obligated to address the issue, let along support reparations or other paths to racial justice. Of course, it is true that white people benefit in measurable ways from systemic and structural racism, but because they have not consented to those systems in any recognizable ways, many do not feel obligated to act to dismantle them.

Real membership in a community always involves more than simply pursuing one's own conception of the good life. Liberalism's one rule against harming others in this pursuit pales in comparison to the challenge we face today, within our nations and across the globe. If human beings are to have hope for the future, we must move beyond the boundaries of the liberal sense of self and neutrality on the question of the good life.

Addressing these problems within liberalism, however, is not simply a matter of theoretical discussion or explication. Changes to the deep structures of liberal democracy—how we think about ourselves, and key concepts like rights and freedoms— requires discussion of actual policies as well. In the next chapters, we turn to some of the key Athenian democratic policies and procedures to see how they lived the theories outlined in this chapter, beginning with the distinctive institution of ostracism.

Chapter Two

Ostracism

On Friday, January 8th 2021, Americans woke up to the news that Twitter had permanently banned Donald Trump from its service. In the announcement, Twitter justified its decision noting 'the risk of further incitement of violence.'[62] Readers will recall that immediately prior to this ban on January 6, following a rally at which Trump spoke, his supporters had stormed and briefly occupied the U.S. Capitol, shocking the nation and threatening the stability of the republic. The stakes were high: President-elect Joseph Biden's inauguration, scheduled for January 20th, was less than two weeks away, and the possibility of further violence was real. Trump, additionally, still held the powers of the office. There was real — and subsequently validated — concern that he and his advisors were considering ways of invalidating the election and keeping his hold on power.

The effect of Twitter's revocation of Trump's account was immediate. Supporters who were used to getting real-time commentary, lies about stolen elections, and sometimes exhortations to action suddenly found themselves cut off. When they tried to access the president's Twitter feed, they could only read the message: 'Account suspended.' Trump's ability to reach out directly to his supporters and mobilize them vanished into the ether. The political temperature of the country dropped markedly, and Biden went on to take the oath of office.

Following Twitter's ban some commentators bemoaned the power of social media companies like Twitter to influence political outcomes so clearly. But it is also likely that had Twitter *not* eliminated Trump's access to the service, we would have seen further instances of political violence both before and after Biden's inauguration. Twitter's action in terminating Trump's account was a form of silencing, of banning. It removed from one part of the political discourse a divisive and potentially dangerous voice. This sort of exclusion of an individual happens rarely in liberal democracies; indeed, contemporary parallels are difficult to come up with. And while there are certainly concerns related to free speech, due process, and the ability of a private company to act so powerfully in the political sphere that need close consideration, we should not neglect the potential benefits associated with this extreme sanction. The Ancient Athenians understood the power of this sort of punishment, and codified it in law. They called it 'ostracism.'

Today we use the word ostracism to describe a form of social exclusion, where the larger group refuses to recognize or interact with an individual, sometimes with damaging psychological consequences for the targeted person. The word has its origins, however, in an Ancient Greek political practice, originating in Athens at the dawn of democracy. Ostracism, or the temporary exile of a citizen, first appears in the late sixth and early fifth centuries BCE in Athens. The term derives from the word *ostrakon* (plural: *ostraka*) the Attic Greek word for a broken piece of pottery, or sherd, on which the citizen would scratch (or paint) the name of the person he wanted removed from the city. Pottery was the primary method of storage and transport for many goods in Athens but, of course, it is also rather fragile. As a result, broken chunks of ceramics littered the streets of Athens; these pottery sherds were the voting mechanism, the ballot, for ostracisms.

Although we have only fragmentary evidence of the ostracisms that took place during the fifth century, several texts from the period clearly describe the procedure for the practice, especially the Pseudo-Aristotelian text *Athenian Constitution*, a

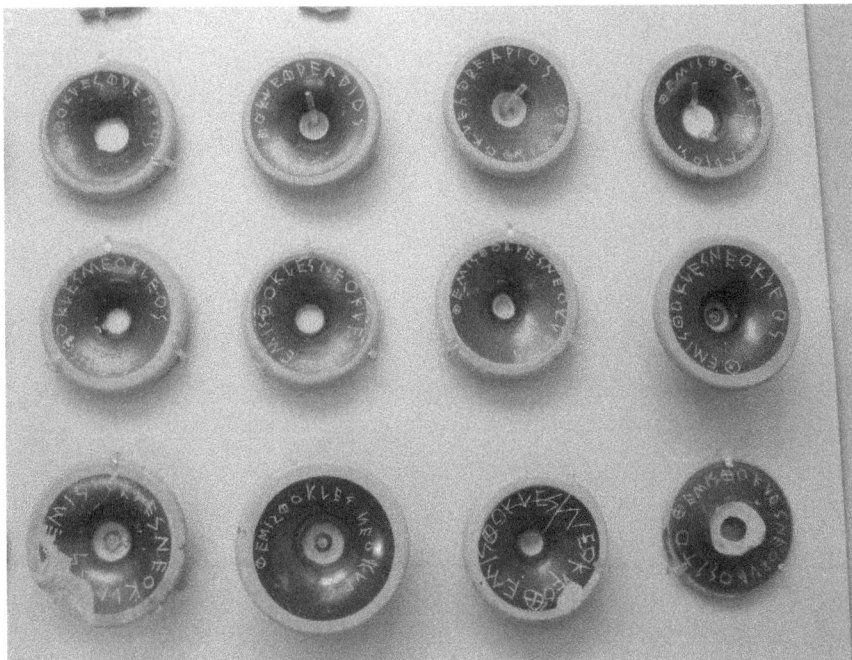

Voting *Ostraka*

Ostrakon of Cimon, an Athenian statesman,
telling his name as 'Kimon [son] of Miltiades'

history and description of the governing laws of Athens. Early each year in mid-January the Athenian *ecclesia*, the main legislative body, also known as the assembly, voted on the question of whether to hold an ostracism. A simple majority vote by hand in favor triggered a second vote two months later (around March on our calendar). The delay between the vote to hold an ostracism and the actual vote itself was probably to prevent precipitous or heated decisions as well as to maximize participation, both important Athenian political goals.

During the time between the initial vote and the ostracism itself, word spread throughout Attica of the coming vote, and individual citizens debated and discussed potential candidates. We do not think Classical Athens had anything like contemporary political parties; most advocacy was likely *ad hoc*, and thus reliant on in-person discussions. But the delay between the announcement of an ostracism, and the vote did leave time for more formal organizing, as indicated by a horde of 190 *ostraka* recently found in a well. All of them had the name 'Themistokles' etched on them, and the writing styles indicate they were prepared by just fourteen people.[63] Since the public nature of ostracism votes makes ballot box stuffing highly unlikely, these were clearly prepared to hand out prior to a vote to those unable to write, thus ensuring their participation in the process. And they may have worked: Themistokles, the famous victorious general at the Battle of Salamis when the Greek fleet defeated a larger Persian force, was ostracized in 471, though it is unclear whether these *ostraka* date from that year.

Normally a vote on an important issue like civic expulsion would take place in an assembly meeting where the Athenians met to decide issues of law and foreign policy. But ostracisms required a special procedure for the vote. Public officials sealed off the main marketplace of Athens, the agora, setting up ten entrances, one for each of the primary political divisions, the tribes, and individual Athenians entered with their inscribed *ostraka* through their tribe's gateway to cast their ballot. The highly stylized ritual of the ostracism vote marked it out from other democratic decision-making processes, and highlighted the drama of the situation.

The agora was a central meeting place for Athenians: a marketplace and a center of discussion, both philosophical and political. During the fifth century, the space held only one central monument, a sculpture commemorating Harmodius and Aristogeiton, two sixth century figures credited with assassinating Athens' last tyrant, Hipparchus. The sculpture was believed to have been set up on the very site of the assassination. Some of our sources, like Thucydides and Aristotle, dispute the details of and motivation for the assassination, but for Athenian democrats, Harmodius and Aristogeiton symbolized resistance to tyrannical and anti-democratic rule in general.[64] It is likely that the statue of the tyrannicides dominated the civic drama of the ostracism, a potent reminder for participants of the importance of the exercise.

A valid ostracism required a minimum of six thousand ballots, though sources disagree about what that number represents. Plutarch reports six thousand as the number for a quorum, while Philochorus states that a minimum of six thousand votes was necessary for a candidate to be ostracized.[65] Philochorus, writing less than a hundred years after the end of Athenian democracy, may have had access to more accurate information than Plutarch, who wrote almost three centuries later. Either way, the number represents a large chunk of the Athenian voting population. Accurate demographics are difficult to come by for this period, but most reasonable estimates would place that number somewhere between one third to one fifth of the total number of voting citizens. The large number of necessary voters ensured both a broad level of democratic participation, and a consensus on the result, as well as insurance against vote fixing.

The 'winner' of the ostracism had ten days to leave Attica or suffer execution. He could take with him his family and any funds or movable property, and neither his property or family suffered formal sanctions if left in Attica. In fact, ostracized individuals could still receive income from properties in Attica while exiled. The sentence of ostracism lasted for ten years, after which the individual could return to the city with his full civic rights restored. We have records of men who did return, and at least one individual, Megacles, returned and was ostracized a *second* time. The Athenian assembly could also recall an ostracized individual for a specific purpose or lift the ban entirely as they did when they recalled Xanthippus and Aristides when Athens was threatened by a Persian invasion in 481 or 480.

Unlike most forms of legal sanction, ostracism was definitely *not* a punishment for violation of a specific law. The legal code in Athens contained provisions for the prosecution and punishment of both ordinary and extraordinary crimes. Accusations of traitorous behavior, for example, resulted in a trial, with permanent banishment or execution as the punishment for a guilty verdict. The law even provided for the treatment of a convicted traitor's bones, which were not allowed burial on Attic soil. Similarly, actual attempts at establishing a tyranny in Athens resulted in either execution for the perpetrator or banishment along with their entire family, as well as confiscation of property. Lesser crimes were punished with execution, loss of citizenship, or fines. The Athenian legal code required individual citizens to prosecute suspected violation of the laws. The accused would then have to defend himself in a formal court trial. By contrast, candidates for ostracism need not have violated a specific Athenian law (though some were accused of crimes). Nor was there a formal prosecution or defense in a law court. Rather, citizens could consider the totality of the individual's actions over time. This marks ostracism out as a distinctive civic practice, and shows that it was designed to address problems which normal criminal laws and associated penalties could not.

Beyond this bare outline of the procedure, we have a series of fragmentary reports and comments, some on the procedure in general, and some relating to specific cases, of which we can definitely identify only nine with certainty, the last of which – that of the politician Hyperbolus – dates to 415.[66] Most scholars agree that while ostracism remained on the books in the fourth century, a different procedure, *eisangelia,* or a formal denunciation of an individual in the assembly or law court, gradually replaced it in practice. Finally, we should also note fragmentary evidence that forms of ostracism were adopted in several other Greek democracies such as Syracuse, Argos, and Megara.[67] And since Aristotle refers to it as a distinctly democratic institution (as opposed to an idiosyncratic Athenian practice), we can safely assume that at least several other democracies during the Classical Period adopted the procedure.

Most scholars date the beginnings of the practice to the traditional birth-date of democracy during the reforms of Cleisthenes in 508/7 BCE, while others place its origins slightly later in the early fifth century in 488.[68] A few ancient commentators even find its origins in the mythical foundation of Athens under Theseus, and there are other mythical parallels to ostracism in stories like Apollonius' *Argonautica,* where 'the Argonauts left Heracles behind … for they feared that he would be too much for the rest of the crew.'[69] In practice, however ostracism originates in the earlier practice of rulers eliminating aristocratic or political competition in their cities. We can find an example of this in Aristotle, who relates a story about Periander and Thrasybulus, the respective tyrants of the Greek city states of Corinth and Miletus. When Thrasybulus sent a servant to Periander for advice, Periander took the servant out into a field and 'said nothing but only cut off the tallest ears of corn till he had brought the field to a level.' The servant had no idea what the message meant, but when it was related to him, Thrasybulus 'understood that he was to cut off the principal men in the state.'[70] Sometimes this meant literally removing the heads of potentially problematic members of the state, but it could also mean exile. So instead of thinking of ostracism as a wholly democratic innovation, we might think of it as a democratic appropriation of the more traditional punishment of banishment or exile, used by tyrants or monarchs to maintain control. Aristotle emphasizes the parallel when he notes that 'oligarchies and democracies are in the same position, for ostracism has in its way this same power of cutting down and banishing the preeminent.'[71]

Like the expulsion involved in banishment, ostracism consisted of the removal of an individual from Athens and its territories but only by a vote of the citizens and only for a defined period of ten years. Ostracism differs from banishment in other important respects. In the Ancient World, banishment relied largely on the whim and word of the monarch, whereas in Athens, ostracism was a collective act of the citizens. Traditional banishment also tended toward the interests of preserving the power of the ruler. It could be employed to remove a potential enemy or source of rebellion or faction within the body politic, but could also be employed in the service of personal vendettas, to seize wealth, or to please a particular individual or group among the nobility. Importantly, banishment fell short of a more final solution, like execution, leaving open the possibility of reconciliation, or reducing the likelihood of permanently alienating the family or faction associated with the exiled person. In this sense, banishment ranks among the less onerous punishments available to rulers in the ancient world, though one ought not underestimate the psychological trauma inflicted, nicely compressed in Bolingbroke's line about 'eating the bitter bread of banishment' in Shakespeare's *Richard II*.[72]

One can easily see how banishment, exercised carefully, might serve as an effective tool in maintaining power in a regime where powerful noble families or individuals might threaten the peace. Aristotle calls it 'not only expedient for tyrants, or in practice confined to them, but equally necessary in oligarchies and democracies.'[73] Exercised for improper 'factious purposes', Aristotle warns, banishment could foster resentment and lead to revolt, as the hapless Richard II learned to his regret.

We can also see connections between the ritual of ostracism and other pre-existing civic practices. Harvard's Classics professor Paul Kosmin, for example, draws some intriguing connections between the action of throwing your *ostrakon* onto the voting pile and stoning, an infrequent but occasional practice in Ancient Athens.[74] Like the ostracized, the bodies of stoning (and other execution) victims were removed from the boundaries of the city to avoid pollution. And *ostraka* frequently contained — in addition to a name — magical curses or symbols, thus linking it with the common casting of lead curse tablets. The act of cutting into ceramic itself was difficult, requiring some degree of force and a sharp, pointed object, thus also implying aggression. In fact, ostracism was sometimes referred to as the *kerameike mastix,* the 'pottery whip' in popular sources. A large number of extant *ostraka* contain names in the dative or accusative cases, pointing toward some sort of aggressive or derogatory pronouncement, now either illegible, lost, or not scratched onto the sherd. Thus an *ostrakon* might have been accompanied by a verbal curse: 'With this sherd I curse Aristides.' We should not view it as surprising that this new civic ritual in a very new democracy borrowed from existing practices to help legitimize it.

Kosmin also points out the symbolism inherent in the civic body assembling with broken sherds of pottery and collectively reassembling them first in a pile and then in a collective civic declaration of exile, signifying the new unity of the polity out of division. Indeed, the initial vote to hold an ostracism signals something wrong in the *polis,* and the second vote itself represents the recovery and reunification of the city.

In its post-classical life, ostracism met with generally negative responses. Many commentators saw the institution as symbolic of the dangers of democratic regimes. The democratic masses, envious of the wealth and privileges of the elite, were unable to recognize the important contribution wealthy and/or aristocratic citizens made to the city, and thus deprived themselves of their advice, counsel, and assistance. An often told anecdote about the Athenian aristocrat Aristides, who was ostracized in the late 480s, has Aristides standing in line to cast his *ostrakon* when a farmer behind him asks if he would inscribe a name on his own pottery sherd, being unable to write himself. Aristides asks what name he would like written and the farmer replies 'Aristides'. Somewhat taken aback, Aristides asks why, and the man replies, 'Because I'm tired of hearing him everywhere called 'The Just'.[75] In the anecdote, Aristides duly inscribes his own name and hands the sherd back to the farmer, thus demonstrating through his actions his own virtue and implicitly condemning the practice. And indeed, some *ostraka* show evidence of a degree of petulance, like one inscribed with 'Agasias, the donkey'[76].

A stronger form of the argument against democracy holds that not only are democrats unable to appreciate the positive virtues of the elite, but they actively oppose their cultivation by imposing a leveling form of political equality as well as a cultural predisposition against expertise and knowledge. As a result, democratic governments were congenitally unable to manage themselves consistently across time, enact wise legislation, or present wholesome models of civic engagement. We can see this attitude in early American political thought, where the much more conservative Roman Republic was the decidedly preferred ancient role model for government. There the power of the masses was curbed, and the people had only a limited voice and role in government. American Founder John Adams, for example, on the subject of ostracism, wrote that

> history nowhere furnished so frank a concession of
> the people themselves of their own infirmities and
> unfitness for managing the executive branch of gov-

ernment, or an unbalanced share of the legislature,
as [ostracism].[77]

In general, criticism of the practice of ostracism paralleled
criticism of the radical nature of Athenian democracy.

Ancient opinion on the practice was only somewhat more
varied, though also largely negative. This is not surprising since
most of our sources for this period are critical of the democracy.
The Athenian historian Thucydides, for example, claims fear
and the insecurity of the democracy drove the practice of
ostracism. And Plutarch, in his biography of Aristides, con-
demns the practice, though he notes that the punishment of
ostracism was relatively mild compared with its possible
alternatives. It was, he writes:

> not a chastisement of base practices, nay, it was spe-
> ciously called a humbling and docking of oppres-
> sive prestige and power; but it was really a merciful
> exorcism of the spirit of jealous hate, which thus
> vented its malignant desire to injure, not in some ir-
> reparable evil, but in a mere change of residence for
> ten years.[78]

More affirmatively, in a discussion of democratic equality in the
Politics, Aristotle notes that the practice of ostracism 'has a
certain political justice to it', and explicitly compares it to the use
of exile by oligarchies:

> Oligarchies and democracies are in the same posi-
> tion, for ostracism has in its way this same power of
> cutting down and banishing the preeminent.[79]

And this gives us insight into the underlying rationale for the
use of ostracism, and why it was such an important democratic
institution. We suspect that Cleisthenes originally introduced
both democratic reforms like opening up public offices to a
larger portion of the population, as well as the law on ostracism
into Athens to constrain his political opponents, who had

oligarchic sympathies and wanted to restrict political power to a small group of aristocrats. By extending various civic rights to the people, or *demos*, Cleisthenes increased his own popularity, and set the stage for a series of reforms that culminated in full-scale democracy by the mid-fifth century. Interestingly, we don't believe Cleisthenes himself used ostracism to rid himself of his political enemies. Rather the threat of the punishment seems to have been enough to control the opposition and dampen the threat of derailing democratic reforms.

Ostracism itself was probably first used in 488, more than a decade after Cleisthenes' likely death, against an aristocrat named Hipparchos.[80] Hipparchos was a relative of the family of tyrants who controlled Athens during the period between 561 and 510, and he was a leader of a prominent conservative faction in Athenian politics, who were generally opposed to Cleisthenes' democratic reforms and friendly with oligarchic governments like Sparta. They were also suspected of having sympathies with Persia, with which Athens was engaged in a power struggle for control of the Aegean and which had recently invaded Greece, and were defeated by the Athenians at the Battle of Marathon.

Hipparchos and his fellow aristocrats were opposed by the popular politician Themistocles, a prominent democratic reformer and later victorious general of the Athenian navy during the battle of Salamis. Among other proposals, Themistocles advocated the dedication of revenue from recently discovered silver mines into the Athenian naval fleet and fortifications. Conservative aristocrats, led at this point by a prominent citizen named Aristides, opposed the use of these funds for the expansion of the fleet. They knew that an expanded navy would represent a tremendous increase in importance for the poorest classes of the city. The Athenians, victorious over the Persians at the Battle of Marathon in 490—less than a decade earlier— fought in hoplite phalanxes, where each soldier was required to provide his own weapons and armor—a considerable expense.

This guaranteed that nearly all soldiers were comfortable members of the Athenian middle class (the very wealthiest could afford horses and thus fought in the cavalry). Themistocles' proposal to expand the fleet meant that the poorest two classes of citizens — and by far the numerical majority — would make up the crews of rowers needed to man the oars; they didn't need armor or weapons, just two strong arms. A Greek warship, a trireme, required about 180 rowers. By the Battle of Salamis in 480, Athens could equip approximately 180 triremes, and in subsequent years the Athenian fleet grew as Athenian domination of the Aegean increased. The growing importance of the navy paralleled growing demands from the lowest class of citizens for increased power in the nascent democracy. It is not an exaggeration to say that while Cleisthenes began the process of democratization, Themistocles accelerated and cemented it by building up the Athenian navy. This growth in power and influence by lower-class members of the city threatened the traditional hold aristocrats like Hipparchos had over the city.

Over a period of about four years during the 480s, Themistocles managed to ostracize not only Hipparchos, but three other powerful aristocratic politicians who opposed his programs as well as further democratic reforms. There is little doubt among scholars that this series of ostracisms was organized by Themistocles but, because ostracisms required substantial citizen-participation, we can also understand this period as the time during which the Athenian *demos* appropriated the power to intervene decisively in elite disputes which threatened to tip the city into violence. Prior to this time period, inter-elite disputes often resulted in the exile of one individual or faction, but exiled members of the community often returned with external help to threaten the city. The Athenians' decision to ostracize Hipparchos and his colleagues including Aristides, represented a decisive moment in fixing Athens' political future. With Hipparchos, Aristides, and others either ostracized or marginalized in the city, further democratic reforms were possible, and

Athens was set on a course that led to victories over the Persians and naval supremacy in the Eastern Mediterranean.

In the hands of the *demos*, ostracism shifted responsibility from one or a few individuals to the city as a whole and made the act of expulsion collective. Compared to older forms of exile, the more moderate terms of ostracism also dampened the possibility that expelled citizens would consider themselves enemies of the city, especially since they retained citizenship, property, and family ties there and – as noted above – a number of the ostracized returned or were recalled to Athens. In brief, ostracism's debut in Athens allowed the *demos* to intervene and decisively resolve both policy and personal disputes between elite members of the polity. What used to be the sole domain of the aristocracy now lay completely within the control of the citizens. It was a major advance for democratic authority in Athens, and it put all members of the aristocracy on notice that the primary faction they had to satisfy was the citizen-body itself.

While ostracism remained a means of controlling inter-elite disputes that threatened the stability of the city, later uses of the practice indicate that the rationale for ostracism expanded, no doubt due to the open-ended nature of the institution: there were no set criteria by which candidates for ostracism could be selected, nor any criteria which prevented an individual from being selected. Despite this lack of formal criteria, however, at least a few *de facto* rules governed its use. Ostracized Athenians were all wealthy, nearly all of them – so far as we can tell – came from aristocratic or noble families, and every one of them had high political profiles. *The Athenian Constitution* tells us that four years after the original series of expulsions associated with Hipparchos, the 'first man to be ostracized not connected with the tyranny was Xanthippus', the wealthy aristocrat and father of the famous fifth century general and politician Pericles.[81] Later ostracisms followed this pattern. So while there was no formal barrier for you scratching the name of your annoying neighbor on your *ostrakon*, in practice unknown or relatively unknown citizens were not viable candidates. Ostracism thus evolved into a method of eliminating potential problems posed to the democracy by the rich and powerful.

It is worth emphasizing that this form of civic penalty worked differently than most other forms of legal enforcement, which tend to affect members of the lower classes dispropor-tionately. Indeed, ostracism solely affected the wealthy and powerful, both as an actuality and a threat. In this sense ostracism was like most other political innovations: designed to control and contain the most potentially dangerous element of the body politic—the wealthy and well-born. As Aristotle puts it, democracies banish those who 'seem to predominate too much through their wealth, or the number of their friends, or through any other political influence.'[82]

Who were the wealthy and powerful individuals affected by ostracism? Lacking precise demographics for Classical Athens, we have to use indirect means to estimate both wealth and its extent. We know, for example, that Athens levied two sorts of taxes on its wealthiest citizens, the *liturgy* and the *eisphora*. Those assigned a *liturgy*—which, typically, required supporting a trireme or chorus in a dramatic festival for the year—came from the wealthiest class, probably numbering between three hundred to twelve hundred citizens in any given year. A more general tax, the *eisphora*, applied to more individuals, maybe as high as six thousand. Athens as a rule *only* taxed very wealthy citizens, and we can think of these two groups as members of the one and ten percent, respectively, though some portion of the *eisphorai* were assigned to resident aliens, or metics (who also paid a poll tax), as well as citizens.

In this context we can also note the long-standing counter-tradition of conservative thought that uses wealth as an indica-tor—even if imperfect—of both moral character as well as the qualities necessary for citizenship and political leadership. Aristotle, for example, points out that wealth provides the opportunity for good education, travel, and other assorted benefits which he argues better prepare the wealthy for political leadership. Plato, Xenophon, Thucydides, and other Athenian thinkers from the Classical Period make similar arguments.[83] The wealthy had what the Greeks called *schole*, or leisure. But unlike its common English translation, leisure, *schole* was not meant simply to indicate free time. Rather, *schole* indicated available time — and resources — used to develop the individual; in this sense, it is closer to its English linguistic descendants: scholar, school, and scholastic. Because they had to labor daily to make enough money to live, the poorer classes didn't have sufficient free time to develop the requisite skills for governing, and hence could be excluded from political participation. This argument, which certainly antedated our Athenian sources, has long echoes in our political tradition. We can see almost identical arguments up to the present day. Edmund Burke, the founder of modern conservative thought, summarizes the argument in florid terms:

> To be bred in a place of estimation; to see nothing low and sordid from one's infancy; to be taught to respect one's self; to be habituated to the censorial inspection of the public eye; to look early to public opinion; to stand upon such elevated ground as to be enabled to take a large view for the wide-spread and infinitely diversified combinations of men of affairs in a large society; to have leisure to read, to reflect, to converse; to be enabled to draw the court and attention of the wise and learned, wherever they are to be found; to be habituated in armies to command and to obey; to be taught to despise danger in the pursuit of honor and duty; to be formed to the greatest degree of vigilance, foresight, and circumspection, in a state of things in which no fault is committed with impunity and the slightest mistakes draw on the most ruinous consequences; to be

> led to a guarded and regulated conduct from a
> sense that you are considered as an administrator of
> law and justice, and to be thereby amongst the first
> benefactors to mankind; to be a professor of high
> sciences, of liberal and ingenious art; . . . These are
> the circumstances of men, that form what I should
> call a *natural aristocracy* . . . A natural aristocracy is
> not a separate interest in the state, or separable from
> it. It is an essential integral part of any large people
> rightly constituted.[84]

In contrast to this line of thought, which emphasizes the importance of wealth and lineage for the state, Athenian democrats recognized these characteristics as always at least potentially dangerous.

The idea that wealth and fame posed a threat to the democracy certainly had its origin in intra-elite disputes over power in the city, which could and did frequently lead to violence or revolution. But Athenians quickly became sensitized to the less overt ways in which wealth and power could endanger their fundamental political commitments. The passage from Plutarch on the ostracism of Aristides, cited above, infers that most Athenians thought of the practice as a 'humbling and docking of oppressive prestige and power.' The key term here is *oppressive* prestige and power. Athenians had no issues with wealth or fame in and of themselves, but they also understood the potential threat these posed to their system of democracy. Among these threats, we can identify a set of interlocking categories.

The first set of problems lies in the sort of psychological power into which wealth translates. Aristotle can help again here with a passage from his *Rhetoric* where he repeats a saying by Simonides of Ceos:

> In answer to Hiero's wife, who asked him whether
> is was better to grow rich or wise, he said: 'Why

rich, for I see wise men spending their days at the
rich men's doors.'[85]

It is a truism that the wealthy or powerful are surrounded by
sycophants and hangers-on, willing to affirm their beliefs,
opinions, and to carry out their wishes. But wealth can also have
subtle effects on people who come into contact with it. At a
minimum, the presence of wealth generates a form of deference
to the holder; citizens might not want to disagree with or oppose
a person in the position to potentially help or harm them in the
future. In more extreme cases, the wealthy can build up a form
of clientism around them by giving out cash payments or
support to friends and political allies, they can create political
and social ties that allow them outsized influence in the political
arena. In Athens, the problem of clientism didn't reach the epic
proportions it did later in Rome, but we do have records of
some notable instances of it. The Athenian aristocrat Cimon, for
example, arguably the richest Athenian of the early fifth
century, provided financial support to his entire *deme*, creating a
set of dependencies which effectively generated a voting bloc for
himself and his policies.[86]

The possession of great wealth does not only affect the poor
and generate sycophancy, of course. It also affects the wealthy
themselves. Aristotle in his *Rhetoric*, gives us a psychological
portrait of the rich worth quoting at length:

> The characters which accompany wealth are plain
> for all to see. The wealthy are insolent and arrogant,
> being mentally affected by the acquisition of wealth,
> for they seem to think that they possess all good
> things; for wealth is a kind of standard of value of
> everything else, so that everything seems purchasa-
> ble by it. They are luxurious and swaggerers, luxu-
> rious because of their luxury and the display of their
> prosperity, swaggerers and ill-mannered because all
> men are accustomed to devote their attention to

> what they like and admire, and the rich suppose
> that what they themselves are emulous of is the ob-
> ject of all other men's emulation.[87]

In this passage, Aristotle makes two claims. The first is that the possession of riches inflates their feelings of self-worth into an extreme and unhealthy form of egotism. Because others defer to them, they mistakenly think that deference is due to their better taste, higher intelligence, or deeper wisdom. In Athens—as in other societies—wealth could lead to acts of hubris. Demosthenes, a fourth century Athenian politician, wrote a speech detailing a series of actions by Meidias, a wealthy political enemy, which culminated in Meidias publicly slapping Demosthenes while he was performing a civic function. Notably, Demosthenes describes the event not as a simple case of assault, but rather as a potential assault on all Athenians:

> For the case stands thus, Athenians. I was the victim
> and it was my person that was then outraged; but
> now the question to be fought out and decided is
> whether Meidias is to be allowed to repeat his per-
> formances and insult anyone and everyone of you
> with impunity.[88]

Meidias' behavior stems from both his high opinion of himself as well as the protection his wealth affords him. We are not sure of the resolution of the dispute, but most scholars argue that instead of facing a trial Meidias settled the case out of court, clearly concerned that his display of *hubris* would not play well with a jury. In an interesting parallel, the oligarchically inclined writer of the *Constitution of the Athenians* warns fellow visiting aristocrats not to strike people in the streets of Athens, because one might accidentally strike a citizen (it is noteworthy in itself that it was sometimes difficult to tell the difference between citizen and slave in Athens), for which they could be charged with assault.[89] Clearly in many of their home cities, their rank and wealth translated into the raw power to assault others, but not in Athens.

The second claim is that wealth also seems to authorize intervention in matters where the rich may actually have no expertise. In contemporary liberal democracies we are no strangers to billionaires attempting to shape or influence public policy and law in areas outside their own expertise. The problem, of course, is not simply that they have an opinion about some law or social policy; many members of a democracy might have similar or competing views. The problem, rather, is that their outsized wealth and the deference other citizens might give them allow them to follow through in enforcing their views in a manner unavailable to nearly all other members of the political community. This eclipses and erodes the bedrock egalitarian principles which underwrite democratic societies.

A related and deeper problem Aristotle raises is that the rich — and perhaps other members of the political community — begin to see wealth as *the* standard of value, displacing knowledge, experience, expertise, and, in the political realm, competing democratic values like equality. Political influence becomes one more thing to buy, and they see no problem with translating their economic power into political power. Oligarchies, Aristotle tells us, are built around a mistaken principle of equality: the rich think themselves unequal in one sense (they have lots of money) and therefore they are or should be unequal in other senses as well, and have proportionately more power in the political realm.[90] But money, as Aristotle points out, is not the standard for political power in a democracy any more than it is in a marathon. Like in a marathon, democracies can distribute awards, distinctions, and power, but only by using an appropriate standard of desert. The fastest runner should win the marathon, while civic honors or prestige should be awarded on the basis of outstanding service to the city, not on the basis of an hereditary title or the accumulation of wealth.

We should finally say a word here about the underlying concept of dignity in democratic societies. It is a fundamental precept of democracies that no one has a natural right to rule over others, and that because of this, each individual should have some role in determining the laws. To the Greeks, this form of self-government marked off a distinctive human capacity, crucial to our flourishing. Furthermore, democracy invests considerable faith in the ability of ordinary individuals to deliberate, debate, and reach good decisions. Aristotle argues explicitly for this capacity, as when he remarks:

> if the people are not utterly degraded, although in-
> dividually they may be worse judges than those
> who have special knowledge, as a body they are as
> good or better.[91]

Each individual member of the citizen body has something to contribute in engaging in debate and discussion over collective self-governance. Accumulated wealth beyond a certain extent has the power to undermine the individual dignity associated with citizenship by minimizing, bypassing, or erasing the capacity to participate. Ostracism was an effective mechanism of reasserting that dignity as well as the power of the *demos,* even in the absence of a clearly violated law. We can see evidence of this in an *ostrakon* from the case of the aforementioned extremely wealthy Megacles, who had a habit of displaying his wealth prominently. On the pottery sherd is written 'Megacles *and* his horses.'[92] Horses were a signal of wealth and privilege in Athens, and Megacles evidently paraded his around just a bit too much for at least this one citizen. Another intriguing pair of sherds come from a vase which originally had the words *megakles kalos* (Megacles is beautiful) inscribed on it. The clear possibility is that the vase was intentionally broken for the ostracism, and the vase Megacles had commissioned for his own political aggrandizement was weaponized against him.[93] A fourth century speech by Demosthenes provides clearer evidence for this point. 'When they caught Themistocles presumptuously setting himself above the people', he writes in a court speech, 'they ostracized him from Athens.'[94]

Of course, Athenian democrats are not the only thinkers who saw a problem in large inequalities of wealth. Machiavelli, writing about two millennia later in the *Discourses* for example, notes that 'corruption and slight aptitude for free life arise from an inequality.'[95] And Jean-Jacques Rousseau was right to promote a general rule that 'no citizen shall ever be wealthy enough to buy another and none poor enough to be forced to sell himself.'[96]

Today in the United States we face wealth inequalities and concentrations not seen in over a century. As of this writing, just three men—Jeff Bezos, Bill Gates, and Warren Buffett—hold more wealth between them than the entire bottom half of the population, and if you pan out from those three to include the richest five percent of Americans, that group holds as much wealth collectively as two-thirds of the rest of the population. It is hard to conceptualize the financial resources controlled by someone like Jeff Bezos (currently estimated at one hundred and fourteen billion dollars), but we can get a sense of the scope of the problem by looking at other measurements. Although salaries are an imperfect indicator of inequality because they do not account for accumulated family wealth, consider the fact that the average employee works for over a month for what an average CEO earns in an hour.

One might think that because of the wealth associated with the Athenian empire, rates of inequality then would be similar to those in the U.S. today. But compared to Classical Athens, the United States today is incredibly unequal. One estimate dating to 321 BCE of the distribution of wealth for Athens shows the top ten percent owned about sixty percent, while the top one percent owned about thirty percent.[97] This is roughly parallel to levels of inequality in the United States in the mid-1950s, when the distribution of wealth was broader. As researcher Geoffrey

Kron puts it, this makes Athens 'not quite Scandinavian, but more like Canada.'

Wealth in the U.S. is not only dramatically unevenly distributed across the population as a whole, it is also unevenly distributed by a number of other important metrics, like race and gender. Between 1984 and 2019, for example, the wealth gap between white and black families quadrupled, and important indicators like household ownership are heavily skewed toward white families. But even within white families, the gap between men and women is large, with men holding on average three times more retirement savings than women. Similar disparities exist between white and Hispanic families and we could break down further inequalities along gender lines.

This wealth inequality translates into substantially disproportionate civic and political power. Like democratic Athens, citizens of the United States are supposed to be equal under the law, but this slogan is much more of an ideal than a reality. From being able to afford legal counsel to having one's voice heard in the halls of Congress or in state capitals, the rich really *are* different from everyone else.

In one recent influential study, political scientists Benjamin Page, Larry Bartels, and Jason Seawright show that the political preferences of the wealthiest one percent of the population rank far more conservatively on both social and economic issues than the general population. One-percent individuals are also much more politically active than the average citizen. The study demonstrates that this difference accounts for nearly all the disparity between the policy preferences of the majority of U.S. citizens and what winds up enacted into law and put into administrative rules.[98]

Martin Gilens and Benjamin Page of Princeton University showed in a 2014 study that 'economic elites and organized interest groups play a substantial part in determining public policy, but the general public has little or no independent influence.'[99] Here the group measured was the 90th income percentile and showed that only when the interests of average citizens and the economic elite align are policies favored by the middle and lower-class put in place or laws passed.

Like in Athens, the problem lies not so much in wealth and inequality itself, but rather in the undue and, by some measures, nearly complete control of the political process. The mechanisms for this control are many: lobbying and advocacy groups, disproportionate influence and coverage in the media, campaign contributions and related expenditures, agency capture, and so on. Some effects are quite subtle. Athenian democrats used to worry about their political leaders being bribed by wealthy outsiders, especially the Persian monarch who had nearly unlimited resources at his disposal. Today in the United States outright bribery rarely ranks as a problem. Instead we see a system where the knowledge that lucrative jobs are given to politicians or bureaucrats after leaving office, where massive political expenditures by nominally independent groups can swing elections even at the local level, and where substantial control of the news media often effectively stifles the ability of Americans to see the truth. As a result, politicians and bureaucrats shape their policies with elite preferences in mind, even if only subconsciously. The gravitational pull of money warps our political discourse, laws, and legislation.

We cannot imitate the Athenian tool of ostracism in contemporary America. Besides the obvious constitutional and legal prohibitions, leaving a country does not have the same effect today as it did in Ancient Athens. Today, one does not have to reside in a country to influence its politics, as Putin's Russia so clearly shows. Similarly, as long as economic borders are porous, the influence of wealth and money will not respect national boundaries.

But there are actions we can take short of ostracism that address the root cause of much of the problem: the permeability of the political realm to money.

Direct and indirect campaign contributions represent one of the clearest targets for mitigating the effects of wealth. Simply put, the wealthy can contribute far more to political campaigns than the average citizen. Even with limits on individual donations, the rich can afford to support more candidates, and can pour unlimited money into nominally non-partisan interest groups which clearly support one candidate or issue.

The Federal Elections Commission currently limits individual contributions to federal candidates to $2,800. This seems like a lot, and it is certainly more than most people can afford. But it pales in comparison with other sorts of possible campaign-related contributions. Individuals can contribute $35,500 to national party committees' main accounts, and an additional $106,500 to special convention accounts. To national party committees' party building accounts they can contribute another $106,500. Add in another $15,000 for state or local party committees and federal PACs. This means the direct campaign-related contributions are 'capped' at $324,500 plus $2,800 per candidate. For many workers, that amount represents a lifetime of earnings, but it is not even the actual amount that one can expend.

If we add in 501c corporations, many of which act effectively as campaign arms for the two main political parties, donation levels are essentially unlimited. What does it say about our democracy when one individual can give more for one campaign than the average person could give over an entire lifetime?

This outsized influence means that one individual can effectively shape an entire campaign or debate on a particular issue.[100] On issues of great public interest, large-scale grass-roots contributions and engagement can make up for this disparity, but many — if not most — issues of law and policy do not rise to this level of interest for the general public, thus leaving a small subset of the monied class free to control outcomes.

Opponents of restricting campaign and other political contributions often equate these contributions with free speech. A financial donation, they argue, is the equivalent of speech and under the U.S. Constitution cannot be regulated, and certainly not restricted by the government. This is the position the U.S. Supreme Court has been moving toward since their 2010 Citizens United decision, which prohibited the government from restricting independent campaign expenditures. Put more abstractly, what opponents of campaign contribution limits are claiming is that when we have a conflict between freedom and equality, freedom trumps equality. But we should note here that freedom does not just trump equality here, it obliterates it. Freedom to speak should not mean the freedom to dominate others.

Clearly, extensive reform is needed in this area to reign in the power of wealth and money in the public sphere. A change in the make-up of the Supreme Court could allow for an overturning of Citizens United and other decisions which treat money as speech. A constitutional amendment clarifying the role and scope of speech in the United States could also open up a wide range of legislative options to control the power of money in politics.

Another way that money finds its way into politics and warps our basic democratic principles is through lobbying (aka 'sleaze'), and here we face a parallel problem to the one we face with individual donations. Individuals, of course, can lobby, but a far bigger problem here are the registered and unregistered lobbyists who not only have an outsized say on the laws themselves, but also on the rules guiding their implementation, which rarely garner enough public interest to counter corporate interests.

We can also attack the effects of wealth inequality on politics more directly by reducing accumulated wealth through taxation. Athens itself, of course, did not attempt to directly reduce the financial holdings of its wealthiest citizens, but was instead concerned with ensuring political, not economic, equality. But, as the passages from Aristotle cited above indicate, the Greeks were aware of the strong connection between wealth and political power. Aristotle, in fact, recommends maximizing the size of the middle class, which he sees as a sobering influence on a regime; large inequalities in holdings raise the risk of instability.[101] Reducing the wealth-gap between the richest and middle class is one way to achieve this. In 1942 the top tax bracket in the United States was set at ninety-four percent on income over $200,000 a year ($2.5 million in today's dollars). Although rates fell slightly after the World War II, top rates did not decline below seventy percent through the 1970s. Today, though, top marginal tax rates cap out at thirty-seven percent, but because of tax shelters and deductions, the actual *taxed* rate is much lower. For the top one percent of earners the effective tax rate is just twenty-nine percent, and for the highest quintile, as low as twenty-four percent.

The high tax rates of the 1940s were an artifact of costs associated with World War II, but we have similar substantial challenges today, such as global warming, decaying infrastructure, and a healthcare system that is unequally distributed and subject to unneeded bureaucratic costs. Revenues from returning rates to their pre-1970s rates would do much to address these collective challenges in addition to reducing the concentrated power of wealth in the United States.

Several candidates in the 2020 Democratic primary field proposed special taxes for accumulated wealth — in addition to payroll taxes. Senator Elizabeth Warren, for example, wants a flat two percent yearly tax on wealth over $50 million, and one percent on wealth over $1 billion. Another approach was taken by Senator Bernie Sanders, who proposed legislation that would limit stock buy-backs. Stocks are owned disproportionately by the wealthiest Americans. The richest one percent of Americans own forty percent of publicly traded shares, and the top ten percent own eighty-five percent of shares. Stock buy-backs have the effect of transferring wealth dramatically upward. Either of these approaches are good starts, but we would need to go further.

Another way of diminishing the influence of wealth is to increase the estate or inheritance tax. Like the payroll tax, estate taxes today are at low levels relative even to the recent past. In 2013, for example, a forty percent tax was imposed on estates holding over five million dollars. Today, though, estates of up to twenty-three million dollars are completely exempt from taxation, and anything over that amount gets taxed at forty percent. As New York University Professor Lily Batchelder points out in a June 24, 2020 *New York Times* editorial, at this rate, a family with an estate of fifty million dollars would have an effective tax rate of just twenty-one percent, and that's without factoring in any tax shelters built into the estate tax, which could easily bring the liability down to zero.[102] Why would we tax inherited wealth at a rate higher than earnings from wages? If anything, the tax code should encourage work.

Batchelder argues persuasively for an optimal estate tax rate between sixty and eighty percent.[103] This would encourage charitable giving and work by heirs to large estates, both beneficial effects. Better yet, we should just tax inheritances like normal income above a certain floor, say, one million dollars.

Cutting off the flow of money into politics does not banish the wealthy and powerful from politics. The point is not to eliminate wealth but to vastly reduce its power to effect changes to legislation and policy.

Chapter Three

Sortition and the Deep Resources of Citizenship

The 2020 U.S. federal elections sent a record number of women and minorities to serve in the U.S. Congress. Among other achievements, Georgia elected its first Black U.S. senator, Raphael Warnock, and California appointed its first Hispanic U.S. Senator, Alex Padilla. Beneath the headlines, news articles filled in the details of demographic and cultural shifts that influenced the results. But anyone looking a bit further at the numbers could see that, despite impressive gains in representation, numbers of women and non-white groups remained well below their proportionate representation in the overall population. Women make up fifty-one percent of the population of the United States, but their share of the seats in the U.S. House of Representatives and the U.S. Senate hovers around twenty-five percent. White, non-Hispanic Americans account for sixty percent of the U.S. population, but hold seventy-seven percent of the seats in Congress.[104] The race and gender gap between political representatives and the general population masks wider and perhaps more significant differences. Financially, for example, U.S. Representatives and Senators are very different from the general population. The average U.S. Senator is forty times richer than the average American, with Members of

Congress having only a somewhat smaller financial advantage. America's politicians are whiter, far richer, and much more likely to be male than the rest of the population.

One might argue that there is nothing wrong with this distribution. After all, Members of the House and Senate hold their offices ostensibly to represent all their constituents, not a particular gender, race or income grouping. And if they fail to adequately represent their states or districts, they can be voted out of office. But a more in-depth look at legislative and policy outcomes suggest otherwise. A much-cited 2014 study by political scientists Martin Gilens and Benjamin Page concludes that average voters have little to no influence on public policies in the U.S. and that the agenda and policy outcomes are largely shaped by elite preferences—matching the interests of the dominant groups in state and federal legislatures.[105] Average voter preferences are generally enacted only when they correspond to elite preferences. Whether intentionally or not, many politicians err in favor of interest groups that seem like themselves and their social and economic peers. This should come as no great surprise to any followers of politics in liberal democracies: John Locke, the intellectual godfather of American constitutionalism, notes that even with the best intentions, 'self-love will make men partial to themselves and their friends.'[106] But while Locke, like James Madison in the *Federalist Papers*, thought that self-interest and self-dealing could be contained through constitutional checks and balances, apparently the best outcome most voters can hope for is a sort-of benign paternalism from the elite. More realistically, as long as representation lags behind population changes, we can expect legislative and policy outcomes that favor the wealthy, those from the dominant racial group, and men.

Part of the problem here rests with liberal democracy's reliance on elections to fill legislative positions. Though relatively new in historical terms, the ballot box now stands in as a proxy for democracy itself. Internationally, even many clearly corrupt regimes feel the need to go through the effort of holding a rigged election to create the appearance of legitimacy.[107] Jean-Jacques Rousseau, a critic of representative democracy, sums up the problem neatly:

> The English people believes itself to be free. It is greatly mistaken; it is free only during the election of the members of parliament. Once they are elected, the population is enslaved; it is nothing. The use the English people makes of its freedom in the brief moments of its liberty certainly warrants their losing it.[108]

Actual democratic practice, however, has deep resources in its history. Reducing democracy to occasional elections obscures more broad-based methods of translating the will of the people into concrete laws and policies. In this chapter we move beyond elections as a means of filling public offices with a look at the Athenian practice of sortition, or selecting officials by lottery.

Athenian democrats took a nuanced view of elections. As in modern liberal democracies, elections in Athens favored certain groups: the rich, the famous, the aristocratic elite, and those already in office. And like today, those four categories often overlapped. In this sense, elections in the ancient word tended to preserve and extend already existing power, creating de facto restrictions on those without it, especially the poorer classes of the city. As a result, Athenians viewed elections with suspicion and limited their use to major military positions (the ten annually elected *strategoi*, or generals), and several other officials, such as the supervisor of the city's water supply, and financial officials like the controllers of the Theoric Fund, which held monies designated to oversee Athenian festivals like the City Dionysia. The specific offices subject to elections change over the fifth and fourth centuries, with a limited growth in the number of elected positions over time, but they are always a small fraction of the total number of public offices.[109] Aristotle argues elections aim at finding the best or most skilled candidates, and so Athens reserved them for positions requiring special technical abilities, experience, or leadership capacities.[110] This explanation seems reasonable given the positions requiring election in Athens.[111] The decision of whom to follow into battle, for example, was clearly an important one, hoplites fighting in a phalanx needed to personally trust their leaders; a lottery could not ensure the selection of an officer others would follow. Oversight of the Theoric Fund, similarly, required a specific skill set and trust from the general population. But these elected positions represented the exception, not the rule, and we should see them as running counter to widespread democratic conceptions of equality. Aristotle makes this plain in Book IV of the *Politics*: 'the appointment of magistrates by lot is thought to be democratic, and the election of them oligarchical.'[112] This is not to say Aristotle thinks elections have no place in democracies. Indeed, concerned with what he sees as potential instability in radical forms of democracy, he recommends the institution of elections as a counter-weight to the democratic emphasis on equality. Imagining most existing cities on a continuum between radical forms of democracy and extreme oligarchies, he advises democracies to make their regimes less extreme by introducing elections, or limiting the persons eligible for election, or even limiting those eligible to cast a ballot. These restrictions, he thinks, makes the regime more stable and approach his realizable ideal of a mixed regime, or polity.[113]

As indicated by Aristotle above, however, democracies like the one at Athens relied on sortition — or a lottery — to distribute almost all political offices instead of elections.[114] Like most Greek institutions, sortition finds its beginnings in older traditions, customs, and narratives. The *Iliad* locates the use of lots in the very origins of Olympian control of the cosmos. In Book 15, during a fit of anger at Zeus' commands, Poseidon recalls that after their victory over their father Chronos and the Titans, he, Zeus, and Hades drew lots for control of the cosmos.

Zeus drew the heavens, Hades the underworld, and he himself the seas.[115] This mythological use of the lot implies both its use to prevent disputes as well as (in the mind of Poseidon, at least) equality between the three gods. Mortals in the epics use chance similarly to aid in difficult decisions. In Book 7 of the *Iliad*, for example, the Greeks at Troy meet Hector's challenge to fight one on one initially with fear. When noone steps forward to fight, they use a lottery to decide which of them must face Hector in single combat:

> So he spoke and each of them marked a lot [*kleron*] as his own one lot / They threw them in the helmet of Atreus' son, Agamemnon. / And the people, holding their hands to the gods, prayed to them. / Then would murmur any man, gazing into the wide sky: / 'Father Zeus, let Aias win the lot, or else Diomedes, Tydeus' son, or the king himself of golden Mykenai.'[116]

In Homer, the Greeks associate the use of a *kleros* here not just with random chance, but with divine intervention, and the selection of Aias seems to validate that assumption.[117] The lottery stones here 'leap' [*ethore*] out of helmets, as if with a will of their own, responding to the urging of the god, and the selection of his lot consequently boosts Aias' courage.[118]

A similar use of *kleros* stones occurs in the *Odyssey*, when Odysseus divides his men into two groups and sends one of those groups to explore Circe's island. Recently scarred by their experiences with the Cyclopes and the Laistrygonians, the crew is terrified of what they might find.

> We shook lots in a helmet made of bronze; / Eurylochus' lot jumped out (*ethore kleros*). / So he went with his band of twenty-two, all weeping. / Those left behind with me were crying too.[119]

In both the case of Odysseus' crew and the Greeks at Troy, the lottery stones mediate a frightening situation with the implication of divine guidance: Aias, the most physically powerful warrior on the Greek side is chosen to fight Hector, and Odysseus stays behind to rescue his crew once they fall prey to Circe.

Later tradition continues the connection between casting lots and the divine. Petitioners approach Apollo's oracle at Delphi in an order determined by lot, and even the priests attending the priestess, or Pythia, may have been selected on the basis of a lottery, though the specifics are uncertain.[120] Some evidence also suggests that the decisions of oracles themselves might have employed lots to determine the will of the gods, a process referred to as cleromancy.[121] This connection between divinity and chance stretches back at least as far as Hesiod, who mentions the birth of the goddess Tyche, luck or chance, from the union of Okeanos (Ocean) and the nymph Tethys,[122] and Pindar calls her a daughter of Zeus and 'savior'.[123] Later, Greeks of the fourth century reified chance or luck in the cult of the goddess Tyche, which spread widely across the Mediterranean by the Hellenistic Period.[124] In Plato's *Laws*, the Athenian Stranger links 'God and good luck' (θεόν καὶ ἀγαθήν τύχην) explicitly with the use of sortition in governing.[125] The use of this practice in political affairs in Athens may have remained linked to the divine, though later evidence for this is scanty, and opposition was not necessarily seen as blasphemous.[126]

Political use of sortition provoked philosophical controversy. Both Socrates in earlier dialogues by Plato and Xenophon as well as the Athenian Stranger in the *Laws* level critiques against the use of lotteries, but in the *Laws*, Plato's last dialogue, we also see a qualified endorsement of their limited use as a means of reducing the potential for civic violence or discontent. In making this endorsement, the Athenian Stranger recommends the 'equality of the lot' (τοῦ κλήρου ἴσῳ) 'because of the peevishness of the many'(δυσκολίας τῶν πολλῶν).[127] We will return to the question of critiques of sortition later in this chapter. But first, we need to consider how sortition in Athens worked, and how the Athenians justified it.

The Aristotelian *Athenian Constitution* locates the origins of the lot as early as the late seventh century in the law code of Dracon, where one of the major organs of government, a *boule*, or council of 401 individuals was selected by lot (κληροῦσθαι) from citizens over the age of thirty. The superseding constitution of Solon possibly extended its use to the major executive office of the archonship, with financial restrictions on eligibility in the early sixth century, though this may also have happened as late as the 480s under the leadership of Themistocles.[128] In either case, a pre-selected pool of ninety citizens (ten from each tribe) made up the candidate pool for nine archon positions. We have only later reports about the law codes and reforms of both Dracon and Solon, but even if the legislative specifics lack reliability, both men likely instituted limited use of lotteries to defuse competition between elites for important political positions, thus potentially preventing violence. In fact, elections were sometimes seen as a cause of revolutions, as Aristotle notes, and the introduction of the lottery reduces the risk of civic turmoil.[129] In Solon's case, the turn to sortition to decide on archons replaced an earlier practice of the Areopagus Council appointing the positions, thus depriving this institution of significant power, and simultaneously dampening potentially factious results.[130] Mere chance replaced favoritism and candidates understood they had an equal chance of selection. Winning or losing no longer indicated inferiority, but rather ill luck.

Defusing elite competition proved a major benefit of sortition. The introduction of the lottery also lessened elite power, as Josiah Ober notes, making it harder for aristocratic families to predictably control offices.[131]

While sortition antedates the establishment of democracy, it was not widely or consistently in use until after the first third of the fifth century. The fragmentary nature of our sources prevent full knowledge of the growing practice, particularly early in the democratic period, but a reasonable time-line would show continued increases in its use through 403, by which time Athenians distributed nearly all political offices via sortition. Indeed, Herodotus — writing in the mid-fifth century — imagines a debate in Persia over which form of government to adopt after the overthrow of the monarchy. The advocate for democracy, Otanes, argues:

> The rule of the multitude [πλῆθος] has in the first place the loveliest name of all, equality [ἰσονομίην] and does in the second place none of the things that a monarch does. It determines offices by lot [πάλῳ], and holds power accountable, and conducts all deliberating publicly. Therefore I give my opinion that we make an end of monarchy and exalt the multitude, for all things are possible for the majority.[132]

As an indication of the relative novelty of the practice, the term translated here as 'lot' in Greek is *palos* [πάλος], which is an echo of the Homeric usage discussed earlier of a marked stone or pebble cast from a shaken helmet, rather than the more common term in Athens, *kleros*. Regardless of how quickly the practice was adopted, by the last part of the fifth century Athens employed the lot widely. M. H. Hansen estimates that in the fourth century Athens filled 1,100 civic positions each year by lot: 500 for the *Boule*, or Council, and some 600 others. By contrast, only 100 positions were filled by elections.[133] The *Athenian Constitution*, dating to the second half of the fourth century, reports:

> The holders of all routine offices in the *polis* are selected by lot except for the treasurer of military funds, the controllers of the Theoric Fund, and the supervisor of the water supply. These are elected ...

all military officials are also elected ... the *Boule* of
500 members is also selected by lot.[134]

We know something of the selection process for three types of
offices – those of the archons, the *Boule,* as well as jurors for the
courts. And in proportion to the importance of the office, the
selection procedure varied in complexity. For the office of the
archonship, or the nine highest political positions in Athens who
oversaw the courts and festivals, the procedure was a form of
double sortition. The initial selection was made in each of the
ten *phylai,* or tribes.[135] Each *phyle* chose ten citizens by lot, and
those names were then sent on to the city, where a second round
of sortition selected one from each of the ten groups, with the
tenth selected individual serving as secretary to the *Thesmothetai,*
the board of six archons selected to oversee the courts.[136]

Originally in charge of the executive, military, and civic-
religious festivals, prior to the fifth century archons in Athens
were elected by and from the aristocracy. Gradually their
responsibilities and control over those three areas was reduced,
or eliminated entirely, as in the case of the Polemarch, the
archon originally in charge of the military. In Classical Athens,
these positions were largely administrative, but still highly
prestigious and coveted offices. After serving their year in office,
former archons joined the Areopagus Council, which oversaw
homicide trials in the fifth century, plus other supervisory
responsibilities in the fourth century.[137]

In order to ensure the legitimacy of this office, Athens shifted
the selection of archons to a double sortition. This made it
effectively impossible for any one person or family to ensure
control of the office, despite the fact that in the first half of the
fifth century the office was open only to members of the top two
economic classes, the *hippeis* and the *pentacosiomedimnoi.* The
lottery also eliminated the effectiveness of bribes or lobbying for
access to the position, and the randomness of the selection
process may have reduced resentment of or resistance to
winners. In 457/6 the office was effectively opened up to

members of the middle-class when the *zeugitai* became eligible to serve, thus vastly expanding the pool of acceptable candidates.[138] The long-term history of the archonship describes, then, an office which shifts from an elite power center to a broadly available administrative position, and one which ensures no one person or family continued control or influence.

We also know some things about the selection of members of the *Boule,* or Council—the administrative magistracy which set the agenda for the *ecclesia.* Probably created to protect the interests of the *ecclesia* against older more elite institutions like the Areopagus Council, this large body of five hundred citizens consisted of fifty members from each tribe, each selected by lot for a one-year term at the deme level.[139] How this happened at the deme level is unclear. In a reasonable inference, P.J. Rhodes imagines *demarchs* – deme officials - recruiting from citizen lists, which were housed in the demes.[140]

Members of the *Boule* took turns serving on a committee, the *prytany,* which sat in more-or-less permanent session on non-festival days of the year (roughly 250 days). The *prytany* dealt with pressing day-to-day matters, some issues of foreign policy, and oversaw financial matters. Most importantly, it brought matters to full meetings of the *ecclesia.* The presiding officer of this body, the *epistates ton prytaneon,* was selected daily by lot. In the fourth century, if not earlier, this latter office was selected by double sortition, like the archons. The *Athenian Constitutions* offers a brief description the complex process:

> One man is picked as chairman of the Prytanies by lot [εἷς ὁ λαχών], and holds office for a night and day; he cannot preside longer, nor can the same man serve twice ... When the Prytanies summon a meeting of the *Boule* or *Ekklesia,* he casts lots for the nine chairmen, one from each tribe except the one supplying the Prytany; he casts lots [kleroi] again among the nine for the man who will actually preside, and he hands over the agenda to them.[141]

Athenian citizens could serve at most twice on the *Boule*, and only once as its presiding officer.[142] These restrictions ensured both broad representation and widespread participation. We should note that Athenians did not have a mathematical understanding of representation and proportionality like statisticians do today. But the elaborate and stratified nature of the sortition process indicates a clear intuitive grasp of this concept. One of the goals was clearly to sample as representative a portion of the population as possible.[143] As an indication of how deeply the *Boule* reached into Athenian life, even Socrates, who famously avoided serving in public office, served at least once on the *Boule* in 406.[144] Hansen estimates that in the fourth century every other citizen served at least once on the *Boule*. Even more surprisingly, approximately a quarter of the citizens served as *epistastes ton prytaneon*, effectively making them head of state, if only for a day.[145]

The complete annual change of *Boule* membership prevented it from devolving into an institution where power resided in the members, instead of the institution itself. As Richard Mulgan points out, the rotating nature and breadth of the membership of the *Boule* helped ensure that its actions reflected the will of the *ecclesia*, and likely prevented it from acquiring an autonomous sense of direction and purpose.[146] In this sense, it differed from other similar institutions in the ancient world like the Spartan *gerousia* (Council of Old Men), or the Roman Senate, both of which had life-long members, and both of which effectively checked the power of other institutions.

In addition to the controls offered by the fluid nature of *Boule* membership, Athenians placed other clear limits on the power of this body. A fragment of a *stele* found on the Acropolis lists a number of restrictions specifically in relation to the *ecclesia*. Among these are decisions of war and peace, impositions of fines, and *atimia* or a form of public disenfranchisement, all of which are powers retained exclusively by the *ecclesia*.[147] Not only was the *Boule* to be representative of the Attic deme structure, it was also clearly designed subordinate to, and reflective of, the *ecclesia*.

While the *Boule* was large, it paled in comparison to the size of the pool of potential jurors needed for the law courts: 6,000 citizens.[148] These Athenian courts met regularly. Hansen estimates the number of meeting days per year somewhere between 175 and 225, so the courts were by far the most regular and prominent sign of Athenian civic life and democracy, and arguably the most important.[149] Juries typically ranged in size from 201 or 401 for financial cases, to 501 for public prosecutions. But we have records of larger juries of 1,001, 1,501, 2,001, and 2,501.[150] Andocides even reports a *graphe paranomon* (a prosecution of a politician who had proposed a law contrary to an existing law) that was judged by 6,000 citizens, apparently the entire jury pool for the day.[151] And the city needed a lot of courts. Athenian citizens had the reputation of being notoriously litigious, and in addition to internal court cases, Athens forced members of the Delian League to resolve some legal disputes in Athenian courtrooms.[152] The number of citizens participating in the law courts and their size provoked good fodder for Athenian comedians. A scene in Aristophanes' play *The Clouds* has Strepsiades shown a map of the world with Athens on it. 'What do you mean?' responds Strepsiades, 'I don't believe it; I don't see any juries in session.'[153]

Like the *Boule* and archonship (as well as other political offices) in Athens, jurors served one-year terms, having been selected at the beginning of the year by sortition from a larger pool of citizens over the age of thirty. Jurors were sworn in and given a bronze (later wood) *pinakion*, or jury ticket, inscribed with their name, their patronymic, deme, and one of ten letters from alpha to kappa.[154] From this original pool of 6,000 jurors, ten sections of 600 were formed. These groups of 600 jurors, in turn, had 60 jurors from each of the ten tribes to ensure an even geographic representation. This much was consistent during the entire democratic period. The rest of the procedure varied depending on when we look. Throughout most of the fifth century, we think groups of these 600 jurors were assigned to specific officers of the court (also determined by lot). Potential jurors simply showed up in the morning, and each court admitted them until full. Characters in Aristophanes' play *Wasps* go to comic lengths to get to court early, thus ensuring both a spot and the daily payment for serving.[155] The character Loathecleon even says jurors wake each other around midnight to claim a seat:

> Loathecleon: You sorry fool, the other jurors will be here to pick up my father any minute now!
>
> Xanthias: What are you talking about? It's hardly dawn.
>
> Loathecleon: Then they've got up late today. Just after midnight's when they usually pick him up, toting torches and warbling sweet old Sidon Songs by Phrynichus; that's how they call him out.[156]

In the first third of the fourth century, the selection process grew more complicated. The *Athenian Constitution* devotes several dense pages to the details.[157] Instead of courts being filled on a first-come-first-served basis, an initial selection of jurors from the pool of citizens who showed up in the morning was followed by a second random selection to determine a subgrouping assigned to a specific official. From those subgroups, jurors were randomly assigned to specific courts. It probably goes without saying that the public officials in charge of organizing this process and even the citizens charged with drawing the lots were also themselves determined by lot: 'to prevent malpractice if the same man should always make the draw.'[158] For those of you keeping track, this entire procedure contains four separate levels of sortition—a quadruple sortition—to empanel a day's juries.

To accomplish all these random assignments, the old Homeric method of *kleroi*, or marked stones shaken in a helmet, would clearly not do. The *Athenian Constitution* provides our best source on this process in the fourth century. We have already mentioned the bronze or boxwood *pinakion*, or jury card, that showed the man was a juror for the year and qualified him to hear cases. Upon arriving at the court site, the prospective juror with his *pinakion* would enter a gate marked for his tribe. Inside the gateway, there were ten boxes, each with a letter, alpha through kappa. He would place his *pinakion* into the box with the letter corresponding to the letter on his *pinakion*. After shaking the box, the *Thesmothete*, or archon in charge, drew one from each in turn and placed them in one of two *kleroteria*.

This device, designed to randomly assign potential jurors to juries, first came into use in the early fourth century.[159] First excavated in the Athenian Agora in the 1930s, the *kleroterion* consisted of a tall stone *stele* with five chiseled parallel columns of slots, one for each tribe (the devices were always paired).[160] Alongside the main column, a tube allowed the official to drop a mixture of black and white *kuboi*, or cubes (like our dice), which he then retrieved one by one from the bottom of the *kleroterion*. A white *kubos* meant that the top row of *pinakia* were selected for jury duty. A black *kubos* indicated that the second row should be chosen. The black *kuboi* eliminated the possibility of tampering with the insertion of the *pinakia* by removing entire rows: there would be no advantage in placing *pinakia* in one row rather than another. The officials repeated the process of drawing *kuboi* until all the jury spots were filled.

This elaborate process took time, though we lack certain knowledge of how much. Hansen thinks the whole process might have taken an hour, though a simulation of the process by Alessandro Orlandini finds that with a bit of practice, empaneling juries for an average day in court took no more than thirty-five minutes.[161]

Attic *Kleroterion*. *Pinakia* (juror identification cards) were shuffled and then inserted into the slots, and white and black balls inserted into the funnel shaped mouth on the left. The crank mechanism released individual balls (*kuboi*) and jury candidates were accepted or rejected depending on which row contained their *pinakion*.

Detail: *Pinakia* and bronze lottery ball (*kubos*)

How many Athenians showed up for jury service? We are unable to answer this question with any degree of precision, though a few things seem clear enough. The appearance of the entire (or near entire) jury cohort of 6,000 likely occurred only for the most important or high profile cases.

Fortunately, most days the courts required far fewer jurors. David Mirhady and Carl Schwarz, working through what statisticians call the 'occupancy problem', calculate that a showing of 2,560 jurors would suffice for ninety-five percent of court days, though even that smaller number represents a significant portion of the citizen population.[162]

We lack precise demographics for the jurors. A purely random sample of citizens would produce a distribution representative of the citizen body across age, class, and geographic lines. But the jury pools would not have mapped precisely onto the population. First off, the formal requirements for serving on a jury were citizenship, of course, and being at least thirty years old. So right away we know that jurors were older. But how much older? A lot, if we are to trust the description in Aristophanes' *Wasps*, where the Chorus, consisting of creaking old men, need to be led by their sons to the courts.[163] Jury service gave Athenian senior citizens a sense of self-importance. Attracted by the power he feels in judging his fellow citizens, Philocleon, one of the main characters of the play, boasts:

> Don't I wield great authority, as great as Zeus? I'm even spoken of in the same way as Zeus. For instance, if we're in an uproar, every passerby says 'Zeus Almighty, the jury's really thundering!' And if I look lightning, the fat cats and VIPs say a prayer and shit their pants.[164]

In Aristophanes' comedy, high-minded civic participation is satirized as merely the vanity of washed-up old men.

Equally or more importantly, the jury payment of three obols, likely instituted by Pericles in the 450s,[165] also lured jurors
in. We can turn to Philocleon again for an example:

> The nicest part of all, which slipped my mind, is
> when I come home with my pay. That's when eve-
> ry one gives me a warm welcome at the door be-
> cause of the money.[166]

Though this also fits with the self-aggrandizement of the
previous quote, there were doubtlessly cases of real need. In an
earlier scene in *Wasps*, a son asks:

> Tell me, then, father, / if the archon doesn't call the
> court / into session today, how / can we buy
> lunch?[167]

A traditional argument, then, is that because they were unable
to work at other jobs, older citizens were more likely to attend
the courts for some income. Younger men could earn from 1.5 to
2.5 drachmas per day, well in excess of the three-obol allowance
for jurors, thus making jury duty less attractive to them. Markle
points out, however, that a man could feed his family (though
certainly not luxuriously) on the three-obol payment.[168] Against
this we have some few scattered mentions in the orators
dividing the juries up roughly into young and old, indicating
that at least they were not uniformly senior citizens, though they
definitely skewed older.[169]

They probably also skewed poorer. Isocrates notes that 'we
see many of our fellow-citizens drawing lots in front of the lawcourts to determine whether they themselves shall have the
necessaries of life.'[170] And the *Athenian Constitution* includes all
6,000 jurors in its count of Athenian citizens 'earning their living
as a result of the tribute, the taxation and the money the empire
brought in.'[171] But we should not assume that all the jurors were
destitute. Even in *Wasps*, where Philocleon revels in his jury pay
and power, his son, Loathecleon, clearly has the means and

desire to keep his father well-fed and housed, and desperately wants to do so. He views his father's participation in the courts as undignified. Philocleon, then, seems more like an aged member of the middle-class than a destitute old man. And in one law court speech, Demosthenes seems to assume that most jurors own some sort of property out in the Attic countryside.[172]

We would also expect members of the jury pool pulled completely at random from the entire population to represent the various geographic areas of Attica: demes close by to the city as well as far away; a mixture of inland and coastal, mountain and plain, urban and rural. But here we need to remember that service on the jury pool was voluntary, unlike contemporary practices in most democracies today, where it makes up one of the few mandatory duties of citizenship. Thus in practice, complete geographic distribution on any given jury was not likely. We have already discussed the lures of higher wages for some workers. We can imagine other opportunity costs. Walking in to the city from outlying demes, for example, on any sort of regular basis for a trial was impractical and unlikely, especially given the early starting times of the jury selection process. In practice, only citizens who lived within walking distance of the courts had regular access to jury service. Despite this, we know from extant *pinakia* that coastal and inland demes likely had higher rates of representation in the fourth century. Though this sample is not representative, Hansen speculates that these individuals represented a wider migration from the outlying areas of Attica into the city itself. The individuals moved, in other words, into the city, but kept their deme identification.[173]

Our sources indicate two main concerns that drove the Athenians to engage in such complex procedures to decide on juries. Demosthenes, in his speech 'Against Boeotus', says that the lottery process represents a sort of equal share in the city when it authoritatively allocates jury slots.[174] The lottery ensured that each eligible and interested citizen had an equal opportunity to serve, and that no one person or group had priority on the basis of wealth, birth or some other criteria, thus echoing broader assumptions about equality and citizen competence.

Athenians also feared possible corruption, either directly through bribes, or indirectly through political advocacy in other forums. Characters in the above mentioned scene in Aristophanes' *Wasps*, for example, state they come for jury service at the direction of the politician Cleon, who tells them, in Douglass Parker's animated translation, to 'Bring a triple ration of ANGER!' and 'Whatever you do, CONVICT that criminal!'[175] Here, the fix is in even before the jury is selected or the trial begins. The jurymen, irritable old men who when angered, can sting like wasps, go to court with the intention of acting as agents of the politician Cleon, and plan on voting to convict regardless of the evidence.

Setting aside the comic element, the possibility of jurors going to court with their minds already made up certainly represents a real possibility. But without advance knowledge of either who will serve, or on which trial — not to mention the sizes of the juries — directly fixing the outcome with either money or political influence posed overwhelming difficulties. But this is not, of course, to say that allegations of bribery never happened.[176] Thus as a final preventative, Athens penalized jury bribery severely; it merited its own law, the *graphê dekasmou*, which imposed the death penalty on those convicted, without the chance to propose an alternative penalty, as was the case with most other crimes.[177]

Beyond the concern about corruption, the close-knit nature of Athenian society made it likely that jurors would know the defendant in many cases at least peripherally, and in higher-profile instances probably had some clear opinion about the person or charges. In this context, we should note that all qualified jurors swore the Heliastic Oath, first reconstructed by Max Fränkel:

> I will vote according to the laws and the votes of the
> *Demos* of Athenians and the Council of the Five
> Hundred, and concerning matters about which
> there are no laws by the most just understanding,
> and for the sake of neither favour nor enmity. And I
> will vote concerning the very matters about which
> the prosecution is, and I will listen to both the ac-
> cusers and defendants, both of them equally. I
> swear these things by Zeus, Apollo, and Demeter,
> and may I have many good things if I swear well,
> but destruction for me and my family if I for-
> swear.[178]

As an indication of how seriously Athenians took this oath,
Demosthenes compares unfavorably positions taken by those
who have not sworn an oath to 'the judgements of sworn
juries.'[179]

Before we turn to criticisms of the use of lottery in Athens, we
need to consider one more group of officials determined by
sortition. These were the one hundred or so lower-ranking
officials who ran Athens on a day-to-day basis. Hansen argues
that we should take Aristotle's estimate of six hundred as a
roughly accurate number for these officials; the *Athenian
Constitution* lists just over two hundred of these explicitly,
though some of these act on subcommittees of the *Boule*.[180]
These officials oversaw various aspects of city administration,
such as the keeping of records, the handling and punishment of
prisoners, waste management and disposal, regulation of
weights and measures, food distribution, and so forth. The
specific mechanism for selecting these officials, or ἔνδημοι ἀρχαὶ,
was likely sortition, though we lack evidence in many cases.[181]
And like jury selection, candidates were not compelled to serve
and drawn from the entire citizen-body, but the pool was rather
limited to those who volunteered to serve.[182] The sheer number
of administrative positions in Athens seems to necessitate some
sort of recruitment campaign at the deme level, though the

orator Lysias speaks of at least one candidate's enthusiasm [*prothumos*] for the lottery.[183]

Significantly, most of these positions consisted not of solitary appointments, but rather appointments to boards of citizens overseeing specific tasks. The appointment of citizens to a board made up of other citizens both broadened responsibility for specific tasks and at the same time reduced reliance on any one person. Use of boards of citizens allowed for the uneven preparedness or participation of individual citizens. Much like group projects in the classroom or office, groups of collaborators often reach better results while at the same time drawing on unequal contributions of effort. Boards also ensured that should one or two members drop off or prove incompetent—whatever the reason—sufficient members remained to complete or perform the task.

While Athens generally limited restrictions on service in office to citizenship and age, they did require incoming officials to undergo an examination, called a *dokimasia*, prior to taking office. For the one hundred city officials just discussed, the *dokimasia* took place in front of a jury, while for archons and some higher-level officials, approval took place in the *Boule*. In either case, each candidate for office needed to answer some basic questions about his citizenship, his membership in a *phratry*, his fulfillment of his religious responsibilities, and his treatment of his parents. Notably, no questions were asked related to expertise or competency related to the specific office. Athenians assumed that an average citizen had the skills necessary to do the requisite work.

Given the sheer number of examinations, we suspect that most of these interviews must have been rather pro forma. Despite this, any member of the citizen-body could appear to challenge the candidate's appointment, which would trigger a secondary round of questions and responses, and then a vote on the candidate's approval. Significantly, three of the extant speeches of Lysias—roughly ten percent—deal with challenges during a *dokimasia*.[184] These speeches are much shorter than standard law court speeches, reflecting the abbreviated time-line for decisions. Lysias tells us that originally Athenians designed the *dokimasia* to prevent oligarchic opponents of democracy from taking office.[185] More generally, though, and like regular court cases, the jury could consider whatever sort of evidence it liked, and speeches often turned on a broad description of the candidate's contributions or harms to the city.

Bribery or other illegal behavior was a concern for many of these public officials, so in addition to the initial scrutiny of office holders, at the conclusion of their term they were required to submit to a *euthyna*, or public review of their tenure of office.[186] Like the initial *dokimasia*, any citizen with evidence of misconduct could come forward and lodge charges. The procedure was complex, and dependent on the specific office, but in general office holders found guilty could be fined immediately or the case might be referred to a public or private suit (with potentially higher penalties).[187] The *euthyna* had to take place prior to a citizen taking another office, so it largely prevented individuals from holding offices in successive years. This tenure of office review, along with other charges, effectively kept political power under the control of the *demos*. This was especially important when it came to the generals, who had armed men at their command. In a compelling comparison with military power at the end of the Roman Republic, Jennifer Roberts argues that Athens' 'rigorous use of the machinery of control' prevented *strategoi*, the generals, from threatening the democracy in the way that Marius, Sulla, and ultimately Caesar did in Rome.[188]

Our discussion up until now shows us that Athenians used an extraordinarily complex set of mechanisms to staff the many offices which kept the city running. No one agency controlled either the process or the nominees, and much preliminary work occurred even earlier at the deme level. Moreover, and rather extraordinarily due to the use of sortition, an average citizen could find himself in charge of an important part of the city's governance. Aristotle in the *Politics* offers a definition of citizenship as 'ruling and being ruled in turn.' That maps nicely onto the democratic experience in Athens.

This system, however, had detractors who pointed out practical political problems as well as philosophical ones. The orator Isocrates argues in his speech *Areopagiticus* that lotteries actually allowed antidemocratic politicians to hold office, something he says would not occur in elections, because the *demos* would not vote for them.[189] Isocrates may be technically correct here. Sortition could result in a citizen with antidemocratic sentiments gaining office, but the odds seem stacked against such an outcome. Not only would the individual have to put himself forward, but he would also have to make it through the random selection process. The lottery did not favor or disfavor any particular individual. But because the number of democratic partisans vastly outnumbered the potentially antidemocratic (taking wealth as a very rough proxy for these political views), the chances of significant representation were small indeed.

In an interesting study, Claire Taylor looked at income-class distribution in the elected office of general (*strategos*) as opposed to the board of treasurers (*Tamiai tes Athenas*), which oversaw, among other things, court costs. This latter office was distributed by lottery, though not the former. Whereas the office of *strategos* did skew strongly in the direction of wealthier, aristocratic citizens (and a geographic concentration in the city of Athens itself), the *tamiai* were distributed as one might expect from random sortition, not significantly favoring a particular geographic region or property class.[190] Self-selection likely played a role here in this difference: because of their resources, wealthier citizens may have more likely pursued elected offices, which one could hold for successive years, and which usually had more substantial, high-profile responsibilities, a manifestation, perhaps, of inter-elite competitions, as Ober argues.[191] We should also not forget that, prior to assuming office, all candidates had to undergo a *dokimasia*, where one of the few things considered was the person's past association with attempts to overthrow or undermine the democracy.

The philosophic and literary tradition of the Classical Period is generally critical of the democracy, and often complaints single out the use of sortition. These criticisms tie in with assumptions about the knowledge levels and skills of citizens empowered through sortition. The conservative author of the *Constitution of the Athenians* says that the city is ruled by the worst [*poneroi*] and—what to him amounts to almost the same thing—the poor [*penates*].[192] Herodotus and Thucydides regularly highlight the volatility of the Athenian *demos*, and their low levels of factual knowledge about the particular policies or proposals on which they decide.[193] How could an average Athenian, Thucydides argues, have the requisite information to make a decision about an expedition to Sicily, which was far away, and about which he knew nothing? In Xenophon's version of Socrates we find this concern directed specifically at the lottery:

> [Socrates] made his companions look down on the established laws, by saying that it is foolish for the rulers of the city to be established in office by lot [ἀπὸ κυαθάμου] when nobody would want to use a pilot chosen by lot [κυαμευτῷ] or a builder or a flutist or anyone for any other task of the sort, although far less harm is caused when mistakes are made in them than when they are made concerning the city. He said that speeches of this sort induced the young to have contempt for the established regime and made them violent.[194]

Socrates' complaint seems superficially justified. Lotteries distribute office based on random selections of citizens, not on the basis of some sort of knowledge or qualification for the position. We would not choose a physician by random selection, so, by analogy, why would we select an official in charge of dealing with prisoners, or regulating commercial transactions in the *agora* by the same method? Lotteries, argues Socrates, misconstrue the appropriate criteria for participation in the affairs of the city. Citizenship alone does not produce the requisite civic knowledge. In this sense, Socrates' charges are similar to those Aristotle offers in the *Politics* about democracy more generally. Democrats make a mistake in assuming that people who are equal in one thing (free birth or citizenship) should therefore have an equal share in other things, in this case rule in the city.[195] For both Socrates and Aristotle, then, the relevant criteria for political authority rests, generally speaking, on knowledge, something democratic sortition in Athens did not take into account.

One possible response to this sort of criticism involves arguing that the offices distributed by lottery in Athens did not require any specialized knowledge. Notably, the *dokimasia* procedure seems to implicitly recognize this: it involved no questions about literacy, numeracy, or civic knowledge one might think relevant to the position. This is Richard Mulgan's position:

> use of the lot, it should be noted, did not imply that superior ability and experience were not discernible, only that they were not required for the job in question.[196]

But this leaves unanswered questions. Some positions did clearly assume some degree of competency and knowledge. The *tamiai*, for example, to whom we already referred, must have needed basic skills in numeracy, and marketplace inspectors must have needed some experience with weights and measures as well as some experience with commerce. These positions certainly did not require the sort of technical knowledge that an epidemiologist working at the Centers For Disease Control in the United States today needs, but nonetheless some knowledge seems necessary — in the case of the *tamiai*, at least rudimentary accounting skills, perhaps.

Setting aside specific knowledge required by individual positions, citizens serving in official capacities more generally did need some knowledge — at a minimum some knowledge of the functioning of Athenian government and the proper role and scope of the various boards on which they served. Here we can turn to work done by Josiah Ober in his 2008 book, *Democracy and Knowledge*. By employing modern techniques of social and political analysis, Ober shows how knowledge flowed in Athenian society through social networks and task-specific work teams which not only transmitted the intellectual capital of democracy from one generation to another, but also provided constant reminders of the proper role for citizens through the (re)commitment rituals of the ephebic oath, as well as civic and religious festivals.[197] In this context, it is worth emphasizing that Athenians serving in public offices had to be at least thirty. As Ober stresses, most Athenians first experienced democratic government in their local demes, each of which operated its own council and replicated on a small-scale the main civic institutions of the city. By the age of thirty, a citizen likely would have participated both in his local deme meetings, as well as Assembly meetings in Athens, and would have acquired knowledge of the various boards and offices in the city. This knowledge would only have grown in subsequent service, as would a citizen's understanding of the wider population, as he came into contact with Athenians from diverse parts of wider Attica. Many Athenian institutions directly fostered this exchange of knowledge across Attica. The *phylai*, or tribal divisions, for example, were purposefully organized by Solon to reflect wide geographic representation, with their memberships made up of non-contiguous spaces divided between coastal, urban, and rural areas of Attica.[198] As Ober notes, the activities of 'marching, fighting, sacrificing, eating, and dancing together' forged strong bonds of civic community and helped transmit knowledge.[199] A candidate for political office, then, very probably had a range of civic experience to draw on when it came to fulfilling the requirements of the position.

We should also remember that most public offices appointed by lot consisted of boards of citizens instead of individuals. A relatively young or less-experienced Athenian who found himself on a board with others would benefit from the advice and experience of older members, and the ignorance, illness, or other incapacitation of any single individual would likely not diminish the efficacy of the board as a whole. Even Aristotle warily approves of the advantages of collectively reached decisions, though likely for much larger groups than a board of ten.[200]

Finally, we can also read sortition as a means of sustaining the dominance of the primary voice of the Athenian *demos*, the Assembly. Today in Western liberal democracies, we imagine different branches of government playing a checking power over each another. Legislatures have long-term interests maintained over and against executive branch claims of authority. Lifetime appointment to judgeships, similarly, ensures against the erosion of judicial authority and power by the other branches. But in Athens, offices were typically held for only a year, and those presiding over meetings (including the Assembly) were determined by lottery, dramatically reducing both the opportunity to intimidate or suborn officials, and also the ability of individuals to build up political power bases. Psychologically, we can guess that distribution of office by chance diminished any sense of superiority among those selected, and — presumably — undue confidence in the value of their own individual opinions as distinct from those of the assembly.

Athenian use of the lottery reflects, then, a broad confidence in the competence of average citizens to perform the work of governing. The emphasis on civic equality and suspicion of accumulated political power made sortition an obvious choice for the distribution of authority. Importantly, Athenians seemed satisfied with the results. The use and complexity of the lottery increased dramatically over the Classical Period and became important not only as a procedural mechanism but also as a form of civic ritual establishing the fairness of the selection process and the city's commitment to civic equality.[201] Perhaps more importantly, though difficult to measure, was the effect of the lottery on the dignity and self-worth of the individual citizen. Aristotle notes in the *Politics* that we can only be fully human within a political community, and that participation in making the laws of one's city—'ruling and being ruled in turn'—proved crucial to human development. Athenian citizens had daily reminders of this as they cycled in and out of law courts, the assembly, and various administrative offices. A telling sign of just how closely Athenians held these privileges is the fact that the bronze jury tokens—the *pinakia*—we have remaining all come from grave caches. Among the most important items Athenians took with them to the tomb were symbols of their citizenship and service.

Liberal democracies today appeal to a core sense of equality not wholly unlike that found in Ancient Athens. We recognize that power most clearly in the theoretical openness of public offices to all citizens. And in one sense, we have fewer restrictions on participation than the Athenians. No liberal democracy today restricts voting or holding office on the basis of financial holdings, property, gender, or class. Most countries allow full voting rights at eighteen, and for countries like the U.K., this is also the minimum eligibility age to stand for any office. Where age restrictions do exist, they tend to affect only higher levels of office, like the office of senator and president in the U.S., South Africa, or Italy.

But significant unequal aspects of citizens' status undermine the theoretical equality of access to public office. Only some individuals are realistic candidates in liberal democracies. As discussed at the beginning of this chapter, racial or gender bias, wealth, fame, education, and other sorts of privilege tilt the electoral playing field dramatically away from the under-resourced and those from groups suffering various forms of discrimination. We have a mismatch between the theoretical promise of equal access to office and the ability to deliver it. This would present less of a problem if representative government actually represented the views of the governed, but the imbalance between majority policy preferences and actual legal and policy outcomes skews strongly in favor of the elite. A lack of visual representation of various groups in legislative bodies also runs the risk of alienating substantial portions of the population from politics, thus increasing minority control over law and policy-making.

Sortition offers clear and real benefits in contrast with electoral distributions. The problem of representation of the actual population, for example, vanishes with large candidate pools, and sortition.[202] It also yields real benefits in terms of resource and time expenditures. Elections in most democracies today are quite expensive and time-consuming. This is particularly a problem in the U.S., which spent close to $15 billion on the 2020 elections, and that number only promises to grow in coming years.[203] Many legislators spend significant amounts of their time raising funds for future elections, and are dependent on large-scale donors. Leaving aside the significant potential for soft corruption, this represents a massive opportunity cost: time given over to fundraising cuts into the real and important work legislators need to do. Because of recurring electoral contests, legislative bodies often have limited time to pass significant legislation. In the U.S., Congressional elections every two years effectively mean that only the first of those two years holds out the possibility of action, thus slowing down an already sclerotic Congress. Sortition, of course, would eliminate the cost and time commitments involved in seating legislators. And, as in Classical Athens, the large potential pool of candidates and random selection would make certain kinds of illegitimate influence peddling much more difficult.

Finally, as discussed earlier, active participation – or even the potential for active participation – places the citizen in an engaged stance relative to the public sphere. Consider a helpful parallel: students in a college class. If the professor lectures for the full class period, attentiveness and active listening drop off substantially. Students lapse into passive receivers of information and are much less likely to ask questions or engage critically with the material. In a more dynamic classroom where the professor uses the Socratic method of asking questions, students need to engage with the materials differently, actively listening and considering their own response, always anticipating a question from the professor or one of their colleagues. Similarly, the potential of serving in office helps reorient the citizen to the public sphere, and drives feelings of engagement. The political sphere appears less like a zero-sum game where winners feel justified because of their electoral victories, but a space reaffirming the dignity of all participants.[204] Holding political office confers significant material and immaterial benefits; we should distribute these benefits fairly.[205]

Of course, in contemporary society we already recognize the utility and fairness of using random chance to determine important issues. Oliver Dowlen describes the appeal of random chance with the term 'blind break': sortition introduces a stage in the decision-making process that eliminates all human influence, whether rational or irrational.[206] Small private disputes are regularly resolved using coin tosses, drawing straws, or card cutting. Ties in some elections at the state and local levels are also resolved in this manner. More significantly, substantial burdens that the state imposes on citizens are distributed randomly: the U.S. uses lotteries for both selective service and jury service.[207] When no one person (or group of people) have legitimate claim to a benefit or a legitimate reason to shirk a responsibility, we often turn to chance to distribute the good.[208]

We also have clear philosophical rationale for the role of chance in public life. John Rawls writes persuasively about the role of chance or luck in determining social and economic positions in his 1971 work *A Theory of Justice*. For Rawls, the role luck plays in opening up access to social, economic, and political goods substantially diminishes strong claims to deserve the resulting benefits.[209] Demographics may not be destiny, but can work as a rough approximation. Certain clear and definable advantages accrue on the basis of birth, education, peer group, and simple genetic luck. These are the sorts of advantages which get leveraged into later social and other benefits like political office. Rawls' point here is that though we may be the holders of various qualities that draw benefits or privileges in our societies, we cannot claim strong and exclusive rights to the rewards. Theorists often read Rawls' arguments as providing the basis for a progressive and redistributive system of taxation, among other progressive policies. But we can also read Rawls' arguments about chance as providing a philosophical basis for the use of sortition.[210] If much of our social capital and hence political potential finds its origins in chance, then no one group has any sort of privileged claim to political benefits. This is exactly the sort of situation calling for sortition.

Frederick Engelstad calls our attention to the importance of understanding the appropriate use of sortition given different social and political circumstances.[211] He reminds us that Classical Athens and Early Modern Florence—another state that used lotteries for some public offices—were very different from modern liberal democracies. Both were relatively small and discrete city states with strong civic ties between citizens, and both enjoyed rather long periods of economic growth when sortition was introduced. In these cities, additionally, sortition accompanied the decline in power of aristocratic elites and corresponding rise in power of the lower classes. Liberal democracies today, by contrast, are diverse, large, and embedded in complex global economic systems. And unlike Classical Athens, many bureaucratic positions in government today do indeed require specialized knowledge or skill sets that the average citizen may not have.

We need, moreover, to take into account the substantial institutional impediments to introducing sortition at any scale: institutional norms surrounding the sanctity of elections run deep, and, more importantly, all liberal democratic constitutions include requirements for elections, thus making any change from the status quo difficult.

Despite these obstacles, recent academic literature is full of examples of small-scale experiments suggesting ways of introducing sortition into legislation and policy-making debates.[212] Citizens' councils, sometimes known as 'minipublics', represent one of the most common attempts to do this. Typically these consist of groups of randomly selected citizens brought together to deliberate and decide on some issue of law or policy. On technical matters, councils bring in experts to explain necessary details. Typically these councils or assemblies write up a report with recommendations for an elected body to consider, or a referendum on which the general public votes. One of the best studied of these efforts, the 2004 British Columbia (Canada) Citizens' Assembly, randomly selected 160 residents to discuss electoral reforms.[213] In this case, the citizens' assembly was authorized by the provincial legislature, which provided funding for the meetings. This money not only compensated recipients for their time, but it also attempted to include individuals who otherwise would not have been able to attend by adding in funding for things like transportation and child care. We should note that despite these efforts, participation rates were not robust. Out of an original stratified sample of 23,034, just 1,715 people indicated a potential willingness to participate, and of these only 964 attended the selection meeting (from which 158 were randomly selected).[214] The voluntary nature of the project makes it unlikely that the final participants were actually fully representative of the wider population. Many of the participants, for example, likely had strong prior interests in constitutional or political issues, thus making the project more interesting to them. Selection bias in a voluntary process like this one makes it very difficult to generate a truly representative assembly. Similar problems likely colored Athenian sortition; citizens residing in or close to Athens, or those with a clear interest in politics likely made up a larger portion of juries and boards. We could address this problem by instituting mandates for participation, much in the same way many countries require judicial jury service.

Once convened, the citizens' assembly divided its sessions into three phases.[215] In the first, they met on weekends with experts who discussed various electoral models. This phase is typical in mini or public assemblies of this sort. Members are not expected to make decisions in the absence of information and data; relevant specialists supply this.[216] Assembly members met in small groups to discuss the material, took meals together, and stayed in the same hotel to build up a sense of community and mutual trust. In the second phase, they took a month to meet with citizens from across the province in public meetings, and heard the arguments of interest groups. Written submissions from the public or interested parties were also accepted at this time.

Finally, members of the assembly met together for two months during the deliberation phase, in which they finalized recommendations later voted on by the entire province. The assembly took a number of steps to guarantee a viable outcome. Small group discussions moderated by a group leader helped individuals not comfortable speaking before large audiences. Regularly changing the membership of the subgroups ensured familiarity with a range of opinion across gender, age, and other factors. In short, every effort was made to ensure a rich and serious debate with workable outcomes.

British Columbia is not alone. Citizen councils have been formed to deal with a number of difficult political issues in Iceland,[217] Belgium,[218] Oregon,[219] on healthcare and Brexit in the U.K.,[220] and on abortion in Ireland,[221] among many others. The specific mechanisms and procedures in all these cases differ.[222] Some councils are restricted to citizens, but others are open to all residents. Some bring together a random selection of people, others select on the basis of stakeholders (proximity, specific interest, *etc.*). What these efforts all have in common, however, is the attempt to generate a space of public debate in which status and power have no place by randomly selecting citizens to deliberate over a matter of public importance. The results should represent not business, interest groups, large donors or other powerful political actors, but rather reflect a true deliberative consensus.

Representative citizen assemblies or councils may work for the toughest and most intractable political dilemmas, but smaller, more targeted groups may offer more efficacy for smaller-scale or less salient issues. John Burnheim, for example, suggests groups of twelve as 'a representative sample of the legitimate interests most strongly affected by the problem to be solved, but not of every group that has an interest in it.'[223] For these problems, for example, we may want to randomly select individuals in proportion to the dangers of making the wrong decision.

Citizen assemblies or minipublics represent only one possible use of sortition in public life. We might also consider following the Athenian example of selecting many of our administrative officials by lottery.[224] Today these positions are largely filled either through election or direct political appointment, and while this arrangement certainly sometimes works, it is also vulnerable to the same sorts of problems we outlined at the beginning of this chapter: potential corruption, favoritism, undue influence, political maneuvering, unrepresentative electoral results, and the growing cost of holding elections.

Instead, boards of randomly selected residents could oversee important aspects of civic life: supervising city or county budgets, police forces, waste management, school and planning boards, and so forth. In these cases, sortition could not replace all civil servants, but rather only those in oversight positions, leaving in place the accumulated experience and expertise of those who actually implement policies. Because sortition always involves at least two steps — determining the pool of potential candidates and then a random selection from that pool — the process could limit access to the initial pool of candidates by some technical criteria. Oversight of a city or county budget might, for example, reserve a certain number of seats for Certified Public Accountants. School boards might similarly reserve seats for adults with children in the district (or seats for students themselves), and a planning board might reserve a seat for a structural engineer or an architect. Generally, however, citizen boards can always access technical expertise through consultation, so limiting equal access in this manner would need good justification.

Moving to lottery-based systems is not easy or quick. To be effective, such systems would at minimum need the initial buy-in of existing legislative bodies, which would have to recognize or accept the results. Legislative bodies could, for example, agree to adopt whatever proposal the citizen assembly produces, or they could agree to debate it and allow a vote on it. They could also agree to put the citizen assembly's proposal up for a public referendum in lieu of taking the matter up themselves. Most elected legislators are understandably unwilling to casually cede their power to another governing body. Substantial efforts, consequently, would have to be made to convince them of both the usefulness and justifiability of citizen assemblies, perhaps by instituting them on a small scale at first, or allowing them to initially address lower-profile issues.

The public would also need to be convinced not only of the efficacy of sortition, but also its legitimacy. For a population of any size, the sampling would need to be done by computer, and ensuring reliability and security would need the same sort of attention we currently pay to the security of voting machines.[225] People would need to be educated about the process, and see themselves reflected in the membership and opinions expressed in deliberations. Importantly, some substantial portion of the proceedings would need to be available for review online. Mini-publics stand in for the larger whole, so the wider population would need time to understand and endorse the procedure. The British Columbia Citizens' Council took several years of advocacy and then legislation to set up, but it did finally get done. Interestingly, private companies have begun to experiment to see if a market exists for organizing these sorts of citizens' councils, an indication of their recent rapid growth.[226]

At a more abstract level, mini publics and sortition help build a more robust democracy. By filling public positions through lotteries and introducing sortition-based minipublics and other discussion groups to assist in the evaluation and making of laws we would actualize our fundamental democratic commitment to equality, substantially broadening the base of meaningful political participation. Citizens in liberal democracies already feel the strong pull of the private life, which draws them away from politics and toward their own pursuits of the good life. Broadening the possibilities of political engagement would help to reorient the public toward civic participation and deliberation, and toward the values and interests we hold in common. But sortition alone, of course, cannot completely reinvigorate civic life in the twenty-first century. To do that, we need to turn to several other practices of Classical Athens for guidance, and those are the subject of the next chapters, where we consider first finances in Ancient Athens, and then how the Athenians build up a sense of civic community and commitment across the population.

Chapter Four

Financing Community

The United States expects to take in roughly $3.8 trillion dollars in the 2021 fiscal year. The vast bulk of this revenue comes in the form of individual income and payroll taxes, which finance the operations of the government. While the U.S., like many liberal democracies, has a slightly graduated income tax, the overall revenue system benefits the wealthy, resulting in a highly regressive tax structure for two primary reasons. First, social security taxes are capped, so individuals are only taxed on the first $137,700 (in 2020 dollars) of income. This effectively means that lower-income earners pay a much larger proportion of their income in social security taxes. Second, and more importantly, no income taxes at all are levied on non-wage revenue sources such as reinvested inherited wealth. For wealthier Americans, such income makes up the vast bulk of earnings, and effectively shields large amounts of holdings from taxation. A variety of tax avoidance strategies available to the wealthy amplify this problem. Consider the example of tech financier Peter Thiel, who transformed a Roth IRA [retirement] account into an untaxed $5 billion dollar tax haven.[227] The wealthiest individuals benefit disproportionally from the economy while paying extremely low levels of taxes. In the United States the average taxpayer shoulders a disproportionate burden of financing the government.

Athens, by contrast, took the opposite approach and required the wealthiest members of society to contribute the vast bulk of revenues financing the operations of the democracy. These revenues were used for expenses we would recognize today: the military, governmental operations, infrastructure projects, some limited forms of welfare, and so forth. But Athenian revenues also financed civic festivals—such as the Festival of Dionysus, which we will discuss in Chapter Five—that helped form and solidify civic bonds and thus generated a common sense of what it meant to be Athenian. This chapter considers the ways Athens financed and sustained its extensive civic activities, and the details and justification for the unique system of taxation they developed to place the monetary burden primarily on the wealthiest members of society. We will also examine the ways in which the city expended resources to ensure widespread and meaningful participation.

We know nothing about the writer of *The Constitution of the Athenians* – commonly identified as 'Pseudo-Xenophon' – but the text assumes the point of view of a critic of the democracy at Athens and gives us a fascinating glimpse into the ideological and financial apparatus that supported a robust Athenian *polis* life. This brief essay, likely dating from the late fifth century, grudgingly admires the manner in which the organization of civic life in Athens helped sustain democracy and minimized political dissent from oligarchic or tyrannical elements in the city.[228] A key insight of the text concerns what we might call the democracy's conception of distributive justice. The author of *The Constitution of the Athenians* argues that the regime's success depends on supplying the poorest and least-well-off members with significant goods. Here is the way he describes resource distribution in the text:

> They regularly distribute more to the bad [πένητες],
> to the poor [δημόται] and to those sympathetic to the
> common people [πολλοὶ], than to the good
> [χρηστοῖς], but even here they can be shown to be

> preserving the democracy. For, if the poor, the
> members of the common people, and the worse
> [χείρους] do well and such people become large in
> number, they will increase the democracy.[229]

If one could not tell from the overall argument, the terms the writer uses here to refer to the democratic masses clearly reveal his class preferences. Robin Osborne has translated these terms above in such a way as to represent their political valence, but we should note that a term like *penetes* technically means one who works for his living, or a day laborer, while *demotai* means something more like a plebeian. The 'good', by contrast, are *chrestos*, or useful, and this includes the aristocratic classes and those in favor of more restrictive forms of government. In the world of the writer of *The Constitution of the Athenians*, these groups of undeserving poor claim a disproportionate and unjustified share of the goods which the city has to give out. This all sounds like a fairly typical conservative critique except for the fact that the author acknowledges that distributing goods or money down the economic scale actually preserves and grows the democracy, presumably because the benefits the poor receive allow them to reproduce at higher rates. But we shall see that the benefits to the city go beyond simple increase in numbers.

The Constitution of the Athenians is correct about both Athenian distributive economics in the strict sense and also about the fact that it enhances the democracy. The author, of course, imagines that the distribution of goods gives individual Athenian citizens a narrow pecuniary interest in the preservation and extension of the democracy in a sort of one-to-one transactional approach: he implies that individual citizens support the democracy *because* they receive benefits from it, thus democracy appears as a sophisticated form of bribery, as opposed to a principled preference or ideological position. No doubt individual citizens appreciated the economic benefits Athens conferred on them. Aristophanes, for example, relies regularly on the stingy, money-obsessed citizen: whether it's the payment-focused jurors of the *Wasps,* citizens lining up early to get their Assembly pay in *Assemblywomen,* or the character Strepsiades in the *Clouds,* who sends his son to Socrates' school to learn how to argue and thus profit in the courts. But while some civic participation certainly had monetary motivation, we will see that the actual ways in which these funds were spent and distributed contributed substantially to both widespread participation and generating a robust sense of community.

In the fifth century, a substantial portion of Athenian revenues came from its control of the Delian League, its *de facto* empire in the Eastern Mediterranean. Subject cities paid annual tributes to Athens as well as contributing ships and men to its fleet. These monies allowed Athens to build the largest fleet in Greek history up to that point, a force that enabled it to largely dominate coastal areas and islands in the Aegean. Revenues from the Delian League also financed the rebuilding of the Acropolis, which the Persians destroyed in 480, and other civic buildings. Supplementing imperial revenues, Athens imposed internal taxes on its citizens as well, a practice that grew in importance after the collapse of the Delian League following the loss to Sparta in the Peloponnesian War in 404. Athens was certainly not the first city to tax its inhabitants, of course. Records in Egypt reflect a well-developed tax system as early as 3000 BCE. Taxes there could take the form of forced labor for the very poor, or some percentage of overall wealth.[230] Uniquely, however, Classical Athens did not levy direct taxes on the majority of its citizens, but instead relied primarily on its wealthiest citizens to support both military and civic projects.[231]

For simplicity's sake, we can consider two main forms of taxation in the Classical Period: the liturgy and the *eisphora.*[232] The latter was a direct tax on wealth, affecting only the richest Athenian citizens. Much is unclear both about the regularity of the *eisphora* prior to 347, as well as the assessment method, though in the fourth century — and perhaps in the fifth as well —

the taxation level was tied to the total volume of property in Athens.[233] The *Athenian Constitution* dates the origins of it to the Solonic Period,[234] while Thucydides plausibly claims it was first imposed in 428/7 due to the high costs of the Peloponnesian War.[235] Most scholars today argue that this tax was sporadically levied in the fifth century, and only regularized in the fourth, settling into an overall assessment of ten talents per year by 347.[236] For our purposes, the important thing to note is that the *eisphora* affected only the very wealthiest members of the Athenian civic body — roughly one thousand to twelve hundred individuals, who shouldered the overall tax assessment.[237] The idea that only the wealthiest individuals should pay taxes was deeply embedded in Athenian civic ideology. As the orator and politician Lysias puts it:

> it is the duty of true leaders of the people not to take
> your property in the stress of your misfortunes, but
> to give their own property to you.[238]

We will more thoroughly investigate the justifications and uses of taxing the wealthy once we outline the other main form of taxation in Ancient Athens, the liturgy.

We use the term 'liturgy' today to refer to the formal ritual of a religious service — the sacramental rite, for example, in Christianity. But the word's roots lie in the Attic Greek terms for 'people' (*laos*), and 'work' (*ergon*), so the term in Attic Greek meant something more like 'work of the people'. Athens used the liturgy to finance specific major annual expenses, and assigned them to individual members of the very wealthiest tier of Athenian economic classes. Precise numbers, as usual during this time period, are tricky to come by, but most estimates suggest that only Athenians possessing assets over three or four talents performed liturgies. For scale, consider that one talent represents roughly what an average laborer in Athens would earn in ten years. Liturgical responsibilities, then, attached only to the Athenian one percent, an even smaller percentage than was liable for the *eisphora*. And like the *eisphora*, we begin to have evidence of liturgies early on in democratic Athens, perhaps by the time of Cleisthenes' reforms in 508/7, and certainly by 480.

Athens had many categories of liturgy. The number varied slightly according to annual needs. Some were extremely costly, others less so. For example, a *hestiasis*, or the provision of a banquet, represented a relatively fixed cost tied to a specific event, perhaps even at the deme level. A *gymnasiarchia*, on the other hand, provided for a team at an athletic festival, and likely included travel, payment, and training for the team, and was a more open-ended expense (good trainers could be expensive). Demosthenes reports roughly sixty of these civil or recurring liturgies per year, though the actual number in any given year might have been much higher—Hansen estimates roughly one hundred.[239] For our purposes, we will consider the two most prominent liturgies, which were also the most costly: the *trierarchia*, or the financing of a warship, a trireme, and the *choregia*, the financing of a theatrical production at one of the major annual festivals.

Every year, the ten elected Athenian *strategoi*, or generals, selected the wealthiest Athenian citizens to finance the city's fleet of triremes.[240] The *trierarchia*, a major expense, cost up to one talent, and while appointments formally lasted only a year, the responsibility could stretch into a second year due to extenuating circumstances, such as an ongoing campaign. Prior to the establishment of the *trierarchia*, Athenian warships were privately owned and equipped. Sometime in the 480s, following the first Persian invasion, the city took control of the fleet, retaining private funding but determining the number of required ships and assigning each one to an Athenian citizen.[241] We can think of this as a sort of nationalization of the naval military apparatus through compulsory patronage, and a way to decrease or dampen elite power and prestige in the young democracy. The *trierarchia* channeled competitive impulses among the elite into properly funding their assigned ships, with rewards for speed and efficiency and fines for damage or negligent loss of the valuable hulls. And the costs were high. Trierarchs had to pay for all necessary equipment as well as maintenance of the ships. Some wealthier Athenian citizens kept their own supplies of oars and ropes in storage between serving as trierarchs. Moreover, while the city compensated the trierarch anywhere from three obols to one drachma per day for a rower, the trierarch had to hire his crew and officers on the open market, where the competition for good oarsmen was particularly intense. A skilled crew could make the difference between victory and defeat in a battle, as well as more efficient — thus cheaper — operation of the vessel. In brief, the trierarch had a strong financial incentive to select the best crew and equipment he could afford.

Athens would typically pay for part of a naval expedition upfront, but the trierarch received full reimbursement only later, perhaps at the end of his service year. This meant that he had to carry with him sufficient funds to pay and feed his crew as well as maintain the vessel during expeditions. While captaining a vessel certainly required naval skills, arguably it was equally or more important for the trierarch to be a competent financier.[242] Costs associated with this liturgy were sufficiently high that in 411 Athens began to allow two citizens to split the costs of a single ship.[243]

A less expensive, but arguably more prominent liturgy was the *choregia*, or the production of a performance at a major festival such as the City Dionysia.[244] The citizen assigned this liturgy, the *choregos*, acted in effect as an executive producer for a set of performances, hiring actors, chorus members, and providing for costuming, training, and meals (these could be for a group of plays or a dithyrambic chorus). We are familiar with the subjects of some of these expenses in the surviving fifth-century tragedies Sophocles' *Oedipus Tyrannos* and *Antigone*, or Aeschylus' *Oresteia* trilogy, all of which were financed by a *choregos*. At first glance, the costs of a theater production might appear minor alongside the trierarchia, but consider this—albeit rather late—comment by Plutarch:

> If the cost of the production of each drama were reckoned, the Athenian people would appear to have spent more on the production of *Bacchaes* and *Phoenician Women* and *Oedipuses* and the misfortunes of Medeas and Electras than they did on maintaining their empire and fighting for their liberty against the Barbarians.[245]

Moreover—at least according to Plutarch—choregic expenses were different in another way:

> For the generals often ordered their men to bring along uncooked rations when they led them forth to battle; and the commanders, I can swear, after providing barley-meal and a relish of onions and cheese for the rowers, would embark them on the triremes. But the men who paid for the choruses gave the choristers eels and tender lettuces, roast-beef and marrow, and pampered them for a long time while they were training their voices and living in luxury.[246]

Even with some license for exaggeration, the amount of money spent on festivals and the indulgences provided was significant.

While Plutarch implies that overly sensitive and effete artists needed luxurious provisions to produce good performances, wealthy Athenians had good reasons to contribute regularly and lavishly to the city in their liturgies: they provided a form of public relations for the liturgist. Consider the orator Lysias, who details his liturgical expenses since he entered politics at the beginning of a court speech:

> I was certified of age in the archonship of Theopompus: appointed to produce tragic drama, I spent

thirty minae and two months later, at the Thargelia, two thousand drachmae, when I won a victory with a male chorus; and in the archonship of Glaucippus, at the Great Panathenaea, eight hundred drachmae on pyrrhic dancers. Besides, I won a victory with a male chorus at the Dionysia under the same archon, and spent on it, including the dedication of the tripod, five thousand drachmae; then, in the time of Diocles, three hundred on a cyclic chorus at the Little Panathenaea. In the meantime, for seven years I equipped warships, at a cost of six talents.[247]

This expense list—if accurate—represents a not so small fortune spent on public service, and probably is not atypical of the costs incurred by members of the liturgy-bearing class. These citizens were allowed to ask for relief from successive years of major liturgies, though the majority of them probably bore at least some liturgical duty most years. Importantly, in the speech quoted above, Lysias defends himself against accusations of bribery. He begins the speech not by addressing the charges themselves, or by producing evidence that he did not take bribes (though he does get to these points), but rather by proudly listing off his largesse to the city over his lifetime. He hopes his substantial contributions to the city will favorably dispose the jury toward him. Lysias' strategy in this speech reflects the performance of liturgies as a form of insurance against indictment, prosecution, and conviction in court, as well as an aid in pushing forward proposals in the Athenian assembly. More generally, jurors and assemblymen, we suspect, looked more favorably on proposals or speeches from those who contributed to Athens, and an orator might not only celebrate his own contributions, but also those of his ancestors.[248] Lysias is far from unique in making this sort of appeal and reflects a tendency of Athenian court cases to take into account not just the guilt or innocence of a defendant, but also his overall contributions to civic life in Athens.[249]

Such rhetorical strategies also, as Josiah Ober demonstrates, channeled competition among elites toward public goods, and away from potentially divisive projects, resulting in benefits all citizens could enjoy.[250] A triumphant *choregos* not only gained bragging rights and a useful appeal in a court case, but the city also allowed him the privilege of setting up a monument to his victory, which usually included the tripod awarded as a trophy, permanently putting his victory on display and generating what David Whitehead calls 'the burden of honor.'[251] The city made parallel awards for the trierarch who first had his ship ready at the start of a new sailing season. Consider Apollodorus' boast about his own trierarchy in his speech *Against Polycles*:

> I was the first to man my ship, hiring the best sailors possible by giving to each man large bonuses and advance payments. More than that, I furnished the ship with equipment wholly my own, taking nothing from the public stores, and I made everything as beautiful and magnificent as possible, outdoing all the other trierarchs. As for rowers, I hired the best that could be had.[252]

Ironically, Apollodorus argues, he provisioned his trireme so well, that the next assigned trierarch, Polycles, didn't want to take it on, worried about the expense. The court speech quoted above represents an attempt to reclaim the expenses related to serving beyond his term when the new trierarch failed to step in and take over the ship.

Ober's insight about the productive channeling of elite competitive instincts should be understood in connection with the decline of elite political power in Athens as the democracy matured. As Athens began to distribute political offices more broadly, details of birth or wealth no longer sufficed as a basis for claiming political or military power and authority. Elite desires for victory, prestige, and honor, if simply frustrated or denied, might have resulted in more violent attacks on or revolts against the young democracy. Instead, the city encouraged competition in a manner that not only minimized the potential threat the elites posed, but also asserted the control of the *demos,* all the while gratifying the competitive quest for honor and prestige. A jury of citizens awarded the prizes in the Festival of Dionysus, and the *demos* itself—whether in the law courts or assembly—validated the contributions of the elite. Athenian civic ideology reinforced the value of these taxes: the vast majority of references to liturgical responsibilities are couched in patriotic language, or in boasts about supererogatory contributions. But—as Matthew Christ points out—we need to view extant evidence with a bit of skepticism. Most of what we know about these forms of taxation comes from public orations, either from the assembly or law courts. Wealthy orators naturally had an interest in publicizing their tax burdens widely, whereas shirkers wanted to escape notice. Additionally, the city itself had an obvious interest in emphasizing widespread compliance. Thus, the number of Athenians who successfully avoided taxation might be higher than our sources would imply.[253]

In fact, we know from multiple sources that despite the boasts about their generosity and service in the Assembly and law courts, Athens' wealthiest citizens unsurprisingly did not necessarily embrace handing over a small fortune for a civic festival or trireme every year. In an understated way, Isocrates describes liturgies as 'burdensome to those to whom they are assigned, although conferring upon them a kind of distinction.'[254] More pointedly, a comic fragment from the fourth century playwright Antiphanes has a rich man lamenting that when:

> having decked out his chorus in golden robes when elected as *choregos*, he will be forced himself as a result to wear rags, or being named trierarch, he will hang himself'.[255]

And in his *Memorabilia*, Xenophon has Callias retort to another character's claim to not have assets, that he should consider himself fortunate since 'the city does not command you and treat you as a slave . . . people do not feel resentful at your not making them a loan.'[256] Not surprisingly, then, we do have some evidence that the rich attempted to conceal their assets and thereby avoid liturgical requirements.[257]

For the Athenians, concealment of wealth presented a major problem. There was no centralized land registry, so accurate assumptions about holdings relied on word of mouth and local knowledge. Liquid or transportable assets must have been even harder to estimate.[258] Athens additionally lacked the capacity to undertake large-scale financial audits. In lieu of more traditional means of assessing taxation levels, Athens instead opted for a legal procedure called *antidosis*, which left regulation of the payment of liturgies to the wealthy themselves. The procedure worked in the following manner. Once liturgies had been assigned for the year, if an individual felt as though another member of the community had more assets but no comparable tax burden, he could challenge that other person to assume the liturgy. If the person refused, he would then offer to exchange all his property (both land and personal property) and assets with those of his opponent, and then assume the tax burden himself. If the offer was rejected, the matter was decided by an Athenian jury, that would decide in a trial which person would take on the burden of the liturgy.[259]

The *antidosis* procedure has clear advantages in prompting the rich to police one another, rather than leave the matter up to the *demos*. A wealthy Athenian likely knew more about his peer's assets than Athenian citizens at large, and the procedure spared the city the effort and expense of keeping track of the holdings of the rich.[260] Indeed, with the potential of an *antidosis* always looming over them, rich Athenians likely kept close track of their colleagues' financial assets.[261] Additionally, the procedure probably also enhanced compliance, since to dispute a liturgy in court possibly appeared as a *de facto* refusal to shoulder one's communal burdens, and may have turned public opinion against both litigants.[262]

Athens thus developed a method not only to place the primary responsibility of direct taxation on its wealthiest members, but also developed a mechanism which placed the primary burden of enforcement on those same tax payers. We can think of the latter as primarily an efficient means of ensuring tax compliance. But Athens' decision to hold its wealthiest members primarily responsible for tax revenues also reflects a different understanding of property than we have today in liberal democracies, where private property is one of the most important of human rights. Indeed, John Locke, one of the intellectual founders of liberalism, locates the natural right to property in the state of nature, antecedent to any sort of social arrangements.[263] For the liberal tradition, property is not an end in itself, but rather an efficient means of pursuing other ends the individual might desire. Human beings retain the right to private property in civil society because most think of it as a 'human' right (close to what Locke called a 'natural' right), not given by the state but, rather, inhering in human beings independent of political affiliation or situation. The twenty-first century state should then—all other things being equal—recognize and protect that right legally. Takings of property—or other assets—in the form of taxes needs special justification, since individuals have a primary and antecedent claim of ownership on their wealth.

As noted earlier, however, the Greek world had no conception of human or natural rights in this strong sense, so ownership of property or other assets sat more firmly under the control of the community. The Greeks did, of course, recognize the importance of property to living well. Aristotle makes this connection early on in the *Politics*, noting that 'no man can live well, or indeed live at all unless he is provided with the necessaries', which we attain most efficiently through property.[264]

Similarly, in critiquing Socrates' proposal to hold property in common in Plato's *Republic*, Aristotle points out the advantages of allowing people to hold property privately, and the disadvantages of communal ownership.[265] But, importantly, Aristotle—and other Greek thinkers—assume as a matter of course that the choice of whether to hold property collectively or individually was one that was made by human beings living in community together, and not one determined by a natural or human right. The decision to protect or allow private property was a pragmatic, collective one, not an ideological one.

We can note a hint of the different conception of property in Athens from another aristocratic complaint about the financial burdens borne by wealthy citizens. In Xenophon's *Economics*, Socrates lists the problems of wealth for Critobulus:

> I observe that already the state is exacting heavy contributions from you: you must keep horses, pay for choruses and gymnastic competitions, and accept magistracies; and if war breaks out, I know they will require you to maintain a ship and pay a level of taxes that you won't easily afford. Whenever you seem to fall short of what is expected of you, the Athenians will certainly punish you as though they had caught you robbing them.[266]

Here, Socrates complains that Athens viewed the assets of the rich as not privately held, but rather something over which the community had some claim. And we see this language echoed in the speeches of democratic politicians, where holdings of the wealthy are viewed as a potential asset for the community. As the speaker in a court speech attributed to Lysias says:

> you ought, therefore, to see the surest revenue for the state in the fortunes of those who are willing to perform public services. So, if you are well advised, you will take as great care of our property as of your own personal possessions.'[267]

This appeal to the jury to respect the speaker's property is underwritten by the assumption that the property is also a shared resource for Athens, that can be called upon when needed.

Socrates' complaint about communal claims on property reflects a common trope raised by wealthy citizens and anti-democratic thinkers about the threat of economic equalization and forced redistribution of resources under democratic governments. Athenian emphasis on political equality implied this possibility, and such seizures did happen in some cities, particularly during or following revolutions. At Athens, however, and despite the fact that no formal barrier existed to this sort of legislation no such steps were ever taken. Indeed, the politician Lysias argued that property confiscation and redistribution was far more likely to occur under an oligarchy:

> champions of oligarchy, who in speech make war
> on the people, but in fact are aiming at your proper-
> ty; and this they will acquire when they find you
> destitute of allies.'[268]

Redistribution of property did surface in Athenian comedy. Aristophanes' *Assemblywomen,* for example, shows the women of Athens forcibly communizing the goods of the city to equalize them once they have taken power in the city. But the fact that this was viewed as comedy, and not a serious proposal indicates the relative safety of property holdings in the city. Instead, the Athenians used the liturgical system and *eisphora* as a sufficient means to exercise the city's claim on accumulated holdings and served as the basis for the provision of critical public goods for the city.

Some contemporary economists have proposed a system similar to liturgies for difficult-to-provide public infrastructure in liberal democracies today.[269] Of course, we already have many examples of private voluntary expenditures on public goods: Andrew Carnegie's funding of public libraries in the

nineteenth and early twentieth centuries, J. Paul Getty's funding
of the Getty Villa, or John D. Rockefeller's founding of the
University of Chicago, for example. Or consider the more recent
acquisition and development of Little Island in the Hudson
River off Manhattan, at an estimated expense of $380 million by
Barry Diller.[270] Many wealthy individuals currently set up trusts
or foundations to expend a portion of their wealth on good
causes. They key difference, though, between contemporary
charitable expenditures and the Athenian system is the voluntary nature of such donations today. While charitable donations
do generate tax reductions, nothing compels the rich today to
part with their money and, should they choose to do so, the
expenditures typically reflect donor priorities rather than public
needs or interests. Consider the contrast between contemporary
voluntary charitable donations and the Athenian decision in
325/4 to deploy a naval fleet into the Adriatic. The decree
passed by the Assembly — which we have preserved in a
fragmentary stone inscription — includes detailed descriptions of
trierarchic responsibilities, instructions for public oversight of
the work, and rewards for outstanding performance. Notably, it
also includes provisions for fines should any individual shirk
his assigned task.[271] The Athenian *demos* collectively determined
the needs and assigned the task of providing for them.

One might object that wealthy members of liberal democracies today do, in fact, pay taxes, and that charitable giving
represents a supererogatory duty, not an obligatory one. But in
the United States, the wealthiest Americans pay only a fraction
of the taxes paid by average Americans due to legal tax avoidance strategies. A recent ProPublica report analyzing a vast
cache of IRS information showed that the wealthiest taxpayers
paid an effective rate of 3.4% on their earnings.[272] Some, like
Amazon founder Jeff Bezos, paid even less: an effective rate of
1.1%, and investor Warren Buffett paid only 0.1%. The median
U.S. household, by contrast, paid 14% in federal income tax. Part
of the problem here is the official tax rates, which today top out

at 37%. U.S. tax rates have historically been much higher than their present levels, reaching 94% on taxable income over $200,000 ($2.5 million in today's dollars) in 1944. But focusing only on tax rates obscures deeper problems in U.S. tax laws, including the failure to tax non-realized gains on investments, mentioned at the beginning of this chapter, which allows the wealthy to shelter the vast majority of their money.

From this brief overview we can see that the Athenian system of liturgies and the tax structure provided both a substantial portion of the city's revenues as well as important public infrastructure. This system also, however, redistributed money and benefits sharply down toward the lower economic classes. The clearest example of this came in terms of direct wages. As the conservative writer of *The Constitution of the Athenians* writes, the 'common people [*penesteroi*] think that they deserve to take money for singing and running and dancing and sailing in the ships, so that they get more and the rich become poorer.'[273] A typical Athenian warship, a trireme, required roughly 170 rowers, plus a crew of some thirty more. During most of the Classical Period, Athens supported fleets of several hundred triremes, ships which quickly added up to thousands of crew members. Rowers in the fleet likely came from the lowest economic class of the city, those too poor to purchase hoplite weapons and armor and fight in the infantry (the wealthiest Athenians fought in the cavalry, on horseback). Thus the fleet itself represented a major form of redistribution of wealth to the poorest members of Athens. Not surprisingly, rowers in the fleet represented the most radical arm of the democracy. Following an attempted oligarchic coup in 411, it was the sailors in the fleet who were instrumental in restoring the democracy.

Liturgies and other taxes, of course, allowed forms of state-sponsored support of citizens beyond rowing slots on a war-ship. Indeed, tax revenues allowed average Athenians to perform the business of the city on a daily basis. One major challenge to substantive and sustained levels of civic engagement in any society is the fact that work occupies a major portion of the day for most people. A person working one or two jobs or caring for children and family members has little time to devote to public life. Even the simple act of voting in liberal democracies like the United States today can require too much time for many citizens, a problem hampered by the lack of a federal holiday for voting. Moreover, elections in the U.S. are held on Tuesdays, a workday, instead of on a weekend when more people have time off. By contrast, most OECD countries set elections on weekends or holidays, and in Australia, voting is actually compulsory.[274] In the U.S., this minimal duty of democratic citizenship is functionally out of reach for a portion of the population.

The one civic duty which does usually compensate citizens for their time in contemporary liberal democracies, serving as a juror, pays so little and requires so much time off work that most people attempt to avoid it. The U.S. compensates jurors at the federal level at fifty dollars per day (and if the jury sits for more than ten days, at sixty dollars per day). This rate of pay works out to an annual equivalent wage of fifteen thousand dollars a year, well below the poverty rate, and certainly creates a disincentive to set one's regular work life aside, despite the theoretical importance of jury trials.[275] Like in Aristophanes' *Wasps*, jury service risks becoming primarily the interest of retired and older citizens.

Athens, by contrast, compensated its citizens for nearly all the tasks necessary for the functioning of the democracy. The Athenians were certainly not unique in paying citizens for political participation, indeed, many Greek democracies in other cities also paid their citizens to do political work. But Athens was exceptional in the range of payments.[276] Civil magistrates selected through sortition, of course, drew a salary for their work over the course of the year, but so did jurors, who were paid enough for their service to support a family. By the fourth century, even simple attendance at the Assembly merited payment equivalent to roughly a day's wage for a laborer. The Athenian system of payment for public services, the *misthos*, originated in the fifth century under Pericles, probably to blunt the effects of liturgies shouldered by the upper class. Prior to that time, the wealthy often wielded large-scale liturgy expenditures to generate political and social support, in effect generating a form of patronage.[277] Pericles' likely target in introducing the *misthos*, a powerful aristocrat named Cimon, had used his wealth and influence in an attempt to check both Pericles' power as well as the expanding democracy.[278] But we need not think that Cimon, alone, was the problem. A major infrastructure project financed by a single individual in a deme might not surprisingly generate a distinctly undemocratic form of inequality. We see this commonly today in the sorts of perks, privileges, and legal deferences afforded to the donor class in economically developed societies. Athens in the early fifth century was no different. The *Athenian Constitution* reports that the above-mentioned Cimon:

> maintained many of the members of his deme, for any member ... who wished could come to him every day and receive adequate maintenance, and all his estates were unfenced so that anyone who wished could help himself to the fruit.[279]

Cimon's economic beneficence translated readily into political power and support until the Athenians ostracized him in 461.

In practice, instead of the individualized patron–client relationship that developed later in the Roman Republic where clients subordinated their own political interests to those of their patrons, we can think of the liturgy establishing a relationship between the *demos* as a whole and wealthy individuals, where the wealthy could gain recognition for their contributions without endangering the political freedom of the citizens. We can see a literary reflection of this relationship in terms such as *philodemos* (lover of the people), and *philopolis* (lover of the city), which appear throughout the literature of the period.[280] And the *misthoi* ensured that the city itself also appeared as a benefactor for the citizens.

Athenian payment for civic participation effectively undercut the sort of direct political control the elite exerted over poorer citizens, liberating them from the burdens of patronage. In practical terms the *misthos* made participation in the administration of the city not just a theoretical possibility for the poorer classes, but a real option for those not independently wealthy. Aristotle recognizes it as a crucial and common democratic strategy, noting that if combined with *no* incentive for the rich to participate in government, the *misthos* would result in power residing firmly in the hands of the masses.[281] In this context, we should view the various *misthoi* not as substitute for a daily wage, but rather as a tool of democratic politics. Athenian citizens did need other sources of income to support themselves, because *misthoi* were only paid on the day of service. The assembly met roughly forty times per year, and courts were in session some 240 times per year. Even an Athenian serving on both would need independent income to supplement his state pay. So instead of thinking of the *misthoi* as a sort of social welfare program, we should view them as a way of preserving citizen independence, and guaranteeing control of the assembly and other political offices in Athens by the *demos* as a whole, instead of the elites.[282]

Critics of the democracy not surprisingly condemned the *misthoi*. Plato has Socrates connect the moral decline of Athens to Pericles' introduction of assembly pay:

> Are the Athenians said to have become better because of Pericles, or, quite to the contrary, are they said to have been corrupted by him? That's what I hear, anyhow, that Pericles made the Athenians idle and cowardly, chatterers and money-grubbers, since he was the first to institute wages [*misthoi*] for them.[283]

Similarly, Isocrates contrasts an older, more virtuous, Athens which valued self-reliance and frugality, in preference to the dependent, money-obsessed citizens he sees about him, who 'know more accurately the incomes derived from the public offices than those which accrued to them from their own estates.'[284] Other sources simply equate the *misthoi* with bribery.[285] While these complaints explicitly question the moral effect on the citizens of payment, much in the same way conservatives today criticize the moral effects of welfare payments on their recipients, the background concern has also to do with the shift in power from the aristocratic and wealthy classes to the population at large that public payments foster.

Athenian provisions of payment for civic participation extended beyond political activities in the narrow sense. Most prominently, from the mid-fourth century onward, citizens received a payment to attend civic festivals — essentially allowing them to take a day off of work to participate in the life of the city.[286] This payment, the *theorikon*, which the orator Demades called the 'glue of the democracy,' originated as a payment for attending theater performances, but was quickly extended to all other festivals, and there were a lot of those.[287] J. K. Davies estimates that in an average year Athens held some ninety-seven festivals, with up to 110 in a Great Panathenaic year. The Old Oligarch sourly notes that Athens held twice as many festivals as other cities.[288] As with the *misthoi*, most critics of the democracy viewed the festivals and *theorika* payments as either distractions for the masses or simple redistribution of wealth down to the lowest classes. The Old Oligarch complains:

> As to sacrifices, temples, festivals, and sanctuaries, the common people recognize that every poor person is unable to sacrifice and feast, to erect temples, or to live in a great and beautiful city, but they have found a means of achieving this end. The city frequently makes many sacrifices publicly, and the common people enjoy the feasts and obtain a share

in the sacrifices. Some of the rich possess private *gymnasia*, baths, and dressing rooms, but the common people build themselves many palestras, dressing rooms, and public baths for their own use; and the mob enjoys this more than do the few and the fortunate.[289]

Undoubtedly the poorer Athenians did materially benefit from festivals and more generally from Athens' innovative progressive structure of taxation. But more importantly, the *misthoi* and *theorika* helped generate a dense communal network of social and political life, orienting the individual toward the community both physically and emotionally. We turn to this topic in the next chapter, focusing especially on the most important festival of all, the annual City Dionysia, or Festival of Dionysus.

Chapter Five

A Network of Civic Life and Community

In 2001 political scientist Robert Putnam published *Bowling Alone*, an important study documenting the dramatic decline in face-to-face interaction in the American public since 1965.[290] He derived his title from the diminishing number of bowling leagues, but it might just have well been titled 'eating alone', 'watching movies alone', or simply 'living alone'. Americans, it seems, increasingly spend more time apart and engaged in solitary activities than at any other time during the past. Putnam examined multiple possible explanations for this decline such as the isolating effects of suburbanization, time pressures for dual-career families, and the effects of geographic mobility. While all these factors may have played some small role in the decline of civic and social organizations, Putnam settled on technology as the primary culprit. Two decades after the publication of *Bowling Alone*, it seems difficult to argue with his conclusion. In the early 1990s, utopian technophiles promised the internet and emerging digital media would provide for the formation of new virtual communities and connect us to one another in deeper and broader ways. Instead it has divided us and left us more isolated than ever. The media, now fragmented into a bewildering array of sources, each speaking to smaller and smaller groups of people, effectively cuts off our access to views different from our own. We hear from and speak to those who already agree with us, and consume our news in the quiet solitude of our houses and apartments.

The internet has also brought commerce directly into our homes. Instead of going into town to shop, we order from Amazon, or if we do go out, we likely shop at a large commercial hub like Walmart or Target instead of a local butcher or pharmacy. In the face of these large, homogenizing commercial centers, small-town Main Streets, where we used to meet and socialize with our fellow citizens, have diminished or vanished, leaving a hollowed out core bypassed by solitary drivers heading elsewhere. And, of course, the COVID epidemic of 2020–2021 only amplified these changes. We all now know the effects of isolation from months of quarantine.

We can trace the consequences of the emerging digital isolation on civic life in economically developed liberal democracies in many ways—from the spiritual to the economic. From one perspective, we might argue that the balkanization and individualization of liberal democratic societies did not begin with the COVID-19 pandemic, the internet or globalization. It began, rather, with liberalism's emphasis on an atomistic, self-interested conception of the human being, buffered and protected from others by human rights, and viewed as theoretically disconnected from the wider social and political fabric of society.[291] We can see hints of this individual emerging in the Early Modern ideas of Thomas Hobbes or John Locke. These political philosophers saw human beings as primarily interested in satisfying their own desires and needing society and the state to help facilitate this pursuit by either providing the necessary infrastructure or protecting us from one another. Once this conception of the self is paired with the economic changes described above, we see in an acute way the sense of declining community and solidarity in contemporary liberal democracies.

Communitarians have lamented the problems of a diminishing sense of belonging and community for quite a while. They offer a critique we can trace back to Rousseau's description of the devastating effects of inequality and individualism, which lies behind Marx's theories of alienation and appears later in Max Weber's position that the world has been 'disenchanted.' This philosophical critique has parallels in concrete measurements of political participation. Setting aside bowling leagues or shopping centers, rates of voter turnout, for example, are strikingly low. In the U.S., typical voter turnout hovers in the mid-50% range for presidential elections, with participation in mid-terms usually well below that level, reflecting widespread disengagement from common life.[292] It can also show up in a loss of confidence in the common threads that unite people together, as Timothy Carney argues in *Alienated America*, in which he links the loss of a sense of community to the rapid growth of mega-churches in the last two decades, where people can get an ersatz sense of belonging.[293] Thomas Mann, Norman Ornstein, and E.J. Dionne link declines in civic participation and alienation with the election of Donald Trump: 'Many rallied to him out of a sense of a yearning for forms of community and solidarity that they sense have been lost.'[294] Americans, like residents of many other states in the developed world, feel isolated and abandoned. Left unchecked, this feeling can manifest itself in unpleasant political consequences.

This chapter argues that we can look to Athenian civic and democratic norms, and their interlocking customs and civic practices to help imagine remedies for contemporary society. In addition to ostracism, sortition, and financial contributions to participation, the Athenians established a number of public institutions that supported and enriched the broader democratic experience and involvement. We will consider a number of these, especially the political organization of the Athenian state, participation in local deme councils, and major festivals like the City Dionysia. None of these institutions was adequate in itself to establish a robust feeling of belonging, but rather they collectively provided a broad civic base for democratic action, orienting individuals toward the public sphere and reinforcing a sense of community. We will consider Athens' unique system of densely interwoven political and civic relations first, and then turn to arguably the most significant annual city-wide event, the Festival of Dionysus, where political and social issues played out thematically on stage.

Before we consider concrete examples in Classical Athens, though, we need first to clarify briefly what we mean by community and a civic life, two rather broad and sometimes vague concepts, but which Athens had in abundance. For the purposes of this chapter, we can examine five primary criteria which constitute them. First, community and civic life usually surround a particular geographic place: a city, town, neighborhood, or even a specific building like a church or other meeting place. Because community can span across geographic or political boundaries, however, it denotes not just a place, but a set of common interests and viewpoints that link people together. Third, this set of intersectional interests and perspectives lends itself to collective action, and a sense of joint identity. Simply put, this is why neighbors or fellow parishioners often help one another; they feel a sense of responsibility and duty derived from their collective ties. This durable sense of community covers not a particular moment or instance, but extends into both the past and the future. Fifth and finally, a thriving community is also diverse in terms of its social complexity: it contains multiple levels and systems, it offers its members many outlets drawing them into the public sphere. Athens in the Classical Period fulfills all these criteria of community and civic life.

Scholars usually assign the birthdate of Athenian democracy to a set of reforms instituted by the politician Cleisthenes in 508/7 BCE. Cleisthenes came to power in the aftermath of the struggle to remove the tyrant Hippias who, with the aid of the Spartan King Cleomenes, established in 510 an oligarchy in Athens, headed by an aristocrat named Isagoras. On assuming power, and with the help of Cleomenes, Isagoras banished

Cleisthenes along with 700 other prominent families. He also attempted to eliminate aspects of the political structure that constrained his power. The Athenian people revolted, and after a brief siege of the Acropolis, to which Cleomenes, Isagoras and their supporters had retreated, the oligarchs fled the city. Athens recalled Cleisthenes, and he instituted a wide-ranging series of governmental reforms, effectively laying the groundwork for the democracy.[295] We will review the major structural reforms here, focusing on how they helped generate an enhanced sense of community and civic connection, which sustained the political superstructure of the democracy.

Prior to Cleisthenes, Athens — like most Greek poleis during the period — was dominated by a system of four tribes (*phylai*) or loose kinship networks. These tribes dominated political activity, and established loyalties that threatened to undermine or bypass the nascent democracy. Not surprisingly, Cleisthenes eliminated these old tribal political structures, replacing them with ten new tribes, each named after a traditional Attic hero.[296] Instead of geographically compact areas, which could be dominated by specific family groups, and which likely priori-tized insular local concerns, each new tribe drew thirds of its membership from each of three physical regions of Attica: the coasts, inland regions, and, finally, the city of Athens itself. Crucially, this brought members of the new tribes into regular contact with people and concerns different from their own. Within these thirds, or *trittys*, we find the more geographically compact and discrete deme: a town, village in Attica, or a neighborhood of the city of Athens itself. The deme served as the most direct communal interface for Athenian citizens.[297] Symbolically, but importantly, residents of Attica began to identify themselves by their demonymic, thus aligning them-selves with the new political structure instead of identifying by their patronymic, which associated them with their family and the older tribal system.

On the one hand, Cleisthenes' reconstruction of Attica's political and social lines clearly aimed at marginalizing older tribal relationships and orienting citizen loyalty toward the new democratic institutions. Aristotle reports as much, associating such actions with extreme forms of democracy:

> Fresh tribes and brotherhoods should be established; the private rites of families should be restricted and converted into public ones; in short, every contrivance should be adopted which will mingle the citizens with one another and get rid of old connections.[298]

But the new political organization also had arguably the more important effect of bringing Athenians from very different areas, traditional family ties, and economic classes together, to work collectively and administer the government. Nowhere do we find clearer evidence for this than in the *Boule*, or Council.

The Council acted as the executive body of the Athenian government. It set the agenda for Assembly meetings, and performed other administrative tasks such as scrutinizing accounts, meeting initially with embassies, and helping to conduct elections and votes in the Assembly.[299] The new governmental structure provided that each tribe sent fifty citizens annually to serve on the Council. These individuals had to serve for one-tenth of the year—the exact timing of which was determined by lot—on the *prytaneis*, a sort of executive body for the Council, which likely met daily, with a third of the members remaining constantly in session to deal with emergencies.

In a fascinating series of studies, Josiah Ober details the sort of connections and civic knowledge acquired by citizens serving on the Council, and especially as members of the *prytaneis*, where much of the day-to-day work of governing Athens was done.[300] The men serving in a *prytaneis* ate, slept, and worked together as part of a team for most of the year. Coming from

different demes and from different parts of Attica, they ex-
changed information about regional concerns and viewpoints
with older and more experienced citizens, instructing younger
less experienced men on procedure and institutional history. At
the end of their service year, *Boule* members returned to their
home demes with both more knowledge and an expanded set of
contacts across Attica. Instead of being familiar only with their
local issues and colleagues, they returned with an enhanced
knowledge of Attica as a whole, anchored by personal relationships.

Because each citizen could serve a maximum of two non-
consecutive terms on the *Boule*, most citizens likely served at
least once in this capacity. Even Socrates, who famously
declared his unwillingness to hold political office, served on the
Boule at least once.[301] Regular turnover on the *Boule* — as well as
in other governmental offices — effectively prevented the sort of
self-serving corporate identity that can develop in an institution
where members remain for long periods of time. It also meant
that whatever sorts of rules or procedures were used needed to
remain relatively simple and transparent, otherwise new
members would not have time to master them. Compare this to
the almost byzantine set of rules governing modern legislative
and bureaucratic bodies, which often require special expertise to
spell out. One other effect of the frequent change among office
holders is that new members of the *Boule* entered on relatively
equal footing. A few members may have served earlier, but not
during the previous year, so no residual power blocs remained
to frustrate new members.

As discussed in Chapter Three, other political offices also
mixed together Athenians from different strata of society. Most
magistrates, for example, did not work alone. Rather, they
served on boards with other citizens. And while they rarely
slept or ate together, they did necessarily work closely with one
another over the course of a year. Given the amount of time
citizen politicians spent together, we must also imagine that

they discussed more than just the political business at hand. Like members of the *Boule*, they likely discussed everyday activities and important events in their lives. Talk about business arrangements, marriages, social engagements, as well as details about the season's olive harvest or pottery production knitted them together.[302] A citizen serving once or twice on the *Boule* and in several other administrative offices would have amassed a significant amount of civic knowledge and personal contacts, which he would then have shared back at the deme level.

We possess less evidence about what went on in the individual demes, but there citizens who had served on the *Boule* or in other administrative capacities would have brought their knowledge and contacts to bear on local issues, educating their fellow demesmen about political and social issues more broadly in Attica. Unlike the main political institutions of Athens, deme government was truly local. The 138 demes in Attica contained 200-300 men on average; most would have known each other personally or via family connections. In the demes citizens got their first taste of democratic government, and they reenacted at a local level many of the democratic procedures through their deme council, which conducted local business, appointed magistrates, and inducted young men into citizenship. At the age of eighteen, young men would be brought before their deme council, identified as citizens by their fathers, and sworn into citizenship by taking the ephebic oath. At the same time, their names were entered onto the official roles, thus giving them broader access to political participation in Athens. Importantly, young men would typically first see or experience politics at the local level before attending the assembly, serving on a jury, or in some other administrative capacity. Participation at the deme level integrated them into the larger network of male citizens, and — as Ober points out — this was as much a virtual network of civic knowledge and connections as it was a concrete one of citizenship and its attendant privileges and duties.[303]

In this sense, Josiah Ober is right to argue that we need to look beyond the formal legal or constitutional structure to understand what made Athenian democracy so resilient. 'Democratic citizenship can be best understood', Ober notes, 'not as a constitutionally guaranteed status, but as a sort of 'social knowledge'.[304] Controlling or hoarding information abets the accumulation of power. It also effectively prevents many organizations from taking advantage of their collective knowledge. In Athens, however, the regular turnover of office holders and the structured mixing of citizens from different geographic, social, and economic levels ensured regular pathways to share information, as well as convey political norms and practices to young members of the polity. It also embodied Aristotle's description of the democratic citizen: one who is 'ruling and being ruled in turn'.[305]

Information sharing and civic connections were not restricted, of course, to formal political offices. Equivalents of Putnam's bowling leagues filled the space between the private sphere of the household and the political structure of Athens. Sailors and rowers working together formed ship companies (*nautai*), merchants grouped themselves into associations (*eis emporian*). There were burial clubs (*homotaphoi*), various cultic groups and associations (*thiasotai* and *orgeones*), and for middle- and upper-class male Athenians, dining clubs were popular (*syssitoi*), most famously described in Plato's dialogue *The Symposium*. Interestingly, many of these organizations mimicked the political rules and procedures of Athenian politics, selecting officers by lottery, inscribing *stelae* with membership lists, rules, and announcements. Robin Osborne calls these sub-state level associations 'mini *poleis*' to indicate the way in which they imitated and reinforced Athenian political norms.[306] Informal socializing, as well, made up a regular part of civic life. In a fascinating study, *Politics and the Street in Democratic Athens*, Alex Gottesman explains how groups of people telling stories or exchanging gossip in the *agora* (marketplace) or in shops influenced public

discourse. Crucially for Gottesman, public spaces in Athens—
what he calls 'the street', functioned as crucial nodes of public
opinion formation, norm enforcement, as well as deliberation.
Unlike many other political and social organizations, the street
admitted the presence and participation of metics, slaves, and—
to an extent—women as well, thus expanding public discourse
and participation to these otherwise marginalized groups.[307] The
point here, of course, is that from the moment they left their
houses, Athenians found themselves immersed in a network of
associations that located them within and oriented them toward
communal life.

The remainder of this chapter investigates one particularly
powerful example of this inclusive effect: the annual Festival of
Dionysus, or the City Dionysia, as the Athenians would have
known it. Held in early spring, this festival had its origins in
pre-democratic Athens, likely in the sixth century as a celebration of the end of winter. It was certainly held and perhaps
enlarged into a major festival under the Peisistratids, a ruling
family of tyrants in the immediate pre-democratic era. By the
fifth century, however, this festival had become a major part of
city life in Athens, arguably the largest and most important
annual festival celebrated.

As its name suggests, the festival is named for the Dionysus,
the god of wine, drunkenness, madness, ecstasy, masks, fluidity,
and the irrational. It was the god's statue—paraded in from its
sanctuary in the nearby deme of Eleutherae—that opened the
festival, and the god presided over the parades, ceremonies, and
theater performances which made up the bulk of the celebrations. Some narratives connect the celebration with Eleutherae's
political union with Athens. As a symbol of their union, the
Eleutherians are said to have brought a statue of Dionysus to the
Acropolis, but the Athenians rejected it. Rejecting divinity was a
dangerous business. In Euripides' play *Bacchae*, the city of
Thebes and its ruler Pentheus rejects the divinity of Dionysus, so
the god possesses the women of the city, turning them into

bacchants – revelers celebrating Dionysus. While possessed by this intoxicating madness, Pentheus' mother, Agave, mistakes her son for a lion and rips him apart with her bare hands, carrying his severed head home to show her father in a ghastly triumph.

Comparatively, the Athenians got off lucky. For refusing his statue, Dionysus punished the Athenians with some sort of genital plague – possibly erectile dysfunction – which the Athenians rid themselves of by accepting Dionysus, and initiating the festival in his honor. Thus, along with the statue of Dionysus, the procession, or *pompe,* initiating the three to four day City Dionysia included large statues of erect *phalloi,* and ended in a revel or *komos* later that night; think of New Orleans' or Brazil's Mardi Gras festival to get a latter-day idea. The whole setting was quite dramatic: the citizens paraded the statue of Dionysus by torchlight, sacrificed bulls, and sang hymns.

Theater performances anchored the activity of the City Dionysia. Athens selected three playwrights every year to compete in the festival, and each of them submitted a trilogy of tragic plays and one comic, or satyr, play. *Choregoi* financed the production of the plays, and they were performed on successive days during the festival. Today we have only a very small fraction of the plays, which probably numbered nearly 1,000 in the fifth century alone. We have thirty-eight surviving plays from the three great tragic writers – Aeschylus, Sophocles, and Euripides – out of approximately 220 they wrote, and only one complete trilogy: Aeschylus' *Oresteia,* first performed in 458. Jurors selected by lot determined first, second, and third prizes, and coveted awards for the *choregoi* as well as the playwright and actors.

As previously discussed, the festival – and especially the productions – were lavish affairs, and tremendously significant, not just for the playwrights and *choregoi,* but also for the Athenian *demos* at large. Consider Demosthenes' complaint about the reactive nature of naval planning in comparison to the elaborate preparations made in advance of each year's City Dionysia:

> And yet, men of Athens, how do you account for
> the fact that the Panathenaic festival and the Diony-
> sia are always held at the right date, whether ex-
> perts or laymen are chosen by lot to manage them,
> that larger sums are lavished upon them than upon
> any one of your expeditions, that they are celebrat-
> ed with bigger crowds and greater splendor than
> anything else of the kind in the world, whereas your
> expeditions invariably arrive too late, whether at
> Methone or at Pagasae or at Potidaea?

Unlike military campaigns, which often had to react quickly in an ad hoc manner to changing situations, elaborate advance planning ensured the success of the City Dionysia:

> everything is ordered by statute; every man among
> you knows long beforehand who of his tribe is to
> provide the chorus or who to equip the gymnasium,
> what he is to receive, when and from whom he is to
> receive it, and what he is to do; nothing here is left
> to chance, nothing is undetermined.[308]

Demosthenes' description of the preparations underlines the importance the festival had in Athenian political and social life. Normal city life came to a halt during the festival: the law courts and most other political institutions shut down and Athens turned its attention not just to the revelry and plays, but also to a series of communal celebrations and instantiations of Athenian democratic ideology. Direct manifestations of this included the awarding of crowns to citizens who had provided Athens with significant service as well as a parade of young men, *ephebes*, whose fathers had been killed in war. The city provided for their upbringing and, upon reaching adulthood, provided them with a set of hoplite armor to mark the occasion. Both groups were also given honorary seats in the Theater of Dionysus to watch the plays.[309] In showcasing these two award ceremonies, Athens reinforced the orientation of individuals in the city to the community, toward service and sacrifice.

The city also displayed tribute from allied cities, demonstrating Athens' military and political power. Greeks and other foreigners came to Athens for the festival from all across the Aegean, which was held at the beginning of the sailing season, after winter when sea travel became safer. In this sense, it served as an effective advertisement of the wealth and power of Athens not only to Athenians, but also to visitors from other *poleis*. We even have some evidence that a specific block of seats at the theater was set aside for foreign visitors.[310]

Theater performances formed the core of the Festival of Dionysus. The three competing trilogies and their attached satyr plays, spread out over three days, were performed in the Theater of Dionysus, a large semi-circular space built into the south slope of the Acropolis. The size of the space grew from its earliest origins in the sixth century throughout the Classical Period, and was further developed in the Hellenistic Period.[311] Figures for the size of the theater vary. In Plato's *Symposium*, Socrates praises the tragic poet Agathon—who had just won first prize—for his calm demeanor in front of 30,000 Greeks at the Theater of Dionysus.[312] Interestingly, Agathon's victory was likely at a lesser festival, the *Lenaia*, and so likely drew a much smaller and less international audience, since it was held in the winter, when travel was difficult. Socrates might also have been teasing Agathon gently with an inflated number. But even accounting for some exaggeration, 30,000 viewers represents a huge percentage of the population of Attica, and should be regarded as an outer limit on the number of attendees. And one wonders what spectators on the fringes of the theater could have understood, given the capacity of the human voice to project so far and over so many.[313] Certainly, the number of actual seats was far fewer. Most scholars today put functional attendance at the theater in the range of 14,000–17,000, with some space for observers outside of the formal seating area.[314]

But even at the lower end of most estimates, the play performances at the Festival of Dionysus likely represent the largest regular gathering in the Greek world during the Classical Period, surpassed only perhaps by the Olympic Games, or the Great Panathenaia, though numbers for those quadrennial events are difficult to assess with any degree of accuracy. Certainly compared to a normal assembly meeting, where about 6,000 Athenians attended, the Festival of Dionysus was huge.

Perhaps more importantly for our purposes here, the audience at the Festival of Dionysus was not limited to adult male citizens, as were most other civic institutions. We have already mentioned foreigners in attendance, but strong evidence suggests that members of the Athenian community normally marginalized in day-to-day political discourse also attended, including metics, women, and slaves. The politician Demosthenes implies that even prisoners were released for the festival.[315] Most of the evidence for these groups is problematic, especially when it comes to slaves. Theophrastus, in his *Characters*, describes the 'shameless man' who purchases tickets to the festival on behalf of foreigners and takes not only his underage son but also his son's tutor (a slave).[316] The 'shameless man' clearly violates a norm against these actions, but the passage also indicates that the norms were violated frequently enough for the example to seem plausible. More concretely, some public slaves — the eight assistants to the *Boule*, for example — evidently had specially reserved seats.[317] Beyond these exceptions, any slaves viewing the performances likely watched from the periphery, and not in formal seating.

The evidence for the presence of women at the Festival of Dionysus is particularly intriguing given their prominent roles in the plays themselves. Most scholars now recognize the likely presence of at least some women, though the extent to which they attended still prompts disagreement.[318] Evidence for their presence in the audience derives largely from chance and problematic mentions. Athenaeus, for example, says that Alcibiades excited both the men and the women when he led the procession into the theater, and a biography of Aeschylus reports that children fainted and women had miscarriages during a performance of his *Eumenides*.[319] We also possess a *scholia* on Aristophanes' *Assemblywomen* noting a proposed piece of legislation by one Phyromachos, intending to formally separate men from women within the theater, and further separating prostitutes from free women.[320] This would imply, of course, that not only were women present, but that they may have even had their own wedge of seats, or *kerkides*. Priestesses also participated in the ceremonial procession, or *pompe*, preceding the plays, and so at least some of those would likely have remained for the actual performances.[321]

The presence of these marginalized groups in the Theater of Dionysus tells us something important about the democracy — something conservative critics of Athens eagerly pointed out, linking it to their more general critique of democracy. Socrates complains in Plato's *Gorgias* about the broad appeal of the musical styles and performances at the festivals, saying:

> Therefore we have now found a form of rhetoric
> aimed at a *demos* such as is composed of children
> and men and women together, slave and free.

Elsewhere in the Minos, he calls the plays 'most soul entrancing' to the *demos*.[322] Aristotle, too, connects theatrical performances to the democracy arguing that theater caters to the tastes and needs of manual workers.[323] A character in Plato's dialogue the *Laws* even proposes that theater culture and the musical forms associated with it bring about radical democracy, thus potentially corrupting more sober forms of political association.[324]

But what is the connection here between theater and politics? On the face of it, the objection seems to relate to the fact that theater, like democracy, allows and promotes participation and entrancement by the wrong sorts of people. Socrates, in Plato's dialogues, argues that most people in a city lack the necessary intellectual capacities to manage public affairs. They may lack the concrete political or economic knowledge to properly introduce or evaluate a legislative proposal, and they also may lack the ability to develop those capacities.

But as the Athenian Stranger implies in Plato's *Laws,* theater's effect may go deeper because of the passions aroused during performance, which awaken and reinforce irrational elements in the soul. In Plato's *Republic,* Socrates notoriously argues that most people are driven by their appetites, and hence think primarily of gratifying themselves, prioritizing financial gain and social prestige, neither of which the Greeks considered good guides to political activity since they ignored the needs of the community as a whole and diminished individual sacrifice. Democracy, Socrates argues, represents one of the worst forms of government (better only than tyranny, into which it easily lapses), because it caters to the whims of the many instead of the knowledge of those better qualified. And like theater, it has broad mass appeal:

> the democratic man is elegant and colorful, just like
> the democratic city. Many men and women might
> envy him his life.[325]

The democratic citizen, like his city, lacks organizing direction in his life, and his meandering pursuit of pleasure prevents him from realizing his — and his city's — full potential. His inability to judge properly, additionally, endangers the physical well-being and freedom of his city.

Another source of this complaint lies in a more abstract rejection of democratic forms of equality. In the same way that the political institutions of the city ignore natural differences between individuals in favor of the random choices of sortition, the Festival of Dionysus even seemed to do away with distinctions between citizens and non-citizens, men and women, as well as between free and enslaved. Both Socrates and Aristotle thus connect the leveling political effects of democratic conceptions of equality with a leveling (and lowering) of intellectual, political, and aesthetic standards, not to mention the practical dangers of a city ruled by the ever-changing whims of the masses.

But, as we have seen, the Athenians invested their festivals — especially the Festival of Dionysus — with enormous importance. The writer of the *Constitution of the Athenians* was right to note that festivals and the liturgies which supported them provided otherwise unobtainable entertainment and luxuries to the masses, but they did more than that. Recent trends in scholarship originating in structuralist approaches to the plays have pointed out the close link between Athenian democratic ideology and the dramatic festivals, not only in terms of the parades and ceremonies, which celebrated individual contributions and symbolized the power of Athens, but in the performances of the plays themselves.[326] On this reading, theater is necessarily entangled in the production and reification of civic ideology: both parasitic on the democracy and constitutive of its values. As Simon Goldhill puts it: 'theater is not so much a commentary on *ta politika* as a part of it.'[327] The most sophisticated versions of this approach emphasize the fact that Athenian tragedy and comedy question, criticize, and subvert civic norms as much as they celebrate them.[328]

Structuralist-oriented readings of Athenian theater recognize the special importance of the contestatory nature of drama itself, which necessarily presents opposing positions and hence opens up space for deliberation and debate, mirroring basic aspects of democratic citizenship.[329] Theater, then, 'practices democracy,' as Peter Burian argues in an analysis of agonistic speech in several tragedies.[330] Free speech, *parrhesia*, and debate in the plays symbolically enact the free speech of the Athenian assembly, *agora*, and public sphere of the citizens. In the best cases, free speech and agonistic debate are used to craft good

laws and public policy, as well as make good citizens. The
orator Demosthenes acerbically remarks in a letter that *parrhesia*
'is thought capable of making even stupid people tolerable.'[331]
But when corrupted — as in the case of Euripides' *Orestes* — it can
subvert.[332] As Burian puts it:

> The Greeks knew that freedom of speech can be
> used to attack freedom. They also knew, as we
> should, that without free speech, there is no free-
> dom.[333]

Paradoxically, democratic discourse both instantiates and
endangers democracy; it simultaneously challenges and
reinforces it, generating the theoretical space necessary for
reflection on political norms.

Theater performances in this sense did more than simply
unite Athenians together spatially in the Theater of Dionysus.
They also linked them together ideologically, and provided a
form of continuing critical reflection on being Athenian. Though
we have only a small fraction of the plays produced during the
Classical Period, a startling number of them deal directly or
indirectly with issues facing the democracy. Some plays
describe not-so-distant historical events. Aeschylus' *Persians*, for
example, portrays the after effects of the Battle of Salamis on the
Persian court. Given the magnitude and importance of the
Athenian naval victory, we might expect some military trium-
phalism in a play like the *Persians*, but instead we see a deeply
sympathetic work which focuses on the (imagined) devastating
psychological consequences on the Persian king Xerxes, his
mother, and the losses to his army. The play has baffled many
modern critics, some of whom saw it as an extended and
puzzling dirge. But more recent readings of the play emphasize
the way in which Aeschylus' description of Persian monarchy
and society constitutes an inverted mirror of Athenian characteristics.[334] Indeed, the play is less interesting for what it says
about goings-on at the Persian court of Xerxes — likely wholly

invented by Aeschylus — than how it serves as a subtle reminder of what it means to be Athenian: the play clearly credits the victory at Salamis to its democratic form of government. The Persian queen mother, Atossa, while waiting to hear the results of the invasion of Greece, asks about Xerxes' opponents: 'Who is set over Athenians as shepherd and is master of their host?' To which the Chorus answers: 'Of no man are they called vassals or slaves.'[335] Athenians are free and fight willingly; they collectively made the decision to face Xerxes' forces. The Persian king, by contrast, rules absolutely, and treats his subjects like slaves. A series of other parallels help distinguish the Athenians from the Persians: Persian opulence, decadence, and wealth take the form of gold, while Athens relies on a more sober form — silver from its mines at Laurium.[336] Aeschylus emphasizes Persian emotion in contrast to the firmness of the Greeks.[337] The Persian army rapidly disintegrates into disorder and chaos during the battle, while the Athenians maintain discipline and order.[338] The Persian army, made up of contributions from across the empire, speaks a polyglot of languages, while the Greeks speak a single language.[339] The Greeks use spears, which are associated with bravery and masculinity, while the Persians use more cowardly bows, and Xerxes, symbolically, returns to Persia with his quiver empty.[340] All this rich description tells the viewer less about Persia than it does about Athens — or perhaps more accurately — what Athens desires to think about itself. The *Persians* — like other plays and social interactions — serves as constant reminders for the Athenians of who they are, the values they hold, and the power of the democracy.

Sometimes Greek tragedies cast a critical eye on Athens when its practices fail to live up to its ideals. Many scholars argue that Euripides' *Trojan Women*, for example, levels a devastating critique of Athenian military brutality in the Aegean, and especially the events surrounding the city of Melos. Famously highlighted in Thucydides' *History of the Peloponnesian War*, the Melian Dialogue describes a discussion between the oligarchic rulers of Melos and unnamed Athenian generals. The Athenians ignore Melian claims of innocence, appeals to justice, fairness, and the gods and offer them only the choice between unconditional surrender and destruction. When the Melians—hoping for Spartan or divine aid—refuse, the Athenians take the city, kill all the adult males, and enslave the women and children.

Euripides' play *The Trojan Women*, first performed in 415, about a year after the events at Melos, shows the desperate situation of the women of Troy after the city has been sacked by the Greek forces and the women are awaiting the news of their own fate. For most, this means enslavement to a Greek commander, but for some it means death. Polyxena, one of the princesses of Troy, has her throat cut over the grave of the dead warrior Achilles. And the small child Astyanax, grandson of the king and queen of Troy, is thrown to his death from the walls of the defeated city after being torn from his mother's arms. The play is irremediably bleak, and the Greeks are portrayed as brutal, sacrilegious, duplicitous, and driven only by thoughts of wealth and power. 'Greeks!' Hecuba cries in the play, 'Your Greek cleverness is simple barbarity'.[341] It would have been hard for an Athenian audience watching this play not to have recollected and drawn parallels with their own city's actions on Melos, scarcely a year earlier.

We cannot know for sure why Euripides displaces the events of his play into the Homeric past. Perhaps too direct a condemnation of Athenian behavior might have prompted a dangerous backlash. We know that a now lost early fifth-century play, *The Sack of Miletus* by the poet Phrynichus, which likely subtly critiqued Athenian inability or unwillingness to support an ally in the face of Persian aggression, caused such an uproar that the poet was fined, and forbidden from performing the play again.[342] But, regardless of the immediate political concerns of the poet, centering of the action outside of Athens itself allowed some space for critical reflection, which more immediate political critiques or disputes might have eclipsed. Tragic playwrights wrote many dramas with other Homeric or mythical settings, focusing frequently on the city of Thebes, which Froma Zeitlin calls 'the anti-Athens,' where Athens 'puts itself and its values into question by projecting itself upon the stage to confront the present with the past through its ancient myths.'[343] Some of the most well known tragedies — *Oedipus Tyrannos*, *Antigone*, and Euripides' *Bacchae*, among others — are all set in Thebes.

Athens itself was only rarely the direct subject of tragedies, and then mostly in its mythical past. The final play of our only fully extant trilogy, Aeschylus' *Oresteia*, ends with the trial of Orestes, who is pursued by the Erinyes, or Furies, to Athens after killing his mother. In convening a jury of Athenian citizens to hear the arguments, Athene also symbolically founds the Athenian judicial system, and establishes a uniform standard of justice. The monumental triumph of this act, however, is undermined by several key details in the trial, where the god Apollo speaks on behalf of Orestes and the Erinyes speak for Clytemnestra, Orestes' dead mother. Both Apollo and the Eryines threaten Athens should they lose the case, and Apollo's defense speech takes a sophistic turn when he argues that mothers are not actually related to their children; only the father has a true blood tie to the child. The jury of Athenians splits evenly, and Athene casts the deciding vote for Orestes, after which she has to calm the anger of the Erinyes with the promise of gifts, a permanent home under the Areopagus in Athens, and the threat of violence:

> alone among the gods I know the keys to the cham-
> ber in which [Zeus'] thunderbolt is sealed up. But
> there is no need for that.[344]

Threats of force, duplicitous arguments, and indecision on the part of the jury, complicate the founding act of Athenian justice. But the play offers another interpretive possibility, of course. The jury's split might reflect not indecision but equal recognition of the claims, and we can see Apollo's argument about fathers being the true parent reflected in roughly contemporary biological theories.[345] Similarly, the integration of the Erinyes, and their change into Eumenides, or well-wishers, may represent the integration into Athens (albeit underground) of the claims represented by Clytemnestra and the Erinyes of the household and private sphere. The complexity of the play's end almost necessitates interpretive work and nicely illustrates how the *Oresteia* simultaneously celebrates the Athenian system of justice while attending to the costs and harms done by it.

Unlike tragedies, comedies took regular aim at Athenian politicians and their policies, as well as ordinary citizens. Aristophanes' *Knights*, for example, mercilessly satirizes the popular politician Cleon, a frequent target of Athenian comedy, as a dangerous demagogue.[346] Average citizens are also mocked as money- and power-obsessed jurors—'brethren of the three obols [φράτερες τριωβόλου]', as Paphlagon (Cleon) calls them, referring to a day's jury pay.[347] And Philocleon in *Wasps*, obsessed with his power as a juryman, enjoys 'the tears and wailings of each day's defendants', and calls himself 'master of everyone! [ὅστις ἄρχω τῶν ἀπάντων].'[348] But not only individuals receive comic treatment: basic political dilemmas such as those caused by the difficulties of collective action make for excellent comedy as well.[349] The clear appeal of such comic critiques might imply antidemocratic sentiments, and indeed, Aristophanes is often read as highly critical of democracy as a form of government.[350] But we must remember that the democracy at Athens faced relatively few internal challenges after its establishment, none of which had any long-term success. Instead, then, these parodies of democratic procedures, politicians, and norms should be understood more broadly as reflecting popular understanding of the criticisms, providing a means of collectively acknowledging them, and finally (re)educating the citizens about their proper roles in the democracy.

In the Theater of Dionysus, even topics off-limits to traditional political discourse gained a hearing. Given their second-class
status politically, a surprising number of tragedies feature
powerful or prominent women from Greek mythology: Clytemnestra, Antigone, Helen, Hecuba, Electra, Medea, among others.
In many of these plays, female characters defend values
associated with the family and private sphere which are in
tension with the male-dominated civic space. Or, like Antigone,
they directly challenge the morality of civic edicts. We see a
similar focus in Aristophanes' comedies. Women manage to
stop a war by going on a sex strike in the *Lysistrata*, and the
women of Athens take over the governing of the city in *Assemblywomen*, reorganizing politics and the economy along communal lines, legislatively negating natural distinctions between
men and women. The prominence of these marginalized groups
did not go unremarked, especially when it came to the youngest
and most radical of the classical tragedians, Euripides. Consider
the following exchange between Euripides and Aeschylus in
Aristophanes' play *Frogs*, which portrays the deceased pair
competing for the chair of tragedy in the underworld while they
await the arrival of Sophocles. Euripides, eagerly embracing the
prominent role of women and slaves in his work, starts off with
a description of his plays:

> Euripides: And from the very first lines, I wouldn't
> leave any character idle; I'd have the wife speak,
> and the slave just as much, and the master, and the
> maiden, and the old lady.
>
> Aeschylus: And for such audacity, you surely de-
> serve the death penalty!
>
> Euripides: No, by Apollo, it was a democratic act
> [δημοκρατικὸν γὰρ αὖτ' ἔδρων].[351]

The passage nicely highlights both the transgressive nature of
foregrounding women and slaves, as well as its imagining of a

more inclusive democratic sphere, not restricted to the voices and worldviews of adult male citizens. This openness to viewpoints outside the normal ambit of politics is what Edith Hall calls the 'multifocal form.'[352] In this sense, despite the ventriloquized nature of women's voices in the plays, we can see evidence of the hidden critique of masculine political discourse and decisions: the cost of militarism to the private sphere, the violence done to the innocent in war, as well as the inadequate management of domestic economy. And it is certainly not a mistake that these concerns are raised in the most democratic institution in Athenian civic life, where citizens and non-citizens, men and women, viewed the plays together.

In an important study on Athenian political rhetoric, Nicole Loraux argues Athenian orators 'abolished the frontiers that separate reality from fantasy', and substituted 'for the real city the phantom of an ideal polis, a utopia.'[353] In a similar way, theater had the same effect—offering up to audiences an image of the city both for viewing pleasure, but also for theoretical reflection. Tellingly, Athenian theater explicitly recognized its role as an educator of the people. While the two poets in Aristophanes' *Frogs* disagree about nearly everything— especially the quality of their respective plays—they do agree on the purpose and function of theater. Responding to Aeschylus' question about the qualities one should admire in a poet, Euripides responds: 'Skill and good counsel, and because we make people better members of their communities.'[354] They did this partly by reinforcing the values and norms of the *polis*, but also by holding them up for inspection and critique.

The Festival of Dionysus, we can now conclude, played a crucial role in Athenian civic life. Bringing the whole city together for a few days, it focused attention not only on the successes and strengths of democracy, but also its difficulties, shortcomings, and unresolved issues. Athenians, young and old alike, were given a lesson both in the norms of the democracy, and space within which to reflect critically on them. Other civic festivals across the year continually reinforced this lesson, though at a smaller scale.

In contemporary society we also have artistic productions capable of offering the same sort of reflective space as those of Athenian theater. Sophisticated plays like Tony Kushner's *Angels in America*, or Arthur Miller's *Death of a Salesman* can provide similar nuance and depth in their analysis of contemporary society as can some films or other artistic productions.[355] But these works of art cannot compare with the theater of Athens in terms of their social and political reach. Audiences and viewership are today as balkanized as our politics and we lack a coherent common text and discursive space within which we can think together about those things which unite us as well as the problems we face as a people.

As we discussed at the beginning of this chapter, liberal democracies today face hollowed-out public spheres and high rates of alienation. Socializing—especially recently—takes place primarily online, aggravating existing trends toward isolation and atomization. Athenians, by contrast, lived largely in the presence of others. Ancient Greek has a rich vocabulary for describing different forms of friendship, love, and association, but relatively few words for solitary activity. Indeed, solitary behavior was rare, and socially frowned upon.[356] Today, solitary work and activity seems close to the norm.

Addressing the problem of hyper-individualism and declining rates of communal activities presents real difficulties, especially given the fractured nature of our political systems, troubled most recently by the COVID epidemic, but more frighteningly by the real threat of antidemocratic actors and forces. But we do have possible solutions, and ways of beginning to address our problems. One path forward is suggested by Robert Putnam, with whom we began this chapter. In a 2004 follow-up to his *Bowling Alone* study, Putnam—along with Lewis Feldstein and Donald Cohen—published *Better Together: Restoring American Community*, a description of community building activities across the United States. One general conclusion they draw points to the significance of 'nesting'.[357] This term refers to the importance of small, intimate groups or organizations 'nested' inside of larger societal units. In practical terms, these groups are organizations we all recognize: Putnam's bowling leagues, the Elks Club, baseball or soccer leagues, churches, synagogues, mosques, and other community organizations. Small nested organizations bridge the gap between our individual, local, and homogenous networks and the impersonal nature of wider liberal democratic society. Small groups open up spaces within which we can bond with others, drawing lines of connection to the wider society. The sub-state-level organizations and clubs described above in our discussion of Classical Athens perform the same function, connecting local activity with the wider community. Athenians were members of their local deme, and perhaps a dining club, trade association, or other grouping. Those, in turn, connected them to the wider Athenian community. Liberalism traditionally has paid little attention to these sorts of associations, largely because of its emphasis on the individual as well as the relegation of these groups to the private sphere, traditionally off-limits to political intrusion or inspection in liberal political thought. Consequently, we have to look beyond liberalism for theoretical approaches that recognize the importance of local 'nested' associations. Edmund Burke's conservatism, for example, emphasizes the importance of small groups of individuals:

> To be attached to the subdivision, to love the little
> platoon we belong to in society, is the first principle
> (the germ as it were) of public affections.[358]

And Georg Hegel argues that we should understand the individual primarily as a member of concentric circles of association moving outward to the whole of society. In contemporary political theory, we can turn to communitarians like Charles Taylor or Benjamin Barber for theoretical expositions of the importance of sub-state-level groupings, or Burke's 'little platoons'.

Concretely, in societies like the United States, we can start by reinvesting in local communities, seeding local groups, and providing the spaces where they might meet or form. Neighborhood assembly and action programs can address specific problems. The creation or renovation of collectively held spaces like parks, community centers, and basketball courts can draw people out of their private lives into common spaces. Civic festivals, even local ones, bring large numbers of neighbors together in one space for a common purpose. Neighborhood or town-wide book groups are even better because they promote dialogue and discussion. The town where my university is located holds such an annual event called One Book, One New Paltz. A committee selects a common community read, and the local library makes copies available so all can participate. Participation in it is widespread, and the discussions are vigorous, occurring over several weeks, with members learning to negotiate sometimes difficult differences of opinion. Politically, we can think about revamping local political institutions to make space for boards of citizens instead of elected officials, citizens' assemblies, and use of lotteries to staff non-technical positions.

Political communities need a common set of beliefs and practices to help tie them together, to reinforce norms and convey them to subsequent generations. Athenian democrats and their conservative critics agreed on this. In Plato's *Republic*, for example, Socrates argues for the importance of myths and stories — he calls them 'useful falsehoods' — to help stabilize the social and political order.[359] Rational arguments alone, Socrates says, fail to fully persuade. Democratic Athens used the Festival of Dionysus, among other institutions, toward this same end. In the Early Modern period, philosophers like Jean-Jacques Rousseau call for a 'civil religion', one which reinforces civic responsibilities. 'It is of great importance to the state', Rousseau writes, 'that each citizen have a religion that causes him to love his duties.' The doctrines of Rousseau's civil religion are few, but importantly include 'the sanctity of the social contract and of the laws.' [360] A sense of belonging, connection, and responsibility should be made almost instinctive instead of as a conclusion of reason. As Rousseau points out, even a reputed atheist like Thomas Hobbes understands the importance of religion in reinforcing civic duty.[361] Early liberal thinkers like John Locke also clearly rely on an underlying set of religious beliefs to add force to basic concepts like natural law and natural rights.

Today, of course, the idea of a national religion, 'the reunification of the two heads of the eagle', as Rousseau describes it, seems unlikely.[362] The diversity and plurality of religious belief in liberal democracies defy consolidation, and attempting to do so would violate important considerations of freedom of conscience. Without this important tool, liberal democracies today need to explore options that would generate a national sense of belonging and responsibility.

One such possibility is to follow the examples of countries like Germany and Israel, which require a period of national service upon reaching early adulthood, thus establishing a common experience and bond of citizenship. For years, scholars like Charles Moskos have called for expanded forms of national service, arguing that it could revive a sense of civic obligation and help restore a 'new balance after an indiscriminate weakening of the sense of citizenship duty.'[363] Benjamin Barber commends it as one of the components of his 'strong democracy,' since it channels our need to find a place in a local community. When such options are lacking, he writes, the desire for a sense of belonging 'will breed unhealthy and anti-democratic forms: gangs, secret societies, conspiratorial political groups, hierarchical clubs, and exclusive communities.'[364] One need not squint hard to see membership in politically dangerous groups such as QAnon or the Proud Boys as a perverted expression of the desire for a sense of belonging and community. Importantly, national service need not take a single form, such as service in the military. The Peace Corps, community service, public infrastructure projects, education, and other options could also fulfill the duty. Regardless, it should involve a meaningful amount of time at the beginning of adulthood, as a transition into full citizenship, with no exemptions from service except in the case of physical or mental disabilities.

One could imagine many other ways to develop and enhance community in advanced liberal democracies. The important key component to all of them, though, involves bringing people into contact with others around the common purpose of engaging in a project that directs the individual away from self-interest narrowly conceived. This is what Classical Athens managed to do, and we in liberal democracies need to think about doing the same to blunt the problem of isolation and the hyper-individualism of contemporary society.

Conclusion

Democracies in the modern world face an uncertain future. Beset with internal and external threats, today's governments creak under stacked stresses like climate change, citizen disengagement, hollowed-out civic life, and ideological challenges from both within and without. Liberal democracies, which have only existed a brief few centuries in human history, are in trouble, and could very well not persist into the next. Robert Michels' 'iron law of oligarchy' may yet claim them, if it has not already.

If we are to persist as democratic nations, as democratic peoples, we must rethink and re-invigorate our basic institutions and relationships with one another. It has been the argument of this book that Athenian democratic practices, institutions, and ideologies can serve as a useful reminder of the large range of democratic experience and possibility. Thucydides has the politician Pericles in his famous 'Funeral Oration' call Athens a 'school of Hellas', and he was right.[365] Athens clearly has the potential to reach beyond Greece and the ancient world to offer us advice today. We can use it to shake off our assumptions about the range of the possible with democracy. Athens can point the way toward a different, deeper, and much more robust conception of citizenship and community.

We began this book with a discussion of the deep theoretical gap that separates us from Ancient Athenians. While we share with – and indeed derive *from* them – fundamental political terminology and concepts like freedom, equality, and democracy, a closer examination of how they deployed and understood these terms brings into relief differences we would be well advised to think about carefully.

One key connecting thread through that discussion was the fact that the Athenians did not think in terms of natural or human rights, but instead in terms of their position in and duties toward their political community. Instead of individuals, they understood themselves as involved together in a collective project. The rights-based discourse which lies at the root of liberalism, by contrast, encourages us to think of one another as separate, and worse, as potential competitors and perhaps even threats. Our entry into the political world is contoured by the need to protect key aspects of the self from others. We begin, metaphorically, in an agonistic stance. Rights, of course, are extremely important, and many of the most important freedoms we enjoy in liberal democracies are linked to them. But taken to an extreme, they can also be divisive, creating conflicts and tensions that are difficult to resolve, partially because appeals to human rights are in part an attempt to push certain protections out of the realm of the political, and partially because conflicting rights claims are very difficult to resolve.[366]

One lesson we can take away from the Athenian experience is the reminder that other values are just as important to successful democracies. Equality, especially in the political realm, was a primary Athenian value. But equality always sits in tension with freedom, and the free exercise of rights. To the extent that we allow free action, inequalities will result. This might be acceptable or relatively unproblematic in the economic realm — indeed, as we discussed, the Athenians did not object to wealth inequality on principle. But when those inequalities of wealth or status threaten to bleed into the political sphere, core democratic commitments to equality begin to be eroded.[367]

The threat aristocratic inequality posed for Athens helps explain the origins and usage of the topic of Chapter Two, ostracism. The practice of banning one individual from the city for a decade first allowed the young democracy to develop in the absence of potentially destabilizing threats of oligarchic retrenchment. Later use of the procedure both helped mediate potentially violent disagreements between the city's elites as well as placing them squarely under the watchful eye of the *demos*. Ostracism was as much an assertion of the power of the people as it was a tool of democracy. We should also not forget here the relatively gentle coercive strength of ostracism. Alternatives to ostracism, such as death, permanent exile, confiscation of property, and associated penalties for families and associates all set the stakes of the penalty too high. Ostracism — as the Athenians practiced it — held out the promise of a potential reconciliation, of a return to Athens, and one's ancestral homeland. And the fact that it only affected the individual in question — and not his family, friends, or assets, all of which could remain in Athens in good standing — doubtless made temporary exile a more palatable option than violence or civil war. Another important aspect of ostracism was the fact that it was not linked to a particular crime; no specific legal offense triggered an ostracism, and its victim could technically be legally innocent of any such torts. But Athenians knew that amassed power could warp the space of democratic actions, creating inequalities than no laws or procedures could mitigate. Ostracism in this sense was a way for the people to remove potential threats to the city without formal cause.

At the beginning of the chapter on ostracism I described the effect of Donald Trump's 'ostracism' from Twitter in January of 2021. And this helps point the way forward in reimagining this practice in contemporary democracies. We need to consider better and more impermeable firewalls to the accumulation of wealth and power than ineffective campaign finance laws, or lobbying restrictions. A start would be to enforce and then additionally enhance such policies. One step better would be to rethink some of our commitments to freedom of speech which has spawned a whole set of new and intractable problems in the age of the internet.

Ostracism, at root, was a way for Athenians to maintain political equality. But they also enacted political equality in the way they distributed most political and administrative offices of the city. This was the lesson of Chapter Three—on sortition. To a degree not since duplicated, Athens spread power and authority throughout the entire citizen body, filling oversight boards with randomly selected citizens who would actualize the enactments of the assembly. Part of the rationale for this elaborate and time-consuming method or governing the city was a deep suspicion of accreted power. Very few offices in Athens were held by an individual for more than one year, and the mechanisms involved in the selection of office holders effectively prevented widespread corruption or abuse. But sortition also reveals a deep faith in the competence of the average Athenian. Lottery-filled positions required no advance knowledge or special expertise. The city assumed, rather, that average citizens would be able to address administrative issues in the city with competence. When knowledge was required, they might learn from an older colleague on the board, or bring in some of their own expertise from earlier administrative or business experiences.

Instead of having their decisions made by experts or professionals, Athenians deliberated, ratified, and enacted laws themselves. In today's liberal democracies the gap between the political class and the rest of the population has grown wide. We see evidence of this in widespread voter dissatisfaction and a loss of confidence in government. Brexit might be credited solely to the perceived gap between bureaucrats in Brussels and the individual voter in Nottingham, Norwich or York. Athens suffered no such crisis of legitimacy; each Athenian had a role in making and enforcing laws and policies; politics were immediate and personal, not distant. Happily, recent experiments and developments in sortition in nations like Canada, the U.S., the U.K., and France suggest that liberal democracies are slowly attempting to learn from the Athenian experiment. This work is among the most promising for revitalizing democracy.

In Chapter Four we considered how the Athenians financed their massive and expensive investment in the average citizen. The time individuals spent in the assembly, in the law courts, and acting on administrative magistracies in the city (let alone in the army or rowing in the fleet on campaign) required money; a poor Athenian certainly could not afford to leave his own work uncompensated to perform his civic duties. To facilitate widespread participation, Athens publicly funded civic activity, making it possible—or perhaps even attractive—for even the poorest members of the community to participate. Athens viewed its citizens as resources, and wanted to allow each person to contribute, again pointing back to a basic and fundamental commitment to equality.

The city financed this participation partly through revenue from the empire, silver mining by slaves, and also through taxation of the wealthiest members of the community. Our discussion revealed the very different conception of property at work in Athenian democratic ideology, where one's property was always held as a resource for the city, and Athens developed effective means of encouraging (and sometimes enforcing) compliance on the part of the wealthy. We would call the Athenian system today a highly progressive system of taxation —not, however, designed to curtail or reduce individual fortunes, but rather to use them to reinforce practices of equality in the political sphere.

Liberal democracies view property as a fundamental right. But sometimes this threatens to limit the sorts of claim the public sphere has on individual wealth. Real, active democracy is costly, and time-consuming; we need to consider how to fund it. Like Athenians, we might begin to think about individual holdings less as an absolute right, than as an asset the community can partly claim. Contemporary arguments about desert from philosophers like John Rawls support this sort of argument.

In Chapter Five we turned to a consideration of one of the many ways in which Athens enhanced civic ideology and community, the annual Festival of Dionysus. This annual event brought Athenians of all different backgrounds together for several days. And unlike most other civic institutions, which were restricted to men and citizens, the City Dionysia was comparatively open—foreigners, diplomatic visitors, and metics attended, and there were likely both slaves and women viewing these events as well. Not surprisingly, Athenians themselves benefitted from a special fund to purchase tickets to this event so that even the poorest citizen could attend. One might easily say that in democratic Athens the Festival of Dionysus was *the* most democratic institution in that it was the most inclusive. This latter fact is important because the festival was a key means of transmitting knowledge and norms from one person to another and from one generation to the next. On stage in front of them Athenians watched basic aspects of their city critiqued, evaluated, and explained. It was simultaneously a space of learning and evaluating the city. The plays of Aeschylus, Sophocles, Euripides, Aristophanes (and many others which we have lost) allowed space for the residents of Athens to think about what it meant to live in that democratic space, and how they shared a set of common values, norms, and traditions.

The Festival of Dionysus was but one example of the many festivals, associations, and institutions that knit Athenians together on a daily basis. Athens was an intensely personal, face-to-face society; a far cry from our isolated workstations and Amazon deliveries. Today we need to think about ways of revitalizing our sense of community and relearning the ways of citizenship. We concluded our discussion of the City Dionysia with a gesture toward how to begin this process: engaging locally in civic organizations, town halls, neighborhood associations and clubs. At the level of the nation we need to consider some idea of service along the lines of Israel or other states to help link us together across geographic, social, and economic lines. There are resources for this in the modern philosophical tradition in thinkers like Rousseau, Hegel, and the communitarians. But we will need to move beyond the atomistic self at the root of Lockean liberalism if we are to succeed.

* * *

No one of the examples from Athens in this book — or their imagined modern counterparts — alone is enough to address the wide range of difficulties we face today. As we just mentioned, reimagining and reviving democratic culture needs time and work at both the local and national levels. Most importantly, we must change our understanding of citizenship, of our relationship to one another and the wider community. We can no longer afford to think of citizenship as a passive affair, where we are more observers than participants in a spectator democracy, more connected to consumer than political culture, or to think about politics in terms of narrow wins and losses. We also cannot afford the luxury of disgruntled withdrawal. Political engagement must become more than retweeting, liking, or upvoting on social media. And local civic life requires that we leave our homes and screens to venture back out into the public square. Building local bonds of trust through community organization and projects is a slow, if reliable, means of extending community outward.

Beyond the local level we need to advocate for and support broader forms of civic engagement, whether that takes the form of national service, citizen assemblies, funding for community-building activities, or reconfiguring the tax and legal structure along more egalitarian lines. No one person, town, or city can manage the task alone, but that is the promise latent in democracy: we work together.

Bibliography

Aeschylus, *Eumenides*, tr. A. Sommerstein (Harvard, 2009).

Aeschylus, *Persians*, tr. S. Bernardete (Chicago, 1956).

Allen, D., Christesen, P, Millett, P., (eds.), *How to Do Things with History: New Approaches to Ancient Greece* (Oxford, 2018).

Alwine, A., 'Freedom and Patronage in the Athenian Democracy', *Journal of Hellenic Studies*, Vol. 136 (2016), pp. 1-17.

Amandry, P., *La mantique Apollinienne à Delphes: Essai sur le fonctionnement de l'Oracle* (Bocard, 1950).

Anderson, G., *The Athenian Experiment: Building an Imagined Political Community in Ancient Attica, 508-490 B.C.* (University of Michigan, 2003).

Aristophanes, *Clouds,* tr. J. Henderson (Harvard, 1998).

Aristophanes, *Frogs*, tr. J. Henderson (Harvard, 2002),

Aristophanes, *Wasps*, tr. J. Henderson, (Harvard, 1998).

Aristotle, *Politics*, tr. C. Lord, (Chicago, 1984).

[Aristotle], *The Politics and Constitution of Athens*, ted. S. Everson (Cambridge Texts in the History of Political Thought, 1996).

Barber, B., 'Service, Citizenship and Democracy: Civic Duty as an Entitlement of Civil Right,' in W. Evers, (ed.), *National Service: Pro and Con* (Hoover Institution Press, 1990), p. 35-6.

Barry, B., *Political Argument* (Routledge, 2011).

Barry, B., 'Justice Between Generations' in Hacker, P., and Raz, J., (eds.) *Law, Society, and Morality: Essays in Honor of H. L. A. Hart* (Oxford, 1977), pp. 268-284.

Batchelder, L.L., 'What Should Society Expect from Heirs? A Proposal for a Comprehensive Inheritance Tax' (February 23, 2010)., 63 *Tax Law Review* 1 (2009), NYU Law and Economics Research Paper No. 08-42. Available at SSRN: https://ssrn.com/abstract= 1274466.

Bentham, J., *The Rationale of Reward* (Wentworth Press, 2019).

Berent, M., 'The Greek Invention of Politics', *History of Political Thought*, XIX, No. 3, pp. 331-362.

Bers, V., 'Just Rituals: Why the Rigamarole of Fourth-Century Athenian Lawcourts?' in Nielsen, T., Flensted-Jensen, P., Rubinstein, L., *Polis and Politics. Studies in Ancient Greek History* (Museum Tusculanum Press, 2000), pp. 555-564.

Berlin, I., 'Two Concepts of Liberty,' *Four Essays on Liberty* (Oxford, 1969).

Bicknell, P., 'Agasias the Donkey', *Zeitschrift für Papyrologie und Epigraphik,* Vol. 62 (1986), pp. 183-184.

Bishop, J., 'The Cleroterium', *Journal of Hellenic Studies*, Vol. 90 (1970), pp. 1–14.

Blass, F., *Die attische Beredsamkeit* iii (Leipzig, 1893).

Blanshard, A.,' Jurors and Serial Killers: Loneliness, Deliberation, and Community in Ancient Athens,' in D. Allen, P. Christesen, P. Millett (eds.), *How to Do Things with History: New Approaches to Ancient Greece* (Oxford, 2018), pp. 137-157.

Brown, W., *States of Injury: Power and Freedom in Late Modernity* (Princeton, 1995).

Burke, E., *Reflections on the Revolution in France* (Hackett, 1987).

E. Burke, *Appeal from the New to the Old Whigs*, ed. D. Ritchie (Cambridge, 1992), p.168.

Burnheim, J., *The Demarchy Manifesto* (Imprint Academic, 2016).

Burian, P., 'Athenian Tragedy as Democratic Discourse,' in D. M. Carter (ed.) *Why Athens?: A Reappraisal of Tragic Politics* (Oxford, 2011) pp. 95-118.

Calder, W. M., 'Vita Aeschyli 9: Miscarriages in the Theatre of Dionysos', *The Classical Quarterly*, Vol. 38, No. 2 (1988), pp. 554-555.

Carney, T., *Alienated America: Why Some Places Thrive While Others Collapse* (Harper Collins, 2019).

Carson, L., 'Integrating Citizen Deliberation into National Decisions: Ireland's Prime Minister's Office', The NewDemocracy Foundation, https://www.newdemocracy.com.au/2017/05/28/integrating-citizen-deliberation-into-national-decisions/.

Carter, D. M., *The Quiet Athenian* (Oxford, 1986).

Carter, D.M., 'Republicanism, Rights and Democratic Athens', *Polis*, Vol 30, No. 1 (2013), pp. 73-91.

Cartledge, P., *Democracy: A Life* (Oxford, 2018).

Castells, M., *Rupture: The Crisis of Liberal Democracy* (Polity, 2018).

Chou, M., Gagnon, J.P., Pruitt, L., 'Putting Participation on State: Examining Participatory Theatre as an Alternative Site for Political Participation', *Policy Studies*, Vol. 36, No. 5, (2015), pp. 608-622.

Christ, M., 'The Evolution of the Eisphora in Classical Athens', *The Classical Quarterly New Series*, Vol. 57, No. 1 (May, 2007), pp. 53-69.

Christ, M. 'Liturgy Avoidance and Antidosis in Classical Athens', *Transactions of the American Philological Association*, Vol. 120 (1990), pp. 147-169.

Cohen, D., 'Democracy and Individual Rights in Athens', *Zeitschrift der Savigny-Stiftung für Rechtsgeschichte: Romantische Abetilung*, Vol. 114, No. 1, (1997), pp. 31-52.

Connor, W., 'Tribes, Festivals and Processions: Civic Ceremonial and Political Manipulation in Archaic Greece', *Journal of Hellenic Studies*, Vol. 107 (1987), pp. 40-50.

Constant, B., 'The Liberty of the Ancients Compared with that of the Moderns,' in *Political Writings*, tr. B. Fontana (Cambridge, 1988), pp. 310-311.

Crochetière, E., 'Democracy and the Lot: The Lottery of Public Offices in Classical Athens,' *McGill University Masters Theses*, (December, 2013).

Courant, D., 'From Kleroterion to Cryptology: The Act of Sortition in the 21st Century,' in L. Lopez-Rabatel, Y. Sintomer (eds.),

Sortition and Democracy: History, Tools, Theories (Imprint Academic, 2020), pp. 343-371.

Cunningham, E., Saich, T, and Turiel, J., *Understanding CCP Resilience: Surveying Chinese Public Opinion Through Time*, (Harvard Ash Center for Democratic Governance and Innovation, 2020).

Davies, J., *Athenian Propertied Families* (Oxford, 1971).

Dawson, S., 'The Theatrical Audience in Fifth-Century Athens: Numbers and Status', *Prudentia*, Vol. XXIX, No.3 (May, 1997) pp. 1-14.

Demont, P., 'Selection by Lot in Ancient Athens: From Religion to Politics', in L. Lopez-Rabatel, Y. Sintomer (eds.), *Sortition and Democracy: History, Tools, Theories* (Imprint Academic, 2020), pp. 112-129.

Demosthenes, *Letters*, tr. N. W. DeWitt (Harvard, 1923).

Demosthenes, *Orations*, (Harvard-Loeb, 1939).

Dowlen, O., *The Political Potential of Sortition* (Imprint Academic, 2008).

Edmonds, J.M. *The Fragments of Attic Comedy after Meineke, Bergk, and Kock* (E. J. Brill, 1959).

Eisinger, J., Ernsthausen, J., Kiel, P., 'The Secret IRS Files: Trove of Never-Before-Seen Records Reveal How the Wealthiest Avoid Income Tax,' 6/8/21. www.propublica.org/article/the-secret-irs-files-trove-of-never-before-seen-records-reveal-how-the-wealthiest-avoid-income-tax.

Engelstad, F., 'The Assignment of Political Office by Lot,' in P. Stone (ed.), *Lotteries in Public Life: A Reader* (Imprint Academic, 2011), pp. 177-200.

Euben, J.P., 'Political Corruption in Euripides' *Orestes*,' in J.P. Euben (ed.), *Greek Tragedy and Political Theory* (University of California, 1986), pp. 222-251.

Euben, J.P., *The Tragedy of Political Theory: The Road Not Taken*, (Princeton, 1990).

Euben, J.P., *Corrupting Youth: Political Education, Democratic Culture, and Political Theory* (Princeton, 1997).

Euben, J.P, Ober, J., and Wallach, J.R. (eds), *Athenian Political Thought and the Reconstitution of American Democracy* (Cornell, 1995).

Fawcett, P. 'When I Squeeze You with *Eisphorai*': Taxes and Tax Policy in Classical Athens', *Hesperia: The Journal of the American School of Classical Studies at Athens*, Vol. 85, No. 1 (January-March 2016), pp. 153-199.

Ferejohn, J., 'The Citizens' Assembly Model', in M. Warren, H. Pearce (eds.) *Designing Deliberative Democracy* (Cambridge University Press, 2008).

Figueiredo, J, Richter, B. 'Advancing the Empirical Research on Lobbying', *Annual Review of Political Science*, Vol. 17, pp. 163-185.

Finley, M.I., *Democracy Ancient and Modern* (Chatto & Windus, 1973).

Fishkin, J., Review of 'When Citizens Decide: Lessons from Citizens' Assemblies on Electoral Reform', and 'Designing Deliberative Democracy: The British Columbia Citizens Assembly', *Perspectives on Politics*, Vol. 11, No. 2 (June, 2013), pp. 670-672.

Fishkin, J., 'Random assemblies for lawmaking? Prospects and Limits', *Politics and Society*, Vol. 46, No. 3 (2018), pp. 359-379.

Fishkin, J.S., *Democracy When the People Are Thinking* (Oxford, 2020).

Flensted-Jensen, et. al. (eds.), *Polis and Politics. Studies in Ancient Greek History Presented to Mogens Herman Hansen on His Sixtieth Birthday, August 20, 2000* (Copenhagen, 2000).

Fontenrose, J., *The Delphic Oracle, Its Responses and Operations, with a Catalogue of Responses* (University of California, 1978).

Forsdyke, S., *Exile, Ostracism and Democracy* (Princeton, 2005).

Fourniau, J., 'The Selection of Deliberative Minipublics: Sortition, Motivation, and Availability,' in L. Lopez-Rabatel, Y. Sintomer (eds.), *Sortition and Democracy: History, Tools, Theories* (Imprint Academic, 2020), pp. 372-399.

Fournier, P., van der Kolk, H., Carty, R., Blais, A., Rose, J., *When Citizens Decide: Lessons from Citizen Assemblies on Electoral Reform* (Oxford, 2011).

Fränkel, M., *Die attischen Geschworenengerichte. Ein Beitrag zum attischen Staatsrecht* (Berlin, 1877).

Fuks, A., *Social Conflict in Ancient Greece*, (Brill, 1997).

Fukuyama, F., 'The End of History?', *The National Interest*, Vol. 16 (1989), pp. 3–18.

Fukuyama, F., *Identity: The Demand for Dignity and the Politics of Resentment* (Farrar, Straus and Giroux, 2018).

Fuller, R., *Beasts and Gods: How Democracy Changed its Meaning and Lost its Purpose* (Zed Books, 2015).

Fuller, R., *In Defence of Democracy* (Polity, 2019).

Gabrielsen, V., 'The Antidosis Procedure in Classical Athens', *Classica et Mediaevalia*, Vol. 38 (1987), pp. 7-38.

Gabrielsen, V., *Financing the Athenian Fleet. Public Taxation and Social Relations* (Johns Hopkins Press, 1994).

Gastil, J., Knobloch, K., Reedy, H., 'Assessing the Electoral Impact of the 2010 Oregon Citizens' Initiative Review', *American Politics Research*, Vol. 46, No. 3 (2018), pp. 534-563.

Giannantoni, G., 'La prinatia di Socrate nel 406 A.C.,' *Rivista Critica di Storia della Filosofia*, Vol. 17, No., 1 (1962), pp. 3-25.

Gilens, M., Page, B. 'Testing Theories of American Politics: Elites, Interest Groups, and Average Citizens', *Perspectives on Politics*, Vol. 12, No. 3 (2014), pp. 564-581.

Glendon, M.A., *Rights Talk: The Impoverishment of Political Discourse* (Free Press, 2008),

Goldhill, S., 'The audience of Athenian tragedy', in *The Cambridge Companion to Greek Tragedy* (Cambridge, 1997), pp. 54-68.

Goldhill, S., 'Civic Ideology and the Problem of Difference: The Politics of Aeschylean Tragedy, Once Again', *Journal of Hellenic Studies*, Vol. 120 (2000), pp. 34-56.

Goldstein, J. A., *The Letters of Demosthenes* (Columbia, 1968).

Goodin, R., *Innovating Democracy: Democratic Theory and Practice After the Deliberative Turn* (Oxford, 2008).

Gorham, E., *National Service, Citizenship, and Political Education* (SUNY Press, 1992).

Gottesman, A., *Politics and the Street in Democratic Athens* (Cambridge University Press, 2014).

Greely, H., 'The Equality of Allocation by Lot', in P. Stone (ed.), *Lotteries in Public Life: A Reader* (Imprint Academic, 2011) pp. 59-84.

Greene, J., *How Rights Went Wrong: Why Our Obsession with Rights Is Tearing America Apart* (Mariner Books, 2021).

Grönlund, K, Bächtiger, A, Setälä, M (eds.), *Deliberative Mini-Publics. Involving Citizens in the Democratic Process* (ECPR Press, 2014), pp. 41–58.

Hacker, J, Pierson, P. 'Winner-Take-All Politics: Public Policy, Political Organization, and the Precipitous Rise of Top Incomes in the United States', *Politics & Society*, Vol. 38, No. 2 (2010), pp. 152-204.

Hall, E., *Inventing the Barbarian: Greek Self-Definition through Tragedy* (Oxford Classical Monographs, Oxford, 1989).

Hall, E., 'The Sociology of Athenian Tragedy' in P. E. Easterling (ed.), *The Cambridge Companion to Greek Tragedy* (Cambridge, 1997), pp. 93-126.

Hansen, M., *Eisangelia: the Sovereignty of the People's Court in Athens in the Fourth Century BC and the Impeachment of Generals and Politicians* (Odense: University of Southern Denmark, 1975).

Hansen, M.H., 'Prerequisites for Magistrates in Fourth-Century Athens', *Classica et Medievalia*, 32 (1980) pp. 105-125.

Hansen, M.H., 'Seven Hundred Archai in Classical Athens', *Greek, Roman and Byzantine Studies*, Vol. 21, No. 2 (Summer, 1981), pp. 151–173.

Hansen, M.H., *The Athenian Ecclesia II: A Collection of Articles 1983-1989* (Copenhagen, 1989).

Hansen, M.H., *The Athenian Democracy in the Age of Demosthenes* (Blackwell, 1991).

Hansen, M.H., *The Trial of Sokrates from the Athenian Point of View* (Kgl. Danske Videnskabernes Selskab, 1995).

Hansen, M.H., 'The 190 Themistokles Ostraka as Evidence of Large Political Groups' in K. Ascani (ed.), *Ancient History Matters,*

Studies Presented to Jens Erik Skydsgaard on his Seventieth Birthday (L'Erma di Bretschneider, 2002), pp. 193-198.

Hansen, M.H., *The Tradition of Ancient Greek Democracy and Its Importance for Modern Democracy* (Royal Danish Academy of Science and Letters, 2005).

Harvey, F.D., 'Dona Ferentes: Some Aspects of Bribery in Greek Politics', *History of Political Thought*, Vol. 6, No. 1/2 (Summer 1985), pp. 76-117.

Hatzfeld, J. 'Socrate au procés des Arginuses', *Revue des Études Anciennes*, 42, (1940).

Herodotus, *Histories*, tr. A. D. Godley (Harvard University Press, 1920).

Hesk, J., 'Euripidean *Euboulia* and Tragic Politics,' in D. M. Carter (ed.), *Why Athens?: A Reappraisal of Tragic Politics* (Oxford, 2011), pp. 119-144.

Homer, *Iliad*, tr. R. Lattimore (Chicago, 1951).

Homer, *Odyssey*, tr. E. Wilson (W. W. Norton, 2018).

Hornblower, S. 'The Old Oligarch and Thucydides. A Fourth-Century Date for the Old Oligarch' in Flensted-Jensen et. al. (eds.) *Polis and Politics. Studies in Ancient Greek History Presented to Mogens Herman Hansen on His Sixtieth Birthday, August 20, 2000* (Copenhagen, 2000), pp. 263-294.

Isocrates, *Isocrates with an English Translation*, tr. G. Norlin (Harvard, 1980), Vols. I & 2.

Kagan, D., 'The Origin and Purpose of Ostracism', *Journal of the American School of Classical Studies at Athens*, Vol. 30, No. 4, (Oct-Dec. 1961), pp. 393-401.

Kaiser, B., 'The Athenian Trierarchy: Mechanism Design for the Private Provision of Public Goods', *The Journal of Economic History*, Vol. 67, No. 2 (June, 2007), pp. 445-480.

Katz, E., *Embattled: How Ancient Greek Myths Empower Us to Resist Tyranny* (Redwood Press, 2021).

Klosko, G., *The Development of Plato's Political Theory* (Oxford, 2007).

Knox, R.A., 'So Mischievous a Beast'? The Athenian *Demos* and its Treatment of its Politicians,' *Greece and Rome*, Vol. 32, No. 2 (October 1985), pp. 132-161.

Kosmin, P., 'A Phenomenology of Democracy: Ostracism as Political Ritual', *Classical Antiquity* Vol. 34, No. 1 (2015), pp. 121-152.

Kovner, A., 'Jury Democracy Blog', https://alexkovner.com/blog/

Kroll, J., *Athenian Bronze Allotment Plates* (Cambridge, 1972).

Kron, G., 'The Distribution of Wealth at Athens in Comparative Perspective', *Zeitschrift für Papyrologie und Epigraphik*, 2011, Bd. 179 (2011), pp. 129-138.

Lane, M., *The Birth of Politics: Eight Greek and Roman Political Ideas and Why They Matter* (Princeton, 2016).

Landemore, H., *Open Democracy: Reinventing Popular Rule for the Twenty-First Century* (Princeton, 2020).

Lang, A., 'But is it for Real? The British Columbia Citizens' Assembly as a Model of State-Sponsored Citizen Empowerment', *Politics and Society*, Vol. 35, No. 1 (2007), pp. 35-70.

Levitsky, S., Way, L., 'Elections Without Democracy: The Rise of Competitive Authoritarianism', *Journal of Democracy*, Vol. 13, No. 2 (April, 2002) pp. 51-65.

Lewis, D. (ed.), *Inscriptiones Graecae I*, 3rd ed. (Berlin, 1981).

Lopez-Rabatel, L., Sintomer, Y., (eds.) *Sortition and Democracy: History, Tools, Theories* (Imprint Academic, 2020).

Lopez-Rabatel, L, 'Drawing Lots on Ancient Greece — Vocabulary and Tools,' tr. C. Delacroix-Howell, in L. Lopez-Rabatel, Y. Sintomer (eds.), *Sortition and Democracy. History, Tools, Theories* (Imprint Academic, 2020). pp. 152-204.

Loraux, N., *The Invention of Athens: the Funeral Oration in the Classical City* (Zone Books, 2006).

Lysias, *Lysias*, tr. W. R. M. Lamb (Loeb, 1989).

Mann, T., Ornstein, N., Dionne, E., *One Nation After Trump: A Guide for the Perplexed, the Disillusioned, the Desperate, and the Not-Yet Deported* (St. Martin's Press, 2017).

Markle, M., 'Jury Pay and Assembly Pay at Athens,' *History of Political Thought*, Vol. 6, No. 1/2 (Summer 1985), pp. 265-297.

Matheson, S., 'The Goddess Tyche', in *Yale University Art Gallery Bulletin: An Obsession with Fortune: Tyche in Greek and Roman Art* (1994), pp. 18-33.

Mavrogordatos, G., 'Two Puzzles Involving Socrates', *The Classical World*, 105, No. 1 (Fall 2011), pp. 3-23.

McCannon, B., 'Who pays taxes? Liturgies and the Antidosis procedure in Ancient Athens,' *Constitutional Political Economy*, Vol. 28, (2017), pp. 407-421.

Meier, C., *The Political Art of Greek Tragedy* (Johns Hopkins, 1993).

Milano, L., 'Destiny, the Drawing of Lots and Divine Will in Ancient Near Eastern Societies' tr. A. Price, in L. Lopez-Rabatel, Y. Sintomer (eds.), *Sortition and Democracy: History, Tools, Theories* (Imprint Academic, 2020), pp. 29-52.

Mill, J.S., *Utilitarianism* (Hacket, 1979).

Mill, J.S., *On Liberty* (Hackett, 1987), I (p. 10).

Miller, F., *Nature, Justice, and Rights in Aristotle's Politics* (Oxford, 1995).

Miller, J., 'Aristotle's Paradox of Monarchy and the Biographical Tradition', *History of Political Thought*, Vol. 19, No. 4 (Winter, 1998), pp. 501-516.

Miller, J., 'Warning the *Demos*: Political Communication with a Democratic Audience in Demosthenes', *History of Political Thought*, Vol. 23, No. 3 (Autumn, 2002).

Millett, P., 'Patronage and its Avoidance in Classical Athens' in A. Wallace-Hadrill (ed.) *Patronage in Ancient Society* (Routledge, 1989), pp. 15-47.

Mirhady, D., 'The Dikasts' Oath and the Question of Fact', in A. Somerstein and J. Fletcher (eds.), *Horkos: The Oath in Greek Society* (Liverpool University Press, 2008).

Mirhady, D., Schwarz, C., 'Dikastic Participation', *Classical Quarterly New Series*, Vol. 61, No. 2 (December, 2011), pp. 744-748.

Moskos, C., *A Call to Civic Service: National Service for Country and Community* (Free Press, 1988).

Mulgan, R., 'Lots as a Democratic Device of Selection', *Review of Politics*, 46, No. 4 (October 1984) pp. 539-560, p. 547, Repr. In P. Stone (ed.), *Lotteries in Public Life: A Reader* (Imprint Academic, 2011), pp. 113-132.

Mueller, C., Tollison, R., Willett, D., 'Representative Democracy via Random Selection,' in P. Stone (ed.), *Lotteries in Public Life: A Reader* (Imprint Academic, 2011), pp. 47-58.

Ober, J., *Mass and Elite in Democratic Athens* (Princeton, 1989).

Ober, J., *Athenian Legacies, Essays on the Politics of Getting on Together* (Princeton, 2005).

Ober, J., *Democracy and Knowledge: Innovation and Learning in Classical Athens* (Princeton, 2008).

Ober, J., *Demopolis: Democracy in Liberalism in Theory and Practice* (Cambridge, 2017).

Ognyanova, K., Lazer, D., Robertson, R. E., & Wilson, C., 'Misinformation in action: Fake news exposure is linked to lower trust in media, higher trust in government when your side is in power', Harvard Kennedy School, *Misinformation Review* (2020) https://doi.org/10.37016/mr-2020-024.

O'Halloran, B., 'The Political Economy of Classical Athens: A Naval Perspective', *Mnemosyne*, Supplements, Vol. 425 (2019), pp. 164-182.

Olson, S.D. (ed.) *Antiphanes. Sappho – Crysis, Fragmenta Incertarum, Fabularum, Fragmenta Dubia* (Vandenhoeck & Ruprecht, 2021).

Olson, S. D., *Broken Laughter: Select Fragments of Greek Comedy* (Oxford, 2007).

Osborne, R., 'The *Demos* and its Divisions in Classical Athens,' in O. Murray, S. Price (eds.), *The Greek City from Homer to Alexander* (Clarendon Press, 1990), pp. 265-93.

Page, B., Bartels, L., and Seawright, L., 'Democracy and the Policy Preferences of Wealthy Americans', *Perspectives on Politics*, Vol. 11, No. 1 (March, 2013), pp. 51-73.

Parker, R., 'Greek States and Greek Oracles', *History of Political Thought*, Vol. 6, No. 1/2 (1985), pp. 298-326.

Pickard-Cambridge, A. W., *Dramatic Festivals of Athens*, 2nd edition rev. J. Gould and D. M. Lewis (Oxford, 1968).

Picketty, T., *Capital in the Twenty First Century* (Harvard, 2017).

Plato, *Republic*, tr. T. Griffith (Cambridge, 2000).

Plato, *Gorgias*, tr. D. Zel, (Hackett, 1987).

Podlecki, A., 'Could Women Attend the Theatre in Ancient Athens: A Collection of Testimonia', *Ancient World* Vol. 21 (1990), pp. 27-43.

Popper, K., *The Open Society and its Enemies* (Routledge, 1945).

Pseudo-Xenophon, *Pseudo-Xenophon's Constitution of the Athenians*, tr. R. Osborne (London Association of Classical Teachers, 2008).

Putnam, R., *Bowling Alone. The Collapse and Revival of American Community* (Simon & Schuster, 2000).

Putnam, L. Feldstein, D. Cohen, *Better Together: Restoring American Community* (Simon & Schuster, 2004).

Raaflaub, K. (ed.), *War and Peace in the Ancient World* (Wiley-Blackwell, 2006).

Rahi, A.,'Who Does and Does Not Support the Taliban?' *Express Tribune*, 2 September 2021: https://tribune.com.pk/article/97465/who-does-and-does-not-support-the-taliban-in-afghanistan.

Raubitschek, A., 'The Origin of Ostracism', *American Journal of Archaeology* Vol. 55, No. 3 (July, 1951) pp. 221-9.

Rawls, J., *A Theory of Justice*, Rev. Ed. (Harvard, 1971).

Renwick, A., Allan, S., Jennings, W. McKee, R., Russell, M., Smith, G., *A Considered Public Voice on Brexit: The Report of the Citizens' Assembly on Brexit* (Online: The Constitution Unit, 2017), http://citizensassembly.co.uk/wp-content/uploads/2017/12/Citizens-Assembly-on-Brexit-Report.pdf.

Rhodes, P.J., *The Athenian Boule* (Oxford, 1985).

Rhodes, P.J., 'Political Activity in Classical Athens', *Journal of Hellenic Studies*, Vol. 106 (November, 1986), pp. 132-144.

Rhodes, P.J. and Osborne, R., *Greek Historical Inscriptions: 404-323 BC* (Oxford, 2003).

Rhodes, P.J., 'Nothing to Do with Democracy: Athenian Drama and the Polis', *Journal of Hellenic Studies*, Vol. 123 (2003), pp. 104-116.

Rhodes, P.J., *Ancient Democracy and Modern Ideology* (Duckworth, 2003).

Rhodes, P.J., 'Problems in the Athenian Eisphora and Liturgies', *American Journal of Ancient History*, Vol. 71 (2017), pp. 1-19.

Roberts, J., *Accountability in Athenian Government* (Wisconsin University Press, 1982).

Rousseau, J.-J., *The Basic Political Writings*, tr. D. A. Cress (Hackett, 2011).

Sandel, M., *Liberalism and the Limits of Justice* (Cambridge, 1982).

Schedler, A., 'Elections Without Democracy: The Menu of Manipulation', *Journal of Democracy*, Vol. 13, No. 2 (April, 2002), pp. 36-50.

Scullion, S., 'Nothing to Do with Dionysus: Tragedy Misconceived as Ritual', *The Classical Quarterly*, Vol. 52, No. 1 (2002), pp. 102-137.

Sealey, R., 'The Origins of Demokratia,' *California Studies in Classical Antiquity*, Vol. 6 (1973), pp. 253-295.

Segal, S., 'Greek Tragedy and Society: A Structuralist Perspective,' in J. P. Euben (ed.), *Greek Tragedy and Political Theory* (University of California, 1986), pp. 43-75.

Sigmundsdóttir, A., 'The People of Iceland Have Spoken', *The Guardian*, November 16, 2009.

Silverman, D., *The Trierarchy and Athenian Civic Identity*, 1994 Ph.D. Thesis, UC Berkeley. https://www.proquest.com/openview/07d095e73ec7544ccd10c06a1909b064/1?pq-origsite=gscholar&cbl=18750&diss=y

Skocpol, T., *Diminished Democracy: From Membership to Management in American Civic Life* (University of Oklahoma Press, 2003).

Stanton, G. R., 'The Tribal Reforms of Kleisthenes the Alkmeonid', *Chiron*, Vol. 14 (1984), pp. 1-41.

de Ste. Croix, G.E.M., 'Notes on Jurisdiction in the Athenian Empire II', *Classical Quarterly*, Vol. 11, No. 2 (November, 1961), pp. 268-280.

de Ste. Croix, G.E.M., *The Origins of the Peloponnesian War* (Cornell, 1972).

de Ste. Croix, G.E.M., 'Political Pay Outside Athens', *Classical Quarterly*, 25 (1975), pp. 48-52.

Stone, P., (ed.), *Lotteries in Public Life: A Reader* (Imprint Academic, 2011).

Stone, P., 'Sortition, Voting, and democratic Equality', *Critical Review of International Social and Political Philosophy*, Vol. 19, No. 3 (2016), pp. 339-356.

Strauss, L., *Socrates and Aristophanes* (Basic Books, 1966).

Sundahl, M., 'The Rule of Law and the Nature of the Fourth-Century Athenian Democracy', *Classica et Mediaevalia*, Vol. 127, (2003), pp. 127-132.

Taylor, C., 'What's Wrong with Negative Liberty?', *Philosophy and the Human Sciences: Philosophical Papers*, Vol. 2 (Cambridge: Cambridge University Press, 1985).

Taylor, C., *Philosophical Papers* (Cambridge University Press, 2010).

Thucydides, *History of the Peloponnesian War*, tr. R. Crawley (rev.) (Free Press, 1996).

Trigger, B., *Early Civilizations: Ancient Egypt in Context* (American University Press in Cairo, 1993).

Van Reybrouck, D., *Against Elections: The Case for Democracy* (Bodley Head, 2016.

Van Reybrouck, D., 'Belgium's Democratic Experiment', *Politico*, April 25, 2019.

Van Wees, H., *Ships and Silver, Taxes and Tribute: A Fiscal History of Archaic Athens* (I.B. Tauris, 2013).

Vernant, J., *Myth and Tragedy*, tr. J. Lloyd (Zone Books, 1990).

Wallace, R., *The Areopagus Council to 307 B.C.* (Johns Hopkins Press, 1989).

Wallace, R., 'Revolutions and a New Order in Solonian Athens and Archaic Greece,' in K. Raaflaub (ed.), *War and Peace in the Ancient World* (Wiley-Blackwell, 2006), pp. 49-82.

Wallace-Hadrill, A., (ed.) *Patronage in Ancient Society* (London, 1989).

Walsh, P., 'A Study in Reception: The British Debates over Aristophanes' Politics and Influence', *Classical Receptions Journal*, Vol. 1, No. 1 (2009) pp. 55-72.

Walzer, M., *Spheres of Justice: A Defense of Pluralism and Equality* (Basic Books, 1983).

Warren, M., Pearse, H., (eds.), *Designing Deliberative Democracy: The British Columbia Citizens' Assembly* (Cambridge University Press, 2008).

Wasserman, D., 'Let Them Eat Chances: Probability and Distributive Justice,' in P. Stone (ed.), *Lotteries in Public Life: A Reader* (Imprint Academic, 2011), pp. 231-250.

Whitehead, D. *The Ideology of the Athenian Metic* (Cambridge, 1977).

Wilson, P., *The Athenian Institution of the Khoregia: The Chorus, The City, and the Stage* (Cambridge, 2000).

Williams, B., 'The Analogy of City and Soul in Plato's Republic' in E. Lee, A. Mourelatos, R. Rorty (ed.), *Exegesis and Argument: Studies in Greek Philosophy Presented to Gregory Vlastos* (Van Gorcum, 1973).

Whittaker, C. 'The Delphic Oracle: Belief and Behaviour in Ancient Greece: And Africa', *Harvard Theological Review*. Vol. 58, No. 1 (Jan., 1965), pp. 21-47.

Xenophon, *Economics*, tr. E. Marchant, O. J. Todd, rev. J. Henderson (Harvard, 1979),

Xenophon, *Memorabilia*, tr. A L Bonnette (Cornell, 1994).

Zelnick-Abramovitz, R., 'Did Patronage Exist in Classical Athens?', *L'Antiquité Classique*, Vol. 69 (2000).

Zimmerman, Z., 'Freie Arbeit, Preise und Löhne' in E. Welskopf, (ed.) *Hellenische Poleis I* (Berlin Akademie-Verlag, 1974), pp. 92-107.

Zumbrunnen, J., *Aristophanic Comedy and the Challenge of Democratic Citizenship* (University of Rochester, 2012).

End Notes

1   Cunningham, Edward, Tony Saich, and Jessie Turiel, *Under-standing CCP Resilience: Surveying Chinese Public Opinion Through Time* (Harvard Ash Center for Democratic Governance and Innovation, 2020).

2   A. Rahi, 'Who Does and Does Not Support the Taliban?' *Express Tribune*, 2 September 2021: https://tribune.com.pk/article/97465/who-does-and-does-not-support-the-taliban-in-afghanistan.

3   Thomas Piketty calculates that the same of the top income percentile in total income rose from 10% to 20% between 1970 and 2010. It's increased further since then. Picketty, *Capital in the Twenty First Century* (Harvard, 2017).

4   Manuel Castells, *Rupture: The Crisis of Liberal Democracy* (Polity, 2018), p. 85.

5   K. Ognyanova, D. Lazer, R. Robertson, and C. Wilson, 'Misinformation in action: Fake news exposure is linked to lower trust in media, higher trust in government when your side is in power.' *Harvard Kennedy School (HKS) Misinformation Review*, 2020. https://doi.org/10.37016/mr-2020-024.

6   Francis Fukuyama is unclear that liberal democracies can survive this challenge: *Identity: The Demand for Dignity and the Politics of Resentment* (Farrar, Straus and Giroux, 2018).

7   F. Fukuyama, 'The End of History?', *The National Interest* (1989), 16, pp. 3–18.

8   See the discussion in R. Sealey, 'The Origins of Demokratia', *California Studies in Classical Antiquity*, Vol. 6 (1973), pp. 253-295.

9   Ancient historians often make a division between the radical democracy of the fifth century and the more moderate democracy of the fourth due to a set of reforms designed to limit the power of the people. But see M. J. Sundahl, 'The Rule of Law and the Nature of the Fourth-Century Athenian Democracy', *Classica et Mediaevalia*, Vol. 127, (2003), pp. 127-132.

10 Thucydides, *History of the Peloponnesian War,* tr. R. Crawley (rev.) (Free Press, 1998) 2.45.

11 *Ibid.,* 1.70.

12 M. Lane, *The Birth of Politics: Eight Greek and Roman Political Ideas and Why They Matter* (Princeton, 2016).

13 Notable exceptions include M.I. Finley, *Democracy Ancient and Modern* (Chatto & Windus, 1973); J.P. Euben, *The Tragedy of Political Theory: The Road Not Taken,* (Princeton, 1990); J.P. Euben, J. Ober and J.R. Wallach (eds), *Athenian Political Thought and the Reconstitution of American Democracy* (Cornell, 1995); J.P. Euben, *Corrupting Youth: Political Education, Democratic Culture, and Political Theory* (Princeton, 1997); M.H. Hansen, *The Tradition of Ancient Greek Democracy and Its Importance for Modern Democracy* (Royal Danish Academy of Science and Letters, 2005); J. Zumbrunnen, *Aristophanic Comedy and the Challenge of Democratic Citizenship* (University of Rochester, 2012); R. Fuller, *Beasts and Gods: How Democracy Changed its Meaning and Lost its Purpose* (Zed Books, 2015); R. Fuller, *In Defence of Democracy* (Polity, 2019); D. Van Reybrouck, *Against Elections: The Case for Democracy* (Bodley Head, 2016); J. Ober, *Demopolis: Democracy in Liberalism in Theory and Practice* (Cambridge, 2017); P. Cartledge, *Democracy: A Life* (Oxford, 2018). D. Zuckerberg, *Not All Dead White Men: Classics and Misogyny in the Digital Age* (Harvard, 2018); H. Landemore, *Open Democracy: Reinventing Popular Rule for the Twenty-First Century* (Princeton, 2020); J.S. Fishkin, *Democracy When the People Are Thinking* (Oxford, 2020): E. Katz, *Embattled: How Ancient Greek Myths Empower Us to Resist Tyranny* (Redwood Press, 2021). For a more sceptical perspective see P.J. Rhodes, *Ancient Democracy and Modern Ideology* (Duckworth, 2003).

14 Locke, *Second Treatise*, Chapter III, §19.

15 *Ibid.*, II, §9.

16 M. A. Glendon, *Rights Talk: The Impoverishment of Political Discourse* (Free Press, 2008).

17 Some scholars of the text also see it as problematic. See, for example, B. Williams, 'The Analogy of City and Soul in Plato's Republic' in E. Lee, A. Mourelatos, R. Rorty (eds.), *Exegesis and Argument: Studies in Greek Philosophy Presented to Gregory Vlastos* (Van Gorcum, 1973), pp. 196-206.

18 Aristotle, *Politics*, tr. C. Lord, (Chicago, 1984), 1253a1-2.

19 *Ibid.*, 1280b5-12.

20 Plato, *Republic*, tr. T. Griffith (Cambridge, 2000), 359a4.

21 Plato, *Apology*, 24d-25a.

22 Plato, *Laws*, 694c.

23 Demosthenes, *Letters*, III.13 (tr. N. W. DeWitt). There is an alternative manuscript tradition which substitutes *metekontes* for *en parrhesia*. See Demosthenes, *Orations*, Vol. VII (Harvard–Loeb, 1939), p. 234 n. For the use of *en parrhesia*, see J. A. Goldstein, *The Letters of Demosthenes* (Columbia, 1968), p. 217, n. 13. On the authenticity of Demosthenes' letters, see F. Blass, *Die attische Beredsamkeit* iii (Leipzig, 1893), pp. 439-455; Blass upholds the authenticity of the third letter.

24 Thucydides, *Peloponnesian War*, tr. J. Dent (Dutton, 1910), 2.37.

25 Isocrates, *Panegyricus*, 151.

26 Demosthenes, *Against Aristocrates*, 142.

27 E. Hall, *Inventing the Barbarian: Greek Self-Definition through Tragedy* (Oxford Classical Monographs, Oxford, 1989), p. 100.

28 Aristotle, *Physics*, II.2.194a28-9, 8.199b15-18; cf. *Eudemian Ethics* II.1.1219a8.

29 Aristotle, *Politics*, 1.1252b33-4, tr. Jowett.

30 *Ibid.*, 1.1253a13-28.

31 *Ibid.*, 1.1253a26-29.

32 Aristotle seems to endorse a form of idealized monarchy as well as polity, or mixed regime, in the late books of the *Politics*, leading to much speculation about how to reconcile these two incompatible recommendations. See my 'Aristotle's Paradox of Monarchy and the Biographical Tradition', *History of Political Thought*, Vol. 19, No. 4 (Winter, 1998), pp. 501-516.

33 On the chronological division of Plato's dialogues, see G. Klosko, *The Development of Plato's Political Theory* (Oxford, 2007).

34 Plato, *Apology*, 21c.

35 *Ibid.*, 38a.

36 Plato, *Crito*, 46b.

37 Thucydides, *The Peloponnesian War*, tr. R. Crawley, rev. (Free Press, 1996), 2.40. As is often the case, however, there was a substantial gap between the official ideology of the *polis* and the reality on the ground. See, for example, D. M. Carter, *The Quiet Athenian* (Oxford, 1986).

38 For a good discussion of the importance of conformity and unity, see M. Berent, 'The Greek Invention of Politics', *History of Political Thought*, XIX, No. 3, pp. 331-362.

39 K. Popper, *The Open Society and its Enemies* (Routledge, 1945).

40 Leo Strauss is famous for advancing this view: *Socrates and Aristophanes* (Basic Books, 1966).

41 Thucydides, *History*, 2.37.2.

42 J. Bentham, *The Rationale of Reward* (Wentworth Press, 2019), III.i.

43 J. S. Mill, *On Liberty* (Hackett, 1987), I (p. 10).

44 Mill recognized that this was essentially a religious notion: God 'takes delight in every near approach made by his creatures to the ideal conception embodied in them', *On Liberty*, III (p. 59).

45 J. S. Mill, *Utilitarianism* (Hacket, 1979), Ch. 2, p. 10

46 B. Constant, 'The Liberty of the Ancients Compared with that of the Moderns,' in *Political Writings*, tr. B. Fontana (Cambridge, 1988), pp. 310-311.

47 I. Berlin, 'Two Concepts of Liberty,' *Four Essays on Liberty* (Oxford, 1969), pp. 118-172.

48 T. Hobbes, *Leviathan*, I.xiv.2.

49 *Ibid.*, I.xiv.27, II.xxi.3.

50 C. Taylor, 'What's Wrong with Negative Liberty?' *Philosophy and the Human Sciences: Philosophical Papers*, vol. 2 (Cambridge: Cambridge University Press, 1985), 211–29.

51 C. Taylor, 'What's Wrong with Negative Liberty?' p. 214.

52 Plato, *Republic*, tr. A. Bloom (Basic Books, 1968), 557b.

53 *Ibid.*, 361c-d.

54 J. Greene, *How Rights Went Wrong: Why Our Obsession with Rights Is Tearing America Apart* (Mariner Books, 2021).

55 W. Brown, *States of Injury: Power and Freedom in Late Modernity* (Princeton, 1995), pp. 96-98.

56 The existence of natural or human rights, of course, are notoriously difficult to establish. Jeremy Bentham captured the spirit of the critique when he called them 'nonsense on stilts.' Mostly they are simply asserted. Utilitarian attempts to justify them — like the ones found in Mill's *On Liberty* — are equally problematic.

57 But see the debate in D. Cohen, 'Democracy and Individual Rights in Athens', *Zeitschrift der Savigny-Stiftung für Rechtsgeschichte: Romantische Abetilung*, Vol. 114, No. 1, (1997), pp. 31-52; D. M. Carter, 'Republicanism, Rights and Democratic Athens,' *Polis*, Vol 30, No. 1 (2013), pp. 73-91; and F. Miller, *Nature, Justice, and Rights in Aristotle's* Politics (Oxford, 1995).

58 See the discussion in R. A. Knox, 'So Mischievous a Beaste'? The Athenian Demos and its Treatment of its Politicians', *Greece and Rome*, Vol. 32, No. 2 (October, 1985), pp. 132-161.

59 M H. Hansen, *The Trial of Sokrates from the Athenian Point of View* (Kgl. Danske Videnskabernes Selskab, 1995).

60 E. Burke, *Reflections on the Revolution in France* (Hackett, 1987) pp. 84-5.

61 See, for example, the discussion in B. Barry, 'Justice Between Generations' in P. Hacker, and J. Raz (eds.) *Law, Society, and Morality: Essays in Honor of H. L. A. Hart* (Oxford, 1977), pp. 268-284.

⁶² K. Conger, M. Isaac, 'Twitter Permanently Bans Trump, Capping Online Revolt', *New York Times,* 8 January, 2021. https://www.nytimes.com/2021/01/08/technology/twitter-trump-suspended.html

⁶³ For a discussion, see M. Hansen, 'The 190 Themistokles Ostraka as Evidence of Large Political Groups' in K. Ascani (ed.), *Ancient History Matters, Studies Presented to Jens Erik Skydsgaard on his Seventieth Birthday* (L'Erma di Bretschneider, 2002), pp. 193-198.

⁶⁴ Thucydides, *History,* 1.20; Aristotle, *Politics,* 1311a35-b1.

⁶⁵ Plutarch, *Life of Cimon,* 17.2-6; Philochorus, *Lex. Cantab.* 30.

⁶⁶ See the discussion in S. Forsdyke, *Exile, Ostracism and Democracy* (Princeton, 2005), p. 171. Forsdyke, in general, is the best guide to the practice.

⁶⁷ P. Kosmin, 'A Phenomenology of Democracy: Ostracism as Political Ritual', *Classical Antiquity,* Vol. 34, No. 1 (2015), p. 126.

⁶⁸ A. Raubitschek,'The Origin of Ostracism', *Amer Jnl of Archaeology* Vol. 55, No. 3 (July, 1951) pp. 221-9.

⁶⁹ Aristotle, *Politics,* 1284a23-5.

⁷⁰ *Ibid.,* 1284a26-34.

⁷¹ *Ibid.,* 1284a36-7.

⁷² Shakespeare, *Richard II,* Act 3, Scene 1, 21.

⁷³ Aristotle, *Politics,* 1284a34-5.

⁷⁴ P. Kosmin, 'A Phenomenology of Democracy', p. 123.

⁷⁵ Plutarch, *Aristides,* in *Plutarch's Lives,* tr. B. Perrin (William Heinemann, 1914), 7.5-6.

⁷⁶ P. Bicknell, 'Agasias the Donkey', *Zeitschrift für Papyrologie und Epigraphik,* Vol. 62 (1986), pp. 183-184.

⁷⁷ J. T. Roberts, "The Creation of a Legacy: A Manufactured Crises in Eighteenth Century Thought" in Euben, Wallach, Ober (eds) *Athenian Political Thought and the Reconstruction of Democracy* (Cornell, 1994) p. 90.

⁷⁸ Plutarch, 'Aristocrates', *Plutarch's Lives,* tr. B. Perrin (William Heinemann Ltd, 1914), 7.2.

79 Aristotle, *Politics,* 1284b15-16, 1284a36-7.

80 Kagan thinks Cleisthenes uses it first for anti-tyrannical pupuses, and that the procedure goes dormant for some period because of fear of its impact. D. Kagan, 'The Origin and Purpose of Ostracism' *Journal of the American School of Classical Studies at Athens,* Vol. 30, No. 4, (Oct-Dec. 1961) pp. 393-401. Raubitschek, however, prefers enactment in 488, arguing that it is primarily used in conjunction with the election of strategoi. A. Raubitschek, 'The Origin of Ostracism', *American Journal of Archaeology,* Vol. 55, No. 3 (July, 1951) pp. 221-9.

81 [Aristotle], *The Athenian Constitution,* 22.6.

82 Aristotle, *Politics,* 1284a19-21.

83 See, for example, Aristotle, *Politics,* 1292b27ff.

84 E. Burke, *Appeal from the New to the Old Whigs,* ed. D. Ritchie (Cambridge, 1992) p.168.

85 Aristotle, *Rhetoric,* tr. W. D. Ross (Harvard University Press, 1926), 2.16.

86 This is debate about the degree to which Athenian politics were organized in the modern sense. See the discussion in P.J. Rhodes, 'Political Activity in Classical Athens', *Journal of Hellenic Studies,* Vol. 106 (November, 1986), pp. 132-144.

87. *Ibid.*

88 Demosthenes, 'Against Meidias', *Demosthenes III,* tr. J. H. Vince (Harvard, 1935), 7 (p. 11).

89 [Pseudo-Xenophon], *The Old Oligarch,* 1.10.

90 Aristotle, *Politics,* 1301a30-35.

91 Aristotle, *Politics,* tr. B. Jowett (Cambridge, 1996), 1282a14-16.

92 Ballot T1/103.

93 P. Kosmin, 'A Phenomenology of Democracy: Ostracism as Political Ritual', p 152.

94 Demosthenes, 'Against Aristocrates', 23.205-6.

95 N. Machiavelli, *Discourses on Livy,* 1.17.3.

96 J.-J. Rousseau, *On the Social Contract,* II.xi.

[97] G. Kron, 'The Distribution of Wealth at Athens in Comparative Perspective', *Zeitschrift für Papyrologie und Epigraphik*, 2011, Bd. 179 (2011), pp. 129-138.

[98] B. Page, L. Bartels, and J. Seawright, 'Democracy and the Policy Preferences of Wealthy Americans', *Perspectives on Politics*, Vol. 11, No. 1 (March, 2013), pp. 51-73.

[99] M. Gilens, and B. Page, 'Testing Theories of American Politics: Elites, Interest Groups, and Average Citizens', *Perspectives on Politics*, Vol. 12, No. 2 (September, 2014), pp. 564-581.

[100] See, for example, the discussion in L. Powell, 'The Influence of Campaign Contributions on the Legislative Process', *Duke Journal of Law and Public Policy*, Vol. 9, No. 1 (2014) pp. 75-101.

[101] Aristotle, *Politics*, 1295b1 – 33.

[102] L. Batchelder, 'Tax the Rich and their Heirs: How to Tax Inheritances More Fairly', *New York Times* June 24, 2020. https://www.nytimes.com/2020/06/24/opinion/sunday/inheritance-tax-inequality.html

[103] L. Batchelder, 'What Should Society Expect from Heirs? A Proposal for a Comprehensive Inheritance Tax' (February 23, 2010)., 63 *Tax Law Review* 1 (2009), NYU Law and Economics Research Paper No. 08-42. Available at SSRN: https://ssrn.com/abstract= 1274466 or http://dx.doi.org/10.2139/ssrn.1274466.

[104] Pew Research Center data: https://www.pewresearch.org/fact-tank/2021/01/28/racial-ethnic-diversity-increases-yet-again-with-the-117th-congress/

[105] M. Gilens, B. Page, 'Testing Theories of American Politics: Elites, Interest Groups, and Average Citizens', *Perspectives on Politics*, Vol. 12, No. 3 (2014), pp. 564-581. Many other studies show similar results. See, for example, J. Hacker, P. Pierson, 'Winner-Take-All Politics: Public Policy, Political Organization, and the Precipitous Rise of Top Incomes in the United States', *Politics & Society*, Vol. 38, No. 2 (2010), pp. 152-204. See J. Figueiredo, B. Richter, 'Advancing the Empirical Research on Lobbying', *Annual Review of Political Science*, Vol. 17, pp. 163-185 for a good overview of some of these trends.

106 J. Locke, *Second Treatise of Government*, II , §13.

107 A. Schedler, 'Elections Without Democracy: The Menu of Manipulation', *Journal of Democracy*, Vol. 13, No. 2 (April, 2002), pp. 36-50, and S. Levitsky, L. Way, 'Elections Without Democracy: The Rise of Competitive Authoritarianism', in the same issue, pp. 51-65.

108 J.-J. Rousseau, On the Social Contract, in J.-J. Rousseau, *The Basic Political Writings*, tr. D. A. Cress (Hackett, 2011), III.15, p. 219.

109 M. H. Hansen, *The Athenian Democracy in the Age of Demosthenes* (Blackwell, 1991), pp. 159-160.

110 Aristotle, *Politics*, 1317b19-21.

111 See the related discussion in Richard G. Mulgan, 'Lots as a Democratic Device of Selection', *Review of Politics*, 46, No. 4 (October 1984) pp. 539-560, p. 547, Repr. In P. Stone (ed.), *Lotteries in Public Life: A Reader* (Imprint Academic, 2011), pp. 113-132.

112 Aristotle, *Politics*, 1294b7-8, tr. Jowett. Aristotle, *Rhetoric*, 1.1365b32.

113 Aristotle, *Politics*, 1300a30-40.

114 L. Lopez-Rabatel provides a convenient summary of terminology surrounding sortition: 'Drawing Lots on Ancient Greece—Vocabulary and Tools' tr. C. Delacroix-Howell, W. Howell, S. Raillard, in L. Lopez-Rabatel, Y. Sintomer (eds.), *Sortition and Democracy: History, Tools, Theories* (Imprint Academic, 2020) pp. 53-94.

115 Much of later tradition follows Homer. Pseudo-Apollodorus in his *Library* (1.2.1) tells a parallel story. But note that Hesiod—a rough contemporary of Homer, describes Zeus as deciding how to divide things up without the use of chance (*Theogony*, 881-885). For a broader discussion of lots in the Ancient World, see L. Milano, 'Destiny, the Drawing of Lots and Divine Will in Ancient Near Eastern Societies,' tr. A. Price, in L. Lopez-Rabatel, Y. Sintomer (eds.), *Sortition and Democracy: History, Tools, Theories* (Imprint Academic, 2020), pp. 29-52.

116 Homer, *Iliad*, tr. R. Lattimore (Chicago, 1951), 7.175-180.

[117] See also *Iliad* 3.314-324; 7.179-192; 15.189-192; 23.352-357, 861-862; 24.400.

[118] The same language occurs when the Greeks compete for chariot positions at Patrokles' funeral games, 23.352.

[119] Homer, *Odyssey*, tr. E. Wilson (W. W. Norton, 2018), 10.206-210. cf. 9.331.

[120] ἴτων πάλῳ λαχόντες, ὡς νομίζεται, Aeschylus, *Eumenides*, 32; Euripides, *Ion*, 416.

[121] C. R. Whittaker, 'The Delphic Oracle: Belief and Behaviour in Ancient Greece: And Africa', *Harvard Theological Review*, Vol. 58, No. 1 (Jan., 1965), pp. 21-47. pp. 27-8. See also R. Parker, 'Greek States and Greek Oracles', *History of Political Thought*, Vol. 6, No. 1/2 (Summer 1985), pp. 298-326. For the debate over cleromancy at Delphi see P. Amandry, *La mantique Apollinienne à Delphes: Essai sur le fonctionnement de l'Oracle* (Bocard, 1950), pp. 86-119, who reports an inscription referring to lots, and J. E. Fontenrose, *The Delphic Oracle, Its Responses and Operations, with a Catalogue of Responses* (University of California, 1978), pp. 219–223, who argues against the use of the lot at Delphi. The use of lots also appears in the Bible: Acts 1:24-36, on the naming of Judas' replacement, Numbers 26:52-6 on division of land, and Judges 20:8-10 on who goes to battle.

[122] Hesiod, *Theogony*, 360. See also the Homeric *Hymn to Demeter*, 420.

[123] Pindar, *Olympian Ode*, 12.1-2. See also a fragment of Sophocles, which calls Tyche 'divine,' cited in H. L. Jones, *Justice of Zeus*, p. 162, n. 6.

[124] S. Matheson, 'The Goddess Tyche,' *Yale University Art Gallery Bulletin: An Obsession with Fortune: Tyche in Greek and Roman Art* (1994), pp. 18-33.

[125] Plato, *Laws*, 757e.

[126] Demosthenes, 25.10-11, for example, says that Athenian jurors are selected by god. Socrates' criticisms of the lottery, by contrast, were not seen as impious. See P. Demont, 'Selection by Lot in Ancient Athens: From Religion to Politics' in L. Lopez-

Rabatel, Y. Sintomer (eds.), *Sortition and Democracy: History, Tools, Theories* (Imprint Academic, 2020), pp. 112-129.

127 Plato, *Laws*, 757e. See also Aristotle, *Politics*, 1350a8, 1303a14-16.

128 [Aristotle], *Constitution of Athens*, 3.3, 8.1, 22.5. Dates for these constitutions of Dracon and Solon are traditionally given as 622 and 594, respectively.

129 Aristotle, *Politics*, 1305a8, 1303 a 14-16.

130 R. W. Wallace, 'Revolutions and a New Order in Solonian Athens and Archaic Greece' in K. Raaflaub (ed.), *War and Peace in the Ancient World* (Wiley-Blackwell, 2006), pp. 49-82.

131 J. Ober, *Mass and Elite in Democratic Athens* (Princeton, 1989), p. 77.

132 Herodotus, *Histories*, tr. A. D. Godley (Harvard University Press, 1920), 3.80.6.

133 Hansen, *The Athenian Democracy*, p. 230.

134 [Aristotle], *Athenian Constitution*, tr. J. Moore, (Cambridge, 1996), 43.1, (p. 244).

135 [Aristotle], *Athenian Constitution*, 8.1, 22.5.

136 [Aristotle], *Athenian Constitution*, 55.1.

137 Andocides, 1.84. R. Wallace, *The Areopagus Council to 307 B.C.* (Johns Hopkins Press, 1989), pp. 97-113.

138 [Aristotle], *Athenian Constitution*, 26.2.

139 [Aristotle,] *Athenian Constitution*, 62.1. Selection by lot to the Boule seems to have begun after the 410 revolution: Andocides,. 1.96.

140 P. Rhodes, *The Athenian Boule* (Oxford, 1985), p. 7.

141 [Aristotle], *Athenian Constitution*, 44.1-2.

142 [Aristotle], *Athenian Constitution*, 44.3.

143 One of the basic political divisions in Athens was modeled by Cleisthenes on the same principle: being made up of representatives of – broadly speaking – coastal, urban, and inland areas.

144 Plato, *Apology*, 32b. Some argue that Socrates might have served more than one term. J. Hatzfeld, 'Socrate au procés des Arginus-

es', *Revue des Études Anciennes*, Vol. 42 (1940), 165-71. G. Gian-nantoni, 'La prinatia di Socrate nel 406 A.C.', *Rivista Critica di Storia della Filosofia* (1962), pp. 3-25. G. Mavrogordatos, argues that Socrates served only as a result of a manpower shortage in 406: 'Two Puzzles Involving Socrates,' *The Classical World*, 105, No. 1 (Fall 2011), pp. 3-23, p. 10-11.

145 Hansen, *The Athenian Democracy*, pp. 250, 313-4.

146 Richard G. Mulgan, 'Lots as a Democratic Device of Selection', *Review of Politics*, 46, No. 4 (October, 1984) pp. 539-560, p. 549.

147 The listing, from a fragment of an inscription, is partial, and seems to include some restrictions on finances as well, but these are not clear. The restrictions probably come in the wake of the oligarchic regimes of 411-410. *Inscriptiones Graecae* I, 3rd ed. D. M. Lewis (Berlin, 1981), 105. Available online at https://www.atticinscriptions.com/inscription/Koerner/12 (Accessed 25 February, 2021). See also [Aristotle], *Athenian Constitution*, 45.1.

148 [Aristotle], *Athenian Constitution*, 24.3.

149 Demosthenes, 57.56.

150 Juries larger than 2,000 might have required a special decree. Lys 13.35. See also the discussion in M.H. Hansen, *Eisangelia: the Sovereignty of the People's Court in Athens in the Fourth Century BC and the Impeachment of Generals and Politicians* (Odense: University of Southern Denmark, 1975), pp. 207, 215.

151 Andocides, 1.17.

152 Pseudo-Xenophon, *The Athenian Constitution* 3.2, 1.16-18; Thucydides, 1.77.1. See de Ste. Croix, 'Notes on Jurisdiction in the Athenian Empire II', *Classical Quarterly*, Vol. 11, No. 2 (November, 1961), pp. 268-280 for details.

153 Aristophanes, *Clouds*, tr. J. Henderson (Harvard, 1998), 207-8.

154 We know that *pinakia* were often used multiples times due to the visible palimpsest of names on extant pieces. J. H. Kroll, *Athenian Bronze Allotment Plates* (Cambridge, 1972), p. 71.

155 Aristophanes, *Wasps*, 233-4, 300-303, 689.

156 Aristophanes, *Wasps*, 216-221.

157 [Aristotle], *Athenian Constitution*, 63-66.

158 [Aristotle], *Athenian Constitution*, 64.

159 Praxagora seems to refer to one in distributing dinner seating in Aristophanes' *Ecclesiazusae* (681-6), usually dated to 391.

160 Fragments from about seventeen Attic machines are extant. J. Bishop, 'The Cleroterium,' *Journal of Hellenic Studies*, Vol. 90 (1970), pp. 1–14. E. Crochetière, 'Democracy and the Lot: The Lottery of Public Offices in Classical Athens,' *McGill University Masters Theses* (December, 2013).

161 Hansen, *Athenian Democracy*, p. 199. A. Orlandini, 'Kleroterion. Simulation of the Allotment of Dikasti,' Available at academia.edu, and a video of the process is on YouTube: https://www.youtube.com/watch?v=gt9H7nbZjAw

162 D. Mirhady, C. Schwarz, 'Dikastic Participation', *Classical Quarterly New Series*, Vol. 61, No. 2 (December, 2011), pp. 744-748, p. 745.

163 Aristophanes, *Wasps*, 230-233, 248.

164 Aristophanes, *Wasps*, tr. J. Henderson, (Harvard: Loeb, 1998) 620-627; 548-558.

165 [Aristotle], *Athenian Constitution*, 27.-35; Aristotle, *Politics*, 1274a8.

166 Aristophanes, *Wasps*, 605-607.

167 Aristophanes, *Wasps*, 304-6.

168 M. Markle, 'Jury Pay and Assembly Pay at Athens', *History of Political Thought*, Vol. 6, No. 1/2 (Summer 1985), pp. 265-297. See also H. Zimmerman, 'Freie Arbeit, Preise und Löhne,' in E. Welskopf, (ed.) *Hellenische Poleis I* (Berlin Akademie-Verlag, 1974), pp. 92-107.

169 Lycurgus, 1.93; Demosthenes, 20.77.

170 Isocrates, *The Speeches*, tr. G. Norlin, (Harvard, 1929), 7.54; Demosthenes, 24.123.

171 [Aristotle], *Athenian Constitution*, 24.3-4.

172 Demosthenes, 55.26.

[173] Hansen, M. *The Athenian Ecclesia II: A Collection of Articles 1983-1989* (Copenhagen, 1989), pp. 75, 87.

[174] Demosthenes, 39.10-11.

[175] Aristophanes, *Wasps*, tr. D. Parker in *Aristophanes: Three Comedies* (Michigan, 1969), 240 (p. 26).

[176] Aeschines, 1.86; [Aristotle], *Athenian Constitution*, 27.5, 28.3; Diodorus Siculus, 13.64.6; Lysias, 30.10; 13.12; Xenophon, *Hellenica*, 1.6.55.

[177] Isocrates, 8.50; Aeschines, 1 106 and see C. Taylor, 'Bribery in Athenian Politics Part II: Ancient Reaction and Perceptions', *Greece & Rome*, Vol. 48, No. 2 (Oct., 2001), pp. 154-172, p. 156.

[178] M. Fränkel, *Die attischen Geschworenengerichte. Ein Beitrag zum attischen Staatsrecht* (Berlin, 1877). Quoted in D. Mirhady, D., 'The Dikasts' Oath and the Question of Fact', in A. Somerstein and J. Fletcher (eds.), *Horkos: The Oath in Greek Society* (Liverpool University Press, 2008), p. 49.

[179] Demosthenes, 24.78, tr. A. T. Murray.

[180] [Aristotle], *Athenian Constitution*, 47-55. M.H. Hansen, 'Seven Hundred Archai in Classical Athens', *Greek, Roman and Byzantine Studies*, Vol. 21, No. 2 (Summer, 1981), pp. 151-173. Includes a list of known positions. The *Athenian Constitution* (24) claims that over twenty *thousand* Athenians earned their livelihood in public service of one sort or another. But this number—if accurate—likely includes rowers in the fleets, *ecclesia* attendance, and other non-appointed positions.

[181] *Ibid.,* p. 231.

[182] Isocrates, 12.12.

[183] Lysias, 31.33. The *Athenian Constitution* hints at possible corruption of the process at the *deme* level at 62.1. And, as Hansen points out, all the offices for a given year might not have been filled. M. Hansen, 'Prerequisites for magistrates in fourth-century Athens', *Classica et Medievalia*, 32 (1980) pp. 105-125, p. 121.

[184] Lysias, 16, 26, 31.

[185] Lysias, 26.9.

186 For example, Aeschines 1.106; Andocides, 1.147. Demosthenes alludes to the potential cost of bribery: Demosthenes, *Exordia*. 48.2.

187 Hansen has a nice summary in *The Athenian Democracy in the Age of Demosthenes*, pp. 222-4.

188 J. Roberts, *Accountability in Athenian Government* (Wisconsin University Press, 1982), p. 175.

189 Isocrates, *Areopagiticus*, 23.

190 C. Taylor, 'From the whole citizen body? The sociology of election and the lot in Athenian democracy', *Hesperia*, Vol. 76 (April–June, 2007), 323-345.

191 Ober, *Mass and Elite*.

192 Pseudo-Xenophon, *Athenian Constitution*, 4; Aristotle, *Politics*, 1279b39-1280a3.

193 J. Miller, 'Warning the Demos: Political Communication with a Democratic Audience in Demosthenes', *History of Political Thought*, Vol. 23, No. 3 (Autumn, 2002).

194 Xenophon, *Memorabilia*, tr. A L Bonnette (Cornell, 1994), 1.2.9. Aristotle, *Rhetoric*, 1392b4-8.

195 Aristotle, *Politics*, 1280a23-4; 1301a31-2; 1282b15-1283a22.

196 Mulgan, 'Lot as a Democratic Device of Sortition,' p. 121.

197 J. Ober, *Democracy and Knowledge: Innovation and Learning in Classical Athens* (Princeton, 2008), especially chapters 4 and 5.

198 [Aristotle], *Athenian Constitution*, 21.2-3.

199 Ober, *Democracy and Knowledge*, p. 142.

200 Aristotle, *Politics*, 1280b42-1282a17.

201 V. Bers, 'Just Rituals: Why the Rigamarole of Fourth-Century Athenian Lawcourts?', in P. Flensted-Jensen, et. al., *Polis and Politics. Studies in Ancient Greek History* (Museum Tusculanum Press, 2000), p. 557. See also W. Connor, 'Tribes, Festivals and Processions: Civic Ceremonial and Political Manipulation in Archaic Greece', *Journal of Hellenic Studies*, Vol. 107 (1987), pp. 40-50.

202 Much has been written on the technical aspects of proper sample sizes and the question of adequate representation. See, for example, D. Mueller, et. al. 'Representative Democracy via Random Selection', and H. Greely, 'The Equality of Allocation by Lot', in P. Stone, (ed.), *Lotteries in Public Life: A Reader* (Imprint Academic, 2011), pp. 47-58, 59-84; J. Fourniau, 'The Selection of Deliberative Minipublics: Sortition, Motivation, and Availability', in L Lopez-Rabatel, Y. Sintomer (eds.), *Sortition and Democracy: History, Tools, Theories* (Imprint Academic, 2020), pp. 372-399.

203 Open Secrets. https://www.opensecrets.org/elections-overview/cost-of-election?cycle=2020&display=T&infl=N Accessed 23 March 2021.

204 R. Mulgan, 'Lot as a Democratic Device of Selection', in P. Stone, (ed.), *Lotteries in Public Life: A Reader*, p. 123.

205 Jean-Jacques Rousseau (*On the Social Contract*, 4.111) notes the opposite: that holding office can represent a disutility; people may be more inclined to do other things with their time. But here the same argument holds: dis-utilities tied to the public sphere should also be distributed as fairly and as equally as possible.

206 O. Dowlen, *The Political Potential of Sortition* (Imprint Academic, 2008), p. 13.

207 Consider the case described in US v. Holmes, 18 U.S. 412 (1820), where survivors of a shipwreck on a lifeboat were charged with murder for throwing fellow passengers overboard in an attempt to maintain sufficient food and water to survive. The judges ruled that had the men used a lottery to determine who was thrown overboard, they would not have been liable to criminal charges.

208 For a discussion of whether, in fact, lotteries need to map precisely onto equality, see D. Wasserman, 'Let Them Eat Chances: Probability and Distributive Justice', in P. Stone (ed.), *Lotteries in Public Life: A Reader*, pp. 231-250.

209 J. Rawls, *A Theory of Justice*, rev. ed. (Harvard, 1971), pp. 273-277. See the extension of Rawls' argument about desert especially in M. Sandel, *Liberalism and the Limits of Justice* (Cambridge, 1982),

pp. 66-103. See also B. Barry, *Political Argument* (Routledge, 2011), pp. 106-118.

[210] Peter Stone makes a similar connection between Rawls' arguments and sortion: P. Stone, 'Sortition, Voting, and democratic Equality', *Critical Review of International Social and Political Philosophy*, Vol. 19, No. 3 (2016), pp. 339-356.

[211] F. Engelstad, 'The Assignment of Political Office by Lot', in P. Stone (ed.), *Lotteries in Public Life: A Reader*, pp. 197-8. See also J. Fishkin, 'Random assemblies for lawmaking? Prospects and Limits', *Politics and Society*, Vol. 46, No. 3 (2018), pp. 359-379.

[212] J. Ferejohn, 'The Citizens' Assembly Model,' in M. Warren, H. Pearce (eds.), *Designing Deliberative Democracy: The British Columbia Citizens' Assembly* (Cambridge University Press, 2008). Participedia.net provides a convenient overview of many of these efforts.

[213] P. Fournier, H. van der Kolk, R. Carty, A. Blais, J. Rose, *When Citizens Decide: Lessons from Citizen Assemblies on Electoral Reform* (Oxford, 2011). A. Lang, 'But is it for Real? The British Columbia Citizens' Assembly as a Model of State-Sponsored Citizen Empowerment', *Politics and Society*, Vol. 35, No. 1 (2007), pp. 35-70; J.S. Fishkin, 'Designing Deliberative Democracy: The British Columbia Citizens Assembly', *Perspectives on Politics*, Vol. 11, No. 2 (June, 2013), pp. 670-672.

[214] R. Goodin, *Innovating Democracy: Democratic Theory and Practice after the Deliberative Turn* (Oxford, 2008), p. 14. Thanks to Keith Sutherland for bringing these statistics and their importance to my attention. See also I. O'Flynn, I., G. Sood, 'What would Dahl say? An appraisal of the democratic credentials of deliberative polls and other mini-publics,', in K. Grönlund, A. Bächtiger, M, Setälä (eds.), *Deliberative Mini-Publics. Involving Citizens in the Democratic Process* (ECPR Press, 2014), pp. 41–58.

[215] https://participedia.net/method/4258 provides a good overview of this process.

[216] The choice of which experts to select can be tricky; ideally the technical aspects of any projects should be presented without bias by neutral authorities. But, as any good social scientist can tell you, this is easier said than done.

[217] A. Sigmundsdóttir, 'The People of Iceland Have Spoken', *The Guardian*, November 16, 2009, https://www.theguardian.com/ commentisfree/ 2009/nov/16/iceland-national-assembly.

[218] D. Van Reybrouck, 'Belgium's Democratic Experiment', *Politico*, April 25, 2019. https://www.politico.eu/article/belgium-democratic-experiment-citizens-assembly/.

[219] J. Gastil, K. Knobloch, H. Reedy, 'Assessing the Electoral Impact of the 2010 Oregon Citizens' Initiative Review', *American Politics Research*, Vol. 46, No. 3 (2018), pp. 534-563.

[220] A. Renwick, *et al.*, *A Considered Public Voice on Brexit: The Report of the Citizens' Assembly on Brexit* (Online: The Constitution Unit, 2017), http://citizensassembly.co.uk/wp-content/uploads/ 2017/12/Citizens-Assembly-on-Brexit-Report.pdf.

[221] L. Carson, *Integrating Citizen Deliberation into National Decisions: Ireland's Prime Minister's Office*, (The NewDemocracy Foundation), https://www.newdemocracy.com.au/2017/05/28/ integrating-citizen-deliberation-into-national-decisions/

[222] J. Fourniau, 'The Selection of Deliberative Minipubics: Sortition', in L. Lopez-Rabatel , Y. Sintomer (eds.), *Sortition and Democracy*, pp. 372-499.

[223] J. Burnheim, *The Demarchy Manifesto* (Imprint Academic, 2016) p. 39.

[224] See Alex Kovner's interesting thinking on this question at his Jury Democracy Blog: https://alexkovner.com/blog/.

[225] For an overview of security issues surrounding machine-based sortition, see D. Courant, 'From Kleroterion to Cryptology: The Act of Sortition in the 21st Century,' in L. Lopez-Rabatel, Y. Sintomer (eds.), *Sortition and Democracy*, pp. 343-371.

[226] I am thinking here specifically of Peter Macleod's MASS LBP, which markets itself as a one-stop shop for organizing minipublics. MASS LBP claims it is 'founded on the radical proposition that the next stage of democracy is not only one where people can have their say, but where everyone has the opportunity and responsibility to exercise public judgement and act as stewards of the greater common good.' https:// www.masslbp.com/about

227 Justin Elliott, Patricia Callahan and James Bandler, 'How Tech Mogul Peter Thiel Turned a Retirement Account for the Middle Class Into a $5 Billion Tax-Free Piggy Bank' https://talkingpointsmemo.com/news/how-tech-mogul-peter-thiel-turned-a-retirement-account-for-the-middle-class-into-a-5-billion-tax-free-piggy-bank. Accessed 24 June, 2021.

228 Simon Hornblower argues for a later fourth-century date in 'The Old Oligarch and Thucydides. A Fourth-Century Date for the Old Oligarch' in Flensted-Jensen, *et. al.* (eds.) *Polis and Politics. Studies in Ancient Greek History Presented to Mogens Herman Hansen on His Sixtieth Birthday*, August 20, 2000 (Copenhagen, 2000), pp. 263-294.

229 Pseudo-Xenophon, *Pseudo-Xenophon's Constitution of the Athenians*, tr. R. Osborne (London Association of Classical Teachers, 2008), 1.4.

230 See B. Trigger, *Early Civilizations: Ancient Egypt in Context* (American University Press in Cairo, 1993), pp. 44-45.

231 As a caveat, we should note that we have little evidence for the system of finance at the *deme* level. Peter Fawcett notes the existence of *deme* liturgies as well as possible property taxation (the *enktetikon*), though the latter likely applied only to non-demesmen. P. Fawcett, 'When I Squeeze You with *Eisphorai*: Taxes and Tax Policy in Classical Athens', *Hesperia: The Journal of the American School of Classical Studies at Athens*, Vol. 85, No. 1 (January-March 2016), pp.167-8. Athens also relied on indirect taxes on imports and exports, silver mining, and a direct tax on all metics.

232 Liturgies and *eisphorai* were not, of course, the only sort of taxation Athens employed during the Classical Period. Metics, or registered aliens, were assessed an annual tax, and taxes were levied on traded goods, etc.

233 Demosthenes, 14.19, 14.27. See the discussion in Fawcett, 'When I Squeeze You', p. 157.

234 [Aristotle] *Athenian Constitution*, 8.3, though the wording implies only a collection of taxes through the *naukraroi*, an apparent subdivision of the city associated with the maintenance of a ship. See also H. Van Wees, *Ships and Silver, Taxes and Tribute: A*

Fiscal History of Archaic Athens (I.B. Tauris, 2013) who makes the case for a Solonian date.

235 Thucydides, *History of the Peloponnesian War*, 3.19.1.

236 M. Christ, provides an overview in 'The Evolution of the *Eisphora* in Classical Athens', *The Classical Quarterly New Series*, Vol. 57, No. 1 (May, 2007), pp. 53-69.

237 [Aristotle] *Athenian Constitution*, 61.1. Hansen estimates 1,000-1,200 individuals, while Rhodes cites 1,200. 'Problems in the Athenian *Eisphora* and Liturgies', *American Journal of Ancient History*, Vol. 71 (2017), pp. 1-19.

238 *Lysias*, 27.10. Tr. W. R. M. Lamb (Loeb, 1989).

239 Demosthenes, 20.21; Hansen, *Athenian Democracy*, p. 111.

240 The number of trierarchies varied with the size of the fleet. For example, for Demosthenes, IG II2 1627.266-78, the number for one year is 400.

241 Equipping and provisioning the fleet became a formal and organized liturgy in the 370s. V. Gabrielsen, *Financing the Athenian Fleet. Public Taxation and Social Relations* (Johns Hopkins Press, 1994), Part 1. But see D. L. Silverman, *The Trierarchy and Athenian Civic Identity*, who argues for an earlier date of 493/2. 1994 Ph.D. Thesis, UC Berkeley, pp. 101-117. Available: https://www.proquest.com/openview/07d095e73ec7544ccd10c 06a1909b064/1?pq-origsite= gscholar&cbl=18750&diss=y

242 See Barry O'Halloran, 'The Political Economy of Classical Athens: A Naval Perspective', *Mnemosyne*, Supplements, Vol. 425 (2019), pp. 164-182.

243 Demosthenes, 47.22.

244 The *locus classicus* for discussion of the *choregia* is A. W. Pickard-Cambridge, *Dramatic Festivals of Athens* (Oxford, 1968), pp. 85-90, 95-99. But see also the recent update in P. Wilson, *The Athenian Institution of the Khoregia: The Chorus, The City, and the Stage*, (Cambridge, 2000).

245 Plutarch, *On the Glories of Athens*, tr. Goodwin, 6, 348d-349b; cf. *Moralia*, 349a; Demosthenes, 4.35.

246 Plutarch, *On the Glories of Athens*, 6, 350a.

[247] Lysias, 21.1-2, tr. W. R. M. Lamb.

[248] Isocrates, for example, appeals to contributions made by his father: 16.35.

[249] Isocrates, 16.35; Isaeus, 7.37-42; Demosthenes, 21.80, 28.17; cf. Lysias. 24.9, 25.12.

[250] J. Ober, *Mass and Elite in Democratic Athens* (Princeton, 1989), pp. 243-4.

[251] D. Whitehead, *The Ideology of the Athenian Metic* (Cambridge, 1977), p. 81.

[252] Demosthenes, tr. A. Murray (Harvard, 1939), 50.7.

[253] M. Christ, 'Liturgy Avoidance and Antidosis in Classical Athens', *Transactions of the American Philological Association*, Vol. 120 (1990), p. 158.

[254] Isocrates, *Panathenaicus*, tr. G. Norlin (Harvard, 1980), 12.145.

[255] S. Douglas Olson, (ed.) *Antiphanes. Sappho – Crysis, Fragmenta incertarum, fabularum, fragmenta dubia* (Vandenhoeck & Ruprecht, 2021), fr. 204. On the burdens of the liturgy see also: Theophrastus, *Characters*, 26.6; Demosthenes, 38.26; 36.39.

[256] Xenophon, *Symposium*, 4.45.

[257] See, for example: Isaeus, 11.47; Demosthenes, 42.23; Aeschines, 1.101; Lysias, 20.23. V. Gabrielsen, 'The Antidosis Procedure in Classical Athens', *Classica et Mediaevalia*, Vol. 38 (1987, p. 38), and Davies, *Athenian Propertied Families* (Oxford, 1971, p. xxii) tend to minimize the problem, but Christ ('Liturgy Avoidance and Antidosis in Classical Athens', *Transactions of the American Philological Association*, Vol. 120 (1990), pp. 147-169) argues that tax avoidance was common, if not widespread.

[258] See V. Gabrielson, *Financing the Athenian Fleet: Public Taxation and Sociat Relations* (Johns Hopkins,1994), p. 113, for a discussion.

[259] We have one full court speech dealing with *antidosis*: Demosthenes 42, *Against Phainippus*. See also Lysias, 4.1, 24.9; Demosthenes, 20.40, 21.79, 28.17. See Gabrielson, 'The Antidosis Procedure in Classical Athens' for a discussion.

[260] Bryan McCannon argues that *antidosis* represents a good solution to overcoming asymetrical information constraints and might have applications in today's tax law where tax evasion is a major problem. 'Who pays taxes? Liturgies and the *Antidosis* procedure in Ancient Athens,' *Constitutional Political Economy*, Vol. 28, (2017), pp. 407-421.

[261] In Xenophon's *Economics*, Isomachus assumes the always-present possibility of an *antidosis* challenge: 7.3. Ober (*Mass and Elite in Democratic Athens*, p. 223), assumes that such disputes were frequent.

[262] But see Lysias 4, where the speaker mentions his involvement in past antidosis cases. And Christ (('Liturgy Avoidance and Antidosis in Classical Athens') argues that *antidosis* actually aggravated the problem of tax avoidance.

[263] J. Locke, *Second Treatise on Government*, Chapter 5, 'On Property.'

[264] Aristotle, *Politics*, 1253b24-5.

[265] Aristotle, *Politics*, 1262b38 − 1268b14. See also Aristophanes' parody of communal ownership in his play *Assemblywomen*.

[266] Xenophon, *Economics*, tr. E. Marchant, O. J. Todd, rev. J. Henderson (Harvard, 1979), 2.6; Cf. Xenophon, *Symposium* 4.32.

[267] Lysias, 21.23. Cf. Athenogoras's description of the wealthy as *phulakes* (guardians) of the city's wealth in his speech to the Syracusan assembly: Thucydides, 6.39.1. See also Demosthenes, 14.25-8; Lysias 19.61-3.

[268] Lysias, 34.5, tr. W. R. Lamb. And see the discussion of the relationship between revolution and redistribution of land in A. Fuks, *Social Conflict in Ancient Greece*, (Brill, 1997), pp. 61 − 65.

[269] Brooks A. Kaiser, 'The Athenian Trierarchy: Mechanism Design for the Private Provision of Public Goods', *The Journal of Economic History*, Vol. 67, No. 2 (June, 2007), pp. 445-480.

[270] *New York Times*, 20 May, 2021: https://www.nytimes.com/ 2021/05/20/arts/little-island-barry-diller.html? searchResultPosition=1. Accessed 22 May, 2021.

[271] A copy of the inscription and translation can be found in P.J. Rhodes, and R. Osborne, *Greek Historical Inscriptions: 404-323*

BC,(Oxford, 2003), pp, 100-102. See also the commentary on this inscription in J. Ober, *Democracy and Knowledge: Innovation and Learning in Classical Athens* (Princeton, 2008), pp. 124-133.

272 J. Eisinger, J. Ernsthausen, P. Kiel, 'The Secret IRS Files: Trove of Never-Before-Seen Records Reveal How the Wealthiest Avoid Income Tax,' 6/8/21. www.propublica.org/article/the-secret-irs-files-trove-of-never-before-seen-records-reveal-how-the-wealthiest-avoid-income-tax

273 Pseudo-Xenophon, *The Constitution of the Athenians*, 1.13.

274 Some US states (Delaware, Hawaii, Kentucky, Louisiana, Montana, New Jersey, New York, West Virginia, and the territory of Puerto Rico) Delaware, Hawaii, Kentucky, Louisiana, Montana, New Jersey, have introduced state-level holidays for elections, though these only affect public employees.

275 State-level jury compensation varies. Only eight states require employers to continue paying jurors while serving, though again here, the level of compensation varies widely.

276 G.E.M. de Ste. Croix, 'Political Pay Outside Athens', *Classical Quarterly*, 25 (1975), pp. 48-52.

277 See the discussion in R. Zelnick-Abramovitz, 'Did Patronage Exist in Classical Athens?', *L'Antiquité Classique*, Vol. 69 (2000), pp. 65-80. Also, P. Millett, 'Patronage and its Avoidance in Classical Athens', in A. Wallace-Hadrill (ed.), *Patronage in Ancient Society* (London, 1989), pp. 15-47.

278 [Aristotle], *The Athenian Constitution*, 27; Theopompus, FrGrH 115, F87; Plutarch, *Cimon*, 10.1-6.

279 [Aristotle], *The Athenian Constitution*, 27.3-4.

280 Aristophanes, *Knights*, 1152-1155; Isocrates, 8.121, 15.132; Demosthenes, 18.112, 20.143; [Lysias], 20.33-35.

281 Aristotle, *Politics*, 1297a35-8.

282 A. Alwine, 'Freedom and Patronage in the Athenian Democracy,' *Journal of Hellenic Studies*, Vol. 136 (2016), p. 5.

283 Plato, *Gorgias*, tr. D. Zel, (Hackett, 1987), 515e2-4.

[284] Isocrates, tr. G. Norlin, (Harvard, 1980), 7.24. See also [Aristotle], *The Constitution of the Athenians* 25.7, where jury pay is linked to the decline of jury quality, and bribery of court.

[285] See Demosthenes, 24.99 for both senses of the term. And F.D. Harvey, 'Dona Ferentes: Some Aspects of Bribery in Greek Politics', *History of Political Thought*, Vol. 6, No. 1/2 (Summer 1985), pp. 76-117 (pp. 83-4).

[286] Plutarch attributes the establishment of the fund to Pericles, and thus nearly 100 years earlier: *Pericles*, 9.

[287] Plutarch, *Moralia*, 1011B.

[288] J. K. Davies, *Athenian Propertied Families* (Oxford, 1971), pp. xxiii-xxiv; Pseudo-Xenophon, *Constitution of the Athenians*, 3.8.

[289] Pseudo-Xenophon, *Constitution of the Athenians*, 2.9-10.

[290] R. Putnam, *Bowling Alone: The Collapse and Revival of American Community* (Simon & Schuster, 2001). See also: T. Skocpol, *Diminished Democracy: From Membership to Management in American Civic Life* (University of Oklahoma Press, 2003).

[291] See Charles Taylor's clear and concise diagnosis of these problems in his essay 'Atomism,' in *Philosophical Papers* (Cambridge University Press, 2010), pp. 187-210.

[292] 'Voter Turnout in Presidential Elections : The American Presidency Project'. www.presidency.ucsb.edu. Retrieved January 8, 2021. The US ranked 26 (of 35) OECD countries for turnout: https://www.arcgis.com/apps/MapJournal/index.html?appid=448109665d774cd6a8702bfbd8cc7433. Retrieved January 8, 2021.

[293] T. Carney, *Alienated America: Why Some Places Thrive While Others Collapse* (Harper Collins, 2019).

[294] T. Mann, N. Ornstein, E. Dionne, *One Nation After Trump: A Guide for the Perplexed, the Disillusioned, the Desperate, and the Not-Yet Deported* (St. Martin's Press, 2017), p. 45.

[295] Both [Aristotle's] *The Constitution of the Athenians* (Ch. 21), and Herodotus' *History* (5.69), contain concise summaries of this period.

296 Supposedly, the new tribal names were chosen from a longer list submitted to the priestess at Delphi, [Aristotle], *The Constitution of the Athenians*, 21.6. Some scholars suggest that Cleisthenes' new arrangement benefitted his own group at the expense of others. See G. R. Stanton, 'The Tribal Reforms of Kleisthenes the Alkmeonid', *Chiron*, Vol. 14 (1984), pp. 1-41.

297 This general overview sets aside many of the complexities of Cleisthenes' redistricting. See Greg Anderson, *The Athenian Experiment: Building an Imagined Political Community in Ancient Attica, 508-490 B.C.* (University of Michigan, 2003) for a detailed description of Cleisthenes' plan.

298 Aristotle, *Politics*, tr. Jowett (revised) (Cambridge, 1996), 1319b23-27 (VI.4). Cleisthenes' redistricting might have also been motivated by the need to muster an army, given recent incursions in Attica by Sparta.

299 Mogens Herman Hansen provides a good overview of these: *The Athenian Democracy in the Age of Demosthenes* (Blackwell, 1991), pp. 246-265.

300 See especially, *Athenian Legacies, Essays on the Politics of Getting on Together* (Princeton, 2005); and *Democracy and Knowledge: Innovation and Learning in Classical Athens* (Princeton, 2008).

301 Plato, *Apology*, 32b. Though we lack clear evidence, demes likely selected citizens by lot to serve on the *Boule*. Deme representation on the *Boule* was roughly proportionate to population. There is some dispute over whether this changes over time. Ober, *Democracy and Knowledge*, p. 3; Hansen, *The Athenian Democracy in the Age of Demosthenes*.

302 See Ober's description of these dense networks: *Democracy and Knowledge*, pp. 146-151.

303 Ibid., p. 140.

304 Ober, *Athenian Legacies*, p. 33. Mogens Herman Hansen's work best exemplifies the alternative approach, which focuses on the legal structure of the democracy. Ober and Hansen resorted to an arm-wrestling competition to resolve their differences, but it is unclear who was the victor.

305 Aristotle, *Politics*, 1277b7.

306 R. Osborne, 'The Demos and its Divisions in Classical Athens,' in O. Murray, S. Price (eds.), *The Greek City from Homer to Alexander* (Clarendon Press, 1990), p. 276.

307 A. Gottesman, *Politics and the Street in Democratic Athens* (Cambridge University Press, 2014), p. 83.

308 Demosthenes, tr. J. Vince, 4.35-6.

309 Aeschines, 3.154.

310 See the fragment of Alexis' *Gynaikokratia* [The Rule of Women]: '[We] have to sit in the last *kerkides*, like foreigners.' J. M. Edmonds, *The Fragments of Attic Comedy after Meineke, Bergk, and Kock* (E.J. Brill, 1959), fr. 41, p. 394-5.

311 A. Pickard-Cambridge, *Dramatic Festivals of Athens*, p. 17.

312 Plato, *Symposium*, 175e.

313 Christian Meier limits the effective 'audience' of a play to about 10,000, which he argues is the number that can actually hear and understand the speech of the actors, *The Political Art of Greek Tragedy* (Johns Hopkins, 1993), p. 59.

314 Thus A. Pickard-Cambridge, *Dramatic Festivals of Athens*, p. 19; S. Goldhill, 'The Audience of Athenian Tragedy', *The Cambridge Companion to Greek Tragedy* (Cambridge, 1997), p. 56. S. Dawson, by contrast, estimates only 3700 attendees: 'The Theatrical Audience in Fifth-Century Athens: Numbers and Status', *Prudentia*, Vol. XXIX, No.3 (May, 1997), p. 7.

315 Demosthenes, 22.68.

316 Theophrastus, *Characters* 9.5. Aeschines also comments that early festivals included a ceremony where slaves were manumitted, implying their subsequent attendance at the performance.

317 Pickard-Cambridge, *Dramatic Festivals of Athens*, p. 20.

318 For the most recent comprehensive study, see D. K. Roselli, *Theater of the People: Spectator and Society in Ancient Athens* (University of Texas, 2011); J. Henderson, 'Women and the Athenian Dramatic Festivals', *Transactions of the American Philological Association* (1974-2014) Vol. 121 (1991), pp. 133-147. Anthony Podlecki agrees that women attended, but only from elite

households: 'Could Women Attend the Theatre in Ancient Athens? A Collection of Testimonia', *Ancient World*, 21 (1990), pp. 27-43. S. Goldhill, 'The Audience of Athenian Tragedy,' takes a more nuanced view, calling the evidence 'inconclusive' (p. 66).

319 Athenaeus, *Deipnosophistae*, 12.47; *Vita Aeschyli*, 9. The latter is often discounted as hyperbole, but see the discussion in W. Calder, 'Vita Aeschyli 9: Miscarriages in the Theatre of Diony-sos', *The Classical Quarterly*, Vol. 38, No. 2 (1988), pp. 554-555, who points out a later parallel. See also, Aristophanes, *Peace* 963-5; Alciphron, *Ep.* 2.3.10.

320 *Schol. Ar. Ecclesiazusae*, 22.

321 Goldhill, 'The Audience of Athenian Tragedy', argues that because these women were priestesses, and virgins, they likely had special status granting them the privilege to attend, p. 65.

322 Plato, *Gorgias*, 501e-502d; *Minos*, 321a.

323 Aristotle, *Politics*, 1341b17.

324 Plato, *Laws*, 700-701d. We can see echoes of this complaint later in texts like Jean-Jacques Rousseau's *Letter to D'Alembert on the Theatre,* where he complains that the introduction of theatre endangers citizen virtue.

325 Plato, *Republic*, tr. T. Griffith, 561e3-4.

326 Jean-Pierre Vernant's *Myth and Tragedy*, tr. J. Lloyd (Zone Books, 1990) is pivotal here. See also Charles Segal, 'Greek Tragedy and Society: A Structuralist Perspective', in J.P. Euben, *Greek Tragedy and Political Theory* (University of California, 1986), pp. 43-75. Much work focuses on specific aspects of the festivals them-selves. Peter Wilson, for example, focuses on the function of the *Choregos* in *The Athenian Institution of the Khoregia: The Chorus, The City, The State* (Cambridge, 2000), or see Simon Goldhill's analysis of the ritual ceremonies beginning the Festival of Dio-nysus in 'Civic Ideology and the Problem of Difference: The Politics of Aeschylean Tragedy, Once Again', *Journal of Hellenic Studies*, 120 (2000), pp. 34-56.

327 Goldhill, 'Civic Ideology', p. 35.

[328] R. Rehm, *Radical Theatre. Greek Tragedy and the Modern World*,(Duckworth, 2003); S. Goldhill, *Reading Greek Tragedy* (Cambridge, 1986); M. Griffith, 'Brilliant Dynasts: Power and Politics in the Oresteia', *Classical Antiquity*, Vol. 14, No. 1, (1995), pp. 62-129.

[329] Not all scholars agree with this approach, arguing that tragedy is ideologically flexible and able to fit a range of political contexts. P.J. Rhodes notes that there are elements of *polis* life in the tragedy, but little specifically democratic about them: 'Nothing to Do with Democracy: Athenian Drama and the Polis', *Journal of Hellenic Studies*, Vol. 123 (2003), pp. 104-116; S. Scullion, 'Nothing to Do with Dionysus: Tragedy Misconceived as Ritual', *The Classical Quarterly*, Vol. 52, No. 1 (2002), pp. 102-137. For the debate between Rhodes and Goldhill, see P. Burian, 'Athenian Tragedy as Democratic Discourse,' in D. M. Carter (ed.), *Why Athens? A Reappraisal of Tragic Politics* (Oxford, 2011), pp. 95-119.

[330] P. Burian, 'Athenian Tragedy as Democratic Discourse,' in Carter, *Why Athens?*, p. 100.

[331] Demosthenes, *Letters* III.13, tr. N. W. DeWitt (Harvard, 1923). There is an alternative manuscript tradition which substitutes *metekhontes* for *en parrhêsia*. See also *fragmenta adespota* 890 K-A: 'For those who are considering major issues, the wisest advisor is parrhesia.'

[332] On this play see also J.P. Euben, 'Political Corruption in Euripides' *Orestes*,' in J.P. Euben (ed.), *Greek Tragedy and Political Theory* (University of California, 1986), pp. 222-251.

[333] Burian, 'Athenian Tragedy', p. 114.

[334] E. Hall, *Inventing the Barbarian: Greek Self-Definition Through Tragedy* (Oxford, 1991). See also Hall's recent reevaluation of that work 'Recasting the Barbarian' in *The Theatrical Cast of Athens. Interactions between Ancient Greek Drama and Society* (Oxford, 2006), pp. 184-224. Other notable recent contributions to this approach include P. George, *Barbarian Asia and the Greek Experience* (Baltimore, 1994); S. Goldhill, 'Battle Narrative and Politics in Aeschylus' Persae', *Journal of Hellenic Studies* Vol. CVIII (1998), pp. 189-193; S. Saïd, 'Tragedy and Reversal: The Example of the Persians' in M. Lloyd, *Oxford Readings in Classical*

Studies: Aeschylus (Oxford, 2007), pp. 71-92; T. Harrison, *The Emptiness of Asia. Aeschylus'* Persians *and the History of the Fifth Century* (London, 2000); W. Nippel, 'The Construction of the Other,' in T. Harrison, *Greeks and Barbarians* (New York, 2002), pp. 278-310.

335 Aeschylus, *Persians*, tr. S. Bernardete (Chicago, 1956), 243-4.

336 *Ibid.*, 3, 9, 79, 159, 163, 238, 250. And unlike the opulent displays of wealth at the Persian court, Athenians viewing the play would have remembered that Athens — at the direction of Themistokles — decided to invest its newly found wealth in a fleet which was ultimately responsible for the victory at Salamis instead of lavish public building or private handouts, thus linking the use of wealth with military victory or defeat.

337 *Ibid.*, 463, 100ff.

338 *Ibid.*, 471, 481, 594.

339 *Ibid.*, 407.

340 *Ibid.*, 26, 85, 147-149, 239-241, 278, 729, 926, 1016-25.

341 Euripides, *The Trojan Women*, tr. R. Lattimore in *Euripides III* ed. D. Grene, R. Lattimore, (Chicago, 1958), 764.

342 Herodotus, *Histories*, 6.2.10.

343 F Zeitlin, 'Thebes: Theater of Self and Society in Athenian Drama,' in *Greek Drama and Political Theory*, ed. J.P. Euben (University of California Press 1986), p. 116.

344 Aeschylus, *Eumenides*, tr. A. Sommerstein (Harvard, 2009) 826-9.

345 For example, Aristotle, *Generation of Animals*, II 3, 737a28-30.

346 See, for example, Aristophanes' description of Cleon and the Spartan general Brasidas as the 'pestles' of war, *Peace*, 238-285. Some evidence suggests that Cleon prosecuted Aristophanes because of his criticisms. See J.E. Atkinson, 'Curbing the Comedians: Cleon Versus Aristophanes and Syracosius' Decree', *Classical Quarterly*, Vol. 42, No. 1 (1992), pp. 56-64.

347 Aristophanes, *Knights*, tr. J. Henderson (Harvard, 1998), 255.

348 Aristophanes, *Wasps*, tr. J. Henderson (Harvard, 1998), 390, 517.

[349] For more details, see J. Miller, 'Democratic Criticism in Aristophanes', *History of Political Thought* Vol. XL, No. 1 (Spring, 2019), pp. 1-22.

[350] Most contemporary scholars who see Aristophanes as conservative cite the influence of G.E.M. de Ste. Croix, *The Origins of the Peloponnesian War* (Cornell, 1972), pp. 371, 356. See P. Walsh, 'A study in reception: the British debates over Aristophanes' politics and influence', *Classical Receptions Journal*, Vol. 1, No. 1 (2009), pp. 55-72, for a good review of the past century and a half of Aristophanes scholarship.

[351] Aristophanes, *Frogs*, tr. J. Henderson (Harvard, 2002), 948-952.

[352] E. Hall, 'The Sociology of Athenian Tragedy', in P. E. Easterling (ed.), *The Cambridge Companion to Greek Tragedy* (Cambridge, 1997), p. 93.

[353] N. Loraux, *The Invention of Athens: the Funeral Oration in the Classical City* (Zone Books, 2006), p. 336.

[354] Aristophanes, *Frogs*, 1009-1010. Cf. 1053-5, 1500-1; *Acharnians* 643-51. John Hesk, 'Euripidean *Euboulia* and Tragic Politics,' in D.M. Carter (ed.), *Why Athens?: A Reappraisal of Tragic Politics* (Oxford, 2011), pp. 119-144.

[355] Chou, M., Gagnon, J.P., Pruitt, L., 'Putting Participation on State: Examining Participatory Theatre as an Alternative Site for Political Participation', *Policy Studies*, Vol. 36, No. 5, (2015), pp. 608-622.

[356] See, for example, A. Blanshard, 'Jurors and Serial Killers: Loneliness, Deliberation, and Community in Ancient Athens', in D. Allen, P. Christesen, P. Millett (eds.), *How to Do Things with History: New Approaches to Ancient Greece* (Oxford, 2018), pp. 137-157.

[357] R. Putnam, L. Feldstein, D. Cohen, *Better Together: Restoring American Community* (Simon & Schuster, 2004), p. 278-9.

[358] E. Burke, *Reflections on the Revolution in France* (Hackett, 1987), p. 41.

[359] See *Republic*, 377a-378e, and 413b8-415a, for example.

360 J. J. Rousseau, *On the Social Contract,* tr. D. A. Cress (Hackett, 1987), IV.8 (p. 102).

361 For example, T. Hobbes, *Leviathan,* II, xxx.21.

362 Rousseau, *Social Contract,* IV.8 (p. 98). Part of Rousseau's concern, of course, has to do with sources of authority outside of the political sphere. Specifically, he worries about the long-standing threat institutions like Roman Catholicism, with its higher claim to allegiance, has on citizens. But, as Locke power-fully argues, even a set of theological tenets rooted outside of human authority has revolutionary potential.

363 C. Moskos, *A Call to Civic Service: National Service for Country and Community* (Free Press, 1988), pp. 4-8. See also E. Gorham, *National Service, Citizenship, and Political Education* (SUNY Press, 1992). See also M. Castell's analysis of this problem in the EU in *Rupture: The Crisis of Liberal Democracy,* pp. 75-84.

364 B. Barber, 'Service, Citizenship and Democracy: Civic Duty as an Entitlement of Civil Right,' in W. Evers, (ed.), *National Service: Pro and Con* (Hoover Institution Press, 1990), p. 35-6.

365 Thucydides, *History of the Peloponnesian War,* 2.41.

366 On the fomer point, see Wendy Brown's discussion of the paradoxes of rights in *States of Injury: Power and Freedom in Late Modernity* (Princeton, 1995).

367 See Michael Walzer's classic analysis of this problem in *Spheres of Justice: A Defense of Pluralism and Equality* (Basic Books, 1983), especially chapters 4 and 12.

Index

www.ingramcontent.com/pod-product-compliance
Lightning Source LLC
Chambersburg PA
CBHW060422100426
42812CB00030B/3275/J